PATTERN GRADING
FOR WOMEN'S
CLOTHES

The Technology of Sizing

jk

Other books on clothing from Blackwell Science

Pattern Grading for Men's Clothes
Gerry Cooklin
0 632 03305 3

Pattern Grading for Children's Clothes
Gerry Cooklin
0 632 02612 X

Introduction to Clothing Manufacture
Gerry Cooklin
0 632 02661 8

The Technology of Clothing Manufacture
SECOND EDITION
Harold Carr and Barbara Latham
0 632 03748 2

Knitted Clothing Technology
Terry Brackenbury
0 632 02807 6

Fashion Design and Product Development
Harold Carr and John Pomeroy
0 632 02893 9

Fashion Marketing
Edited by Mike Easey
0 632 03459 9

Metric Pattern Cutting
THIRD EDITION
Winifred Aldrich
0 632 03612 5

Metric Pattern Cutting for Children's Wear
From 2 to 14 years
Winifred Aldrich
0 632 03057 7

PATTERN GRADING FOR WOMEN'S CLOTHES

The Technology of Sizing

GERRY COOKLIN

Blackwell Science

© 1992 by
Blackwell Science Ltd
Editorial Offices:
Osney Mead, Oxford OX2 0EL
25 John Street, London WC1N 2BL
23 Ainslie Place, Edinburgh EH3 6AJ
350 Main Street, Malden
  MA 02148 5018, USA
54 University Street, Carlton
  Victoria 3053, Australia
10, rue Casimir Delavigne
  75006 Paris, France

Other Editorial Offices:

Blackwell Wissenschafts-Verlag GmbH
Kurfürstendamm 57
10707 Berlin, Germany

Blackwell Science KK
MG Kodenmacho Building
7-10 Kodenmacho Nihombashi
Chuo-ku, Tokyo 104, Japan

First published 1990
Reprinted 1994, 1996, 1999

Set by Best-set Typesetter Ltd, Hong Kong
Printed and bound in the United Kingdom
at the University Press, Cambridge

The Blackwell Science logo is a
trade mark of Blackwell Science Ltd,
registered at the United Kingdom
Trade Marks Registry

DISTRIBUTORS

Marston Book Services Ltd
PO Box 269
Abingdon
Oxon OX14 4YN
(Orders: Tel: 01235 465500
           Fax: 01235 465555)

USA
Blackwell Science, Inc.
Commerce Place
350 Main Street
Malden, MA 02148 5018
(Orders: Tel: 800 759 6102
                  781 388 8250
           Fax: 781 388 8255)

Canada
Login Brothers Book Company
324 Saulteaux Crescent
Winnipeg, Manitoba R3J 3T2
(Orders: Tel: 204 837-2987
           Fax: 204 837-3116)

Australia
Blackwell Science Pty Ltd
54 University Street
Carlton, Victoria 3053
(Orders: Tel: 03 9347 0300
           Fax: 03 9347 5001)

A catalogue record for this title
is available from the British Library

ISBN 0-632-02295-7

Library of Congress
Cataloguing-in-Publication Data
is available

For further information on
Blackwell Science, visit our website:
www.blackwell-science.com

This book is dedicated to the memory of the late
Eng. Eli Sharizli of Shenkar College,
Ramat Gan, Israel. In 1974, he provided the
original impetus to the project which ultimately
led to the development of this grading system.

Contents

Preface

'This research project was undertaken in order to provide measurements which could be used for improving the fit of women's garments and patterns. No scientific study of body measurements used in the construction of women's clothing has ever been reported.

The measurements used have grown up in the industry chiefly by trial and error, based on measurements taken of a few women by various, inaccurate procedures.'

From the introduction to the first USA report on Measurement and Sizes, 1949.

During the past two decades or so, the clothing industry has achieved a series of major technological advances which have made important contributions to the general high quality of ready-to-wear clothing. To a great extent, most of these quality related improvements are concerned with garment function and durability rather than to an issue which is central to that of garment quality, the issue of sizing.

For most people in the clothing industry, sizing quality refers to the dimensional accuracy of the finished garment and as such, the checking of measurements is an integral part of quality control procedures in most factories. However, the fundamental issue of sizing quality is not whether the garments are dimensionally accurate but rather, if the given measurements are in themselves correct. In other words, do the specified measurements for a garment provide a fitting quality standard at the same level as those standards pertaining to other aspects of the garment?

This book will examine the importance of this question, and in so doing, will develop and establish the basic principles of sizing technology and pattern grading for women's outerwear. It is my sincere hope that the theory and practice of this grading system will contribute towards the improvement of sizing quality in general.

I should like to express my thanks to all of my friends and colleagues who gave me their help and encouragement during the planning and preparation of this book.

Gerry Cooklin

Acknowledgements

My thanks are extended to the authors, publishers and institutions who gave their permission to reproduce the following illustrations:

Fig. 1.1 Clothes of the Classic Period
Costume of the Classical World by Marion Sichel, published by Batsford, London, England.
Fig. 1.2 Sewing Machine 1876
Old Sewing Machines by Carol Head, published by Shire Publications, Aylesbury, England.
Fig. 1.4 Ladies Costume
The Cut of Women's Clothes by Nora Waugh, published by Faber and Faber, London, England.
Fig. 1.7 The New-Look 1948 (Christian Dior), Victoria and Albert Museum, London, England.

My thanks are also extended to the following suppliers and agencies for their helpful cooperation and permission to reproduce illustrations of their equipment:

Beta Engineering, Beersheba, Israel
Gerber Garment Technology, Windsor, Conn. USA
Lectra Systems, Bordeaux, France
Neel Agencies, Tel-Aviv, Israel
Schleien Bros, Tel-Aviv, Israel
Steiner GmbH, Zurich, Switzerland

PART 1

INTRODUCTION

Chapter 1

Looking Back

A little history

The first clothes, apart from fig leaves, were made of animal skins roughly sewn together and tied around the body. From the beginning, the first garment makers started from flat skins, thus establishing a precept unchanged since then, that the natural starting point for making a garment is a flat sheet of material.

A great advance occurred when the arts of spinning and weaving were discovered at some unknown date in Neolithic times, and by the beginning of the Bronze Age woven clothes such as linen, silk and wool were in common use. In the ancient world, squares of cloth direct from the loom and without being cut, were draped around the body and held in position by girdles, ornamental brooches and clasps (Fig. 1.1). The first garments which were cut to fit the body and limbs through the provision of sleeves and legs appeared during the Minoan Civilisation (3000–1400 BC).

The earliest known garment patterns date from the 12th century and were used to cut habits for Italian monks. These patterns which were made from slate, consisted of the back, front and sleeve of the garment, and were brought to Italy by Greek and Palestinian traders. About this time, the cutting and making of clothes took on the basic structure that was to last for many centuries.

For men, there were tailors who would produce hand-made bespoke clothing and uniforms. Tailors took many measurements and had to use them accurately because their clients were not prepared to stand around for long periods of time whilst being fitted. According to Guild history, by the 16th century, men's tailors knew a great deal about the proportions of the body and how to draft rudimentary patterns for many different types of garments. Cutting and sewing journals started appearing as early as 1600 and in 1671 a French master tailor, Bensonit Barclay, published the first book on pattern making for men's clothes.

On the other hand, the making of women's clothes

Fig. 1.1. Clothes of the classic period.

4

was carried out exclusively at home, either by members of the household or a visiting seamstress. The basic pattern for the garment was prepared by draping toile onto the body and adjusting the style lines and fitting by means of pins and tack stitches. When the style and fitting were satisfactory, the toile was ripped down and used as a guide for cutting the cloth. Measurements, other than very rudimentary ones taken as a guide for cutting the toile, played a minor role in the cutting of women's garments. Time was of little importance, and the women of those times were quite prepared to spend hours being fitted at every minor stage of making up the garment. Until the middle of the 19th century, the majority of women's clothes continued to be made at home, using draping or very primitive pattern cutting techniques.

About this time saw the emergence of dressmaking salons which made clothes on an individual made-to-measure basis. This period also saw the introduction of the newly invented sewing machine (Fig. 1.2) and also workroom stands made from willow cane, woven in basket fashion. During the 1860s, Stockman Freres of France started producing stock-sized workroom stands based on their extensive knowledge of measurements accumulated over many years of producing papier mâché stands to individuals' measurements. They adopted a size interval which became the basis of most European sizing systems used today.

Stockman Freres knew from their accumulated experience that the most frequently appearing bust girth was 88 cm and that other bust girths could be spaced at 4 cm intervals up and down from this size. The moulds which were used to cast and form the papier mâché stands were equivalent to half of the trunk and they were referred to by this half measurement, i.e. 88 cm girth became size 44, etc. For many years, the stands produced by Stockman Freres and others were the only guide available for producing ready-made garments in different sizes.

The first real ready-to-wear garments for women started to appear towards the end of the 19th century and they were usually very simple and cheap interpretations of the current fashions. Individually hand-made garments were still made for the upper classes and these garments were elaborately trimmed in order to prevent copying and thus retain their exclusivity. The techniques of Pattern Construction and Grading (Fig. 1.3) were still in their infancies and the women of that time who purchased ready-made clothes fully accepted the fact that substantial alterations would be required before the garments had any semblance of a reasonable fit.

The awakening

Until the outbreak of World War I (1914–1918), social traditions still prejudiced many women against wearing

Fig. 1.2. A sewing machine of 1876.

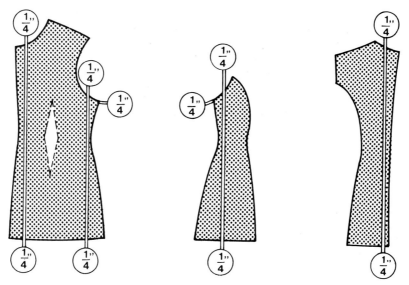

Fig. 1.3. Pattern grading system (1879).

ready-made clothes. The war changed these attitudes very rapidly because women were called upon to serve in the auxiliary services of the warring nations, and one of the first requisites was uniforms. Consequently, for the first time, it became imperative to mass-produce ladies' ready-to-wear clothing of all types.

The uniforms produced during this period were based on the tightly corsetted, artificial hour-glass figure which had been in vogue for many years (Fig. 1.4). As a result, the uniforms required extensive alterations to make them less restrictive and easier to wear in active situations. By the end of the war, many of the conventions regarding women's clothes had broken down and the early 1920s saw the start of an ever increasing demand for ready-to-wear clothing.

Clothing manufacturers of this period realised that more rational methods of pattern construction and grading were required and after many trials found, so it seemed, answers to both of these problems.

For many centuries, artists had used the 'Eight Head' principle when portraying the female body. This principle held that the length of the head is $\frac{1}{8}$th of the total height and that the bust, waist and hip lines were equally spaced down the body at $\frac{1}{8}$th intervals (Fig. 1.5). These length proportions were combined with what were then considered to be the ideal girth measurements of the female body and together they produced garment patterns with the following proportions:

(a) The height of an average woman was assumed to be between 168 cm to 170 cm.

Fig. 1.4. Ladies costume (1904).

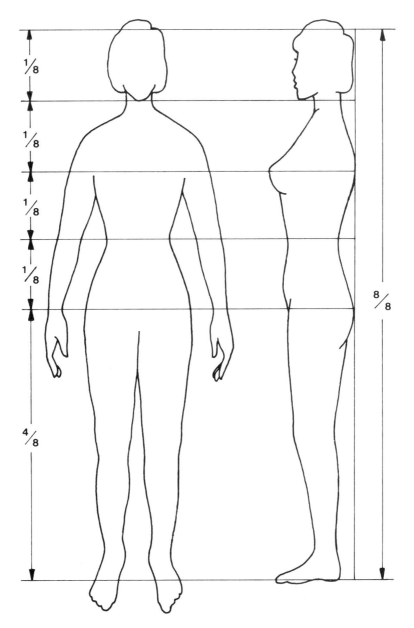

Fig. 1.5. The eight-head principle

(b) The bust girth was 6 cm to 8 cm smaller than the hip girth.
(c) The waist girth was at least 30 cm smaller than the hip girth.

These length and girth proportions were to serve as the basis for pattern construction systems for many years, and they in turn led to the development of what became at that time, a widely accepted pattern grading system called Proportionate Grading (Fig. 1.6).

This grading system was based on the theoretical assumption that there is a fixed relationship between length and girth measurements. In practice, this meant that when the girth increased, the length proportions also increased and vice versa when decreasing girths. As a consequence, when patterns were constructed according to the 'Eight Head' principle and graded by the 'Proportionate Sizing' method, the following results ensued:

The length proportions of the original pattern were

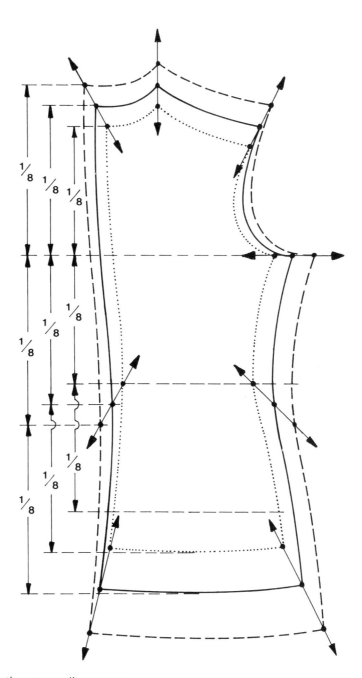

Fig. 1.6. The proportionate grading system

based on a stature of about 10 cm taller than the average woman of that time which meant that the waistline was 3 cm to 4 cm lower than its natural position. This disparity increased every time the pattern size was increased. Consequently, a woman requiring a large size would receive a garment with the waistline at nearly mid-hip level and obviously,

pocket positions and garment lengths were similarly affected. Phillip Kunick[5] writes that 'it would be no exaggeration to say that at least 80% of the garments produced by these systems required shortening in the bodice and skirt sections'.

It took the launching of a new fashion by the French designer, Christian Dior, in 1947 (Fig. 1.7) to compel the clothing industry into developing realistic and accurate sizing data on which to base their pattern construction and grading systems.

The essence of this revolutionary fashion, called the New-Look, was its emphasis on natural body fitting, especially in the trunk section of the body. This meant that the vertical proportions had to be related to the true height of the average woman, and that the girth measurements and proportions had to be realistic and not just suitable for some Grecian goddess. This situation made clothing manufacturers take stock, and the following facts emerged:

(a) The current and foreseeable trends were for naturally fitted and proportioned garments.
(b) With the growing introduction of new merchandising concepts, retailers wanted to maximise their sales areas and not have the expense of maintaining large alteration departments.
(c) Customers were objecting to the additional cost of altering nearly every ready-made garment which they purchased.

The conclusion was clear: pattern construction methods based on accurate sizing combined with precise pattern grading were the pre-requisites for efficient mass production and trouble-free volume sales.

As a result, the next few years saw the rapid development of more rational pattern construction and grading systems and these systems made substantial contributions to the sizing quality of women's clothes. Many of the systems owed their origins to the men's sector, and these origins can be seen in many of the textbooks used today. The major weakness which underlay all of these developments was the fact that there was an almost complete lack of anthropometric data on which to base the systems.

The deficiency was rectified when the results of four large scale anthropometric surveys, carried out between 1956 and 1968, were published. Together, these four reports provided for the first time comprehensive scientific data regarding women's measurements. However, with a few exceptions, the results of these surveys have had a rather limited effect on the sizing systems used by clothing industries

Fig. 1.7. The 'New-Look' (Christian Dior) 1948.

throughout the world. The reasons for this are manifold, but a detailed examination of them is beyond the scope of this book.

TO SUM UP

A pattern grading system cannot be fundamentally correct if the principal propositions have not been derived from authoritative data obtained by scientific methods. Thus, a systematic examination and evaluation of the main findings of these surveys is necessary in order to develop the first principles of sizing technology.

Chapter 2

Sizes and Measurements

Anthropometrical research

Anthropometry, a word coined by the French naturalist George Cuvier (1769–1832) means the measurement of man and is derived from the Greek roots for 'man' and 'measurement'. This discipline has long been used by physical anthropologists for the comparison of man to other primates and for the comparison of different racial groups. Apart from its use for the sizing of clothing, anthropometric data is also used to design car seats and the cockpits of aeroplanes and space vehicles, etc.

During the past century, there have been many small scale surveys designed to determine the sizes and measurements of specific groups within a given population. In the main, however, these surveys were of limited value because of the small samples taken and their lack of scientific method. Therefore, the four large scale surveys carried out between 1956 and 1968 are of major importance because, to a very large extent, they still provide the only authoritative basis for women's measurements and sizes. The surveys are:

(1) *USA* This survey, with various additions, was carried out between 1948 and 1959 and covered a sample of 10 000 women from each of whom 49 measurements were taken. The USA survey is a definitive example of an anthropometric survey specially designed for the clothing industry.
(2) *England* During 1951, about 50 000 women were measured and 37 measurements were taken on each subject. The report published in 1956 contains a detailed analysis of the measurements and size groupings of the entire female population between the ages of 18 and 65.
(3) *West Germany* A large scale survey was carried out by the Hohensteiner Institute in 1970 at the request of the German Association of Clothing Manufacturers. The sample consisted of 10 000 women and 21 measurements were taken from each one. The report which was published in 1973, also contained proposals for a new system of sizing nomenclature which has since been adopted throughout West Germany. The Hohensteiner Institute carried out a repeat survey of the same

size in 1981/82 and the report was issued in 1983. The findings of the second survey regarding measurements and proportions were very similar to those contained in the first report, and the results of both of these surveys were used in the development of this system. (Size charts from both of these surveys and a comparison between them are included in the appendix.)
(4) *France* The French survey was carried out by the Technical Centre for Clothing (CEITH) in 1968 for the Federation of Clothing Manufacturers. During the survey, 26 measurements were taken from each of the 8000 subjects.

All of the surveys used the same basic procedures to take the measurements and apart from standard tape measures, various calibrated instruments were also used. The measurements themselves were taken from specific anatomical landmarks marked on the body with a skin pencil and the subjects wore a specially designed measuring costume. Measurements taken over the clothed areas of the body were adjusted to bring them into line with those taken over nude areas of the body.

Each survey used the same four groupings of measurements:

Group 1: Girth. Measurements taken around the body or limbs such as bust girth, neck girth, etc.
Group 2: Arc. These are measurements which are specific parts of girth measurements. For example, the bust arc anterior is part of the bust girth.
Group 3: Vertical. The majority of these measurements relate to the height of various girth lines from the soles of the feet, such as knee height, waist height and cervical height, etc.
Group 4: Width and length. This group contains the primary and secondary measurements of width and length, such as across back, neck to waist, across chest, etc.

The following tables describe all of the measurements taken during the surveys and their locations are shown in Figs 2.1, 2.2, 2.3 and 2.4. (A glossary of technical terms can be found on page 383.)

10

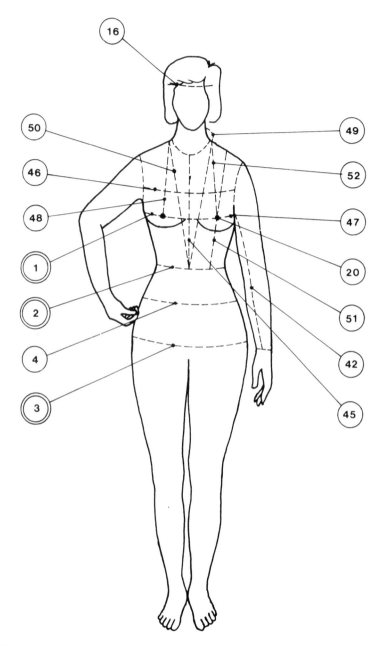

Fig. 2.1. Front view of body.

GROUP 1: GIRTH

1. Bust girth — level of maximum bust girth.
2. Waist girth — average waist level.
3. Hip girth — average hip level.
4. Abdominal extension — level of extension.
5. Chest girth at scye — minimal chest girth level.
6. Thigh — maximum at upper part of leg.

7. Mid-thigh — midway between hip and knee.
8. Knee girth — around the leg and over the knee-cap.
9. Calf girth — around the leg and over the knee-cap.
10. Ankle girth — at the level of maximum girth.
11. Neck girth — at midway level.
12. Neck base — at base of neck.
13. Upper arm — girth at armhole base level.

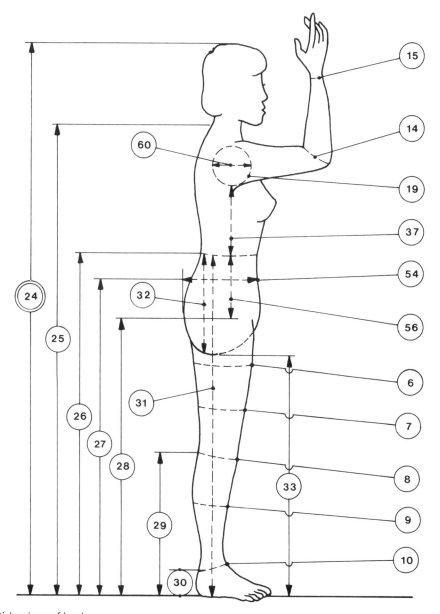

Fig. 2.2. Side view of body.

14. Elbow girth — measured with the arm bent at a right angle.
15. Wrist girth — measured over the distal end of the ulna.
16. Head circumference — at maximum girth level.
17. Sitting spread — measured around both thighs of seated subject.
18. Vertical trunk — mid-shoulder point to crotch.
19. Armhold girth — from the shoulder point through the underarm.

GROUP 2: ARC MEASUREMENTS

All of the arc measurements are taken from an imaginary vertical line extending from the mid-underarm point to the hip bone along one side of the body to a similar line on the other side.

20. Bust arc anterior — front portion of the bust girth.
21. Waist arc anterior — front portion of the waist girth.

12

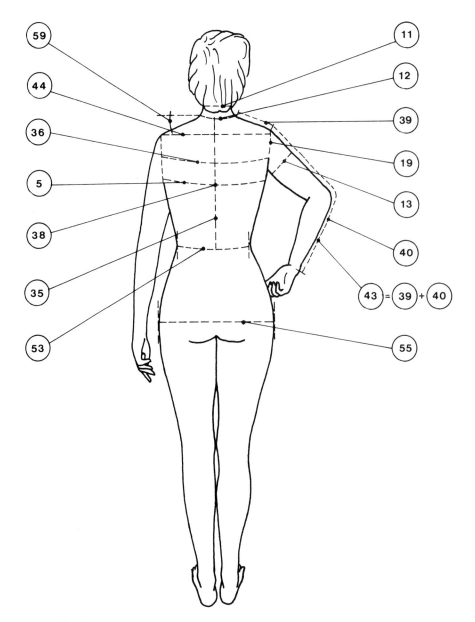

Fig. 2.3. Back view of body.

22. Abdominal extension arc anterior — front portion of abdominal extension girth.
23. Hip arc posterior — back portion of hip girth.

GROUP 3: VERTICAL MEASUREMENTS

(These measurements were taken without shoes.)

24. Height — from crown to soles of feet.
25. Cervical height — from cervical to soles of feet.
26. Waist height — waist level to soles of feet.

27. Abdominal extension — from extension level to soles of feet.
28. Hip height — hip level to soles of feet.
29. Knee height — knee to soles of feet.
30. Ankle height — ankle to soles of feet.
31. Side seam — waist level at side to soles of feet.
32. Body rise — at side from waist level to level of the seat with the subject sitting.
33. Inside leg — base of trunk to soles.
34. Sitting spread height — average height of the most lateral extension of the upper thighs when the subject is standing (see No. 2.4–17)

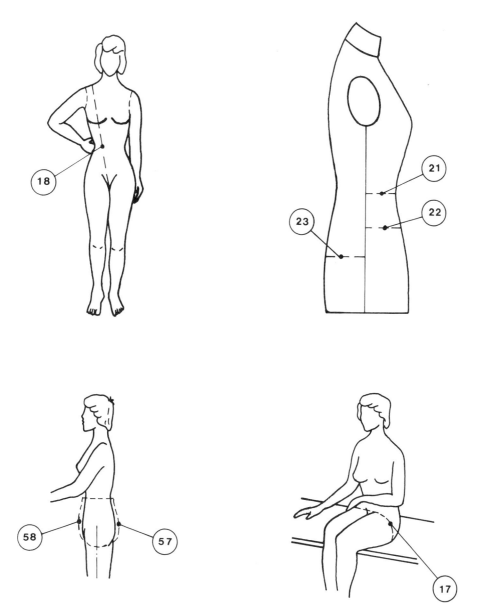

Fig. 2.4. The locations of other measurements.

GROUP 4: WIDTH AND LENGTH MEASUREMENTS

35. Waist length, back — cervical to waist length.
36. Across back — between posterior armscyes.
37. Armscye to waist — underarm mid-point to waist at side.
38. Scye depth — cervical to a point level with the mid-underarm point.
39. Shoulder length — intersections of shoulder line with neck base and armscye.

40. Arm length — from intersection of shoulder and armscye lines, over the elbow to the wrist.
41. Upper arm length — as 40, but taken to elbow.
42. Underarm length — underarm mid-point to wrist line.
43. Neck point to wrist — from neck base on shoulder line to wrist.
44. Interacromion width — between acromion points.
45. Waist length, front — from neckbase to waist level at centre front.
46. Across chest — front of the chest from armscye to

armscye, midway between shoulder and armhole base (same level as across back no. 36).

47. Width of bust prominence — from bust point to bust point.
48. Neck to bust point — from front shoulder point to bust point.
49. Cervical to centre front waist — from cervical to waist level at centre front.
50. Neck point to front waist — from neck point over bust to front waist — vertically.
51. Centre shoulder to front waist — from shoulder line to bust point and then vertically to waist line.
52. Cervical to bust point — from cervical to bust point.
53. Lateral waist width — width of body at waist level.
54. Abdomen seat diameter — greatest depth of body from abdomen to seat.
55. Bitrochanteric width — width of body at hip level.
56. Waist to hip — waist line to hip line at side.
57. Crotch length — centre front waist, through crotch to centre back waist.
58. Crotch length, front — front portion of No. 57 to centre of inner thigh at crotch level.
59. Shoulder slope — slope in relation to horizontal.
60. Scye width — depth between anterior and posterior armscyes.

It is of interest to compare the different measurements which the planners of each survey considered necessary to provide the requisite data for the country concerned (Table 2.1).

In total, the surveys published some 52 size charts together with all of the raw statistics from which they were derived and relevant extracts from these charts appear in the Appendix.

These first four surveys were in their own way, landmarks in the history of the clothing industry. Up until the publication of the studies, the sizing systems in current use were the results of many years development by trial and error methods and it now became possible for the first time to use scientific methods for determining the average measurements for a size based on the bust or hip girth.

The main findings

It is generally accepted by clothing manufacturers that the female population is comprised of five main size groups and one sub-group, with each group having distinctive features of physical development in relation to age and hip girth (Fig. 2.5). The major physical characteristics of these groups are:

Group 1: INFANTS (Age 0–3 years)
The body form has very little definition and is characterised by a protuberant abdomen and stomach.
Group 2: GIRLS (Age 3–9 years)
The body form in this group still lacks definition but tends towards a taller and slimmer development.
Group 3: JUVENILE (Age 9–13 years)
In this group, the waistline has more definition and the larger sizes show the beginnings of bust development.
Group 4: TEENAGE (Age 13–18 years)
The smaller sizes in this group cover body forms which are beginning to take shape but are not yet fully developed. The larger sizes cater to a more well proportioned and developed figure.
Group 5: WOMEN (Age 18–65 years)
This is the group covered by all of the surveys and is characterised by a well proportioned and fully developed figure.
Sub-Group 5A: WOMEN'S-OUTSIZES (Age 18–65 years)
A maturely developed figure where the waist and hip girths are larger in proportion to the bust girth than those in Group 5.

Where there is a viable demand from the market, these five main size groups can each be broken down into sub-groups which cater for specific body forms. For example, Murray Scheier[18] provides detailed measurements of six different size ranges for Women's and Misses garments.

Table 2.1. Measurements used in each survey

Type	Total used in all surveys	USA	England	West Germany	France
1. Girth	19	17	11	7	9
2. Arc	4	4	1	0	0
3. Vertical	11	11	6	5	6
4. Width & Length	26	17	19	9	11
5. Weight	1	1	1	1	1
Totals:	61	50	38	22	27

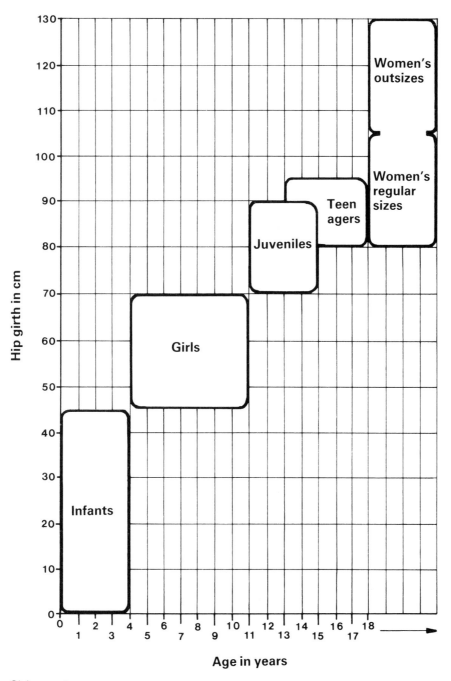

Fig. 2.5. Sizing sectors.

This book deals with Group 5 (Women) only and according to all of the surveys, the sizes in this group can be categorised according to two parameters.

(1) Stature.
(2) The relationship between the bust and hip girths.

STATURE

This refers to the main height groups within a given population and all of the surveys use the same three divisions of short, medium and tall. The groupings and their distributions for each country are set out in Table 2.2.

16

Table 2.2. Height group distributions (all measurements in centimetres)

Country	Short (cm)	(%)	Medium (cm)	(%)	Tall (cm)	(%)	Total
USA	155	46	165	45	175	9	100%
England	150	24	160	55	170	19	98%
West Germany	156	31	164	47	172	22	100%
France	152	28	160	51	168	16	95%

Table 2.2 is presented graphically in Fig. 2.6 and the skew of the USA distribution is the result of an arbitrary decision by the compilers to provide the maximum size range which could be fitted adequately within one height category. Statistically, the USA survey shows a similar height distribution to those of the other surveys. Although the mean height varies from country to country, the average stature range for

sizing purposes is 9 cm between each height group. In countries which have sophisticated sizing systems, the three height group division is generally used.

BUST AND HIP GIRTH RELATIONSHIP (Fig. 2.7)

All of the surveys discovered that for any given hip girth, there can be a number of different bust girths irrespective of the height groups. The main relationships were established as being:

(1) Very small bust — bust girth is 15 cm smaller than the hip girth.
(2) Small bust — bust girth is 10 cm smaller than the hip girth.
(3) Medium bust — bust girth is 5 cm smaller than the hip girth.
(4) Full bust — bust girth is equal to hip girth.
(5) Large bust — bust girth is 5.0 cm larger than the hip girth.
(6) Extra large bust — bust girth is 10 cm larger than the hip girth.

The distribution of these bust and hip girth

Table 2.3. Bust type distribution according to height

Bust type	Height group	USA	England	West Germany	France
(1) Very small	Short	—	1%	—	—
	Medium	—	3%	—	—
	Tall	—	2%	—	—
(2) Small	Short	10%	5%	11%	11%
	Medium	10%	12%	16%	19%
	Tall	1%	5%	7%	6%
(3) Medium	Short	21%	9%	15%	12%
	Medium	21%	20%	23%	23%
	Tall	5%	7%	10%	7%
(4) Full	Short	14%	7%	5%	5%
	Medium	15%	14%	8%	9%
	Tall	3%	4%	5%	3%
(5) Large	Short	—	2%	—	—
	Medium	—	5%	—	—
	Tall	—	1%	—	—
(6) Extra large	Short	—	—	—	—
	Medium	—	1%	—	—
	Tall	—	—	—	—
Totals:		100%	98%	100%	95%

17

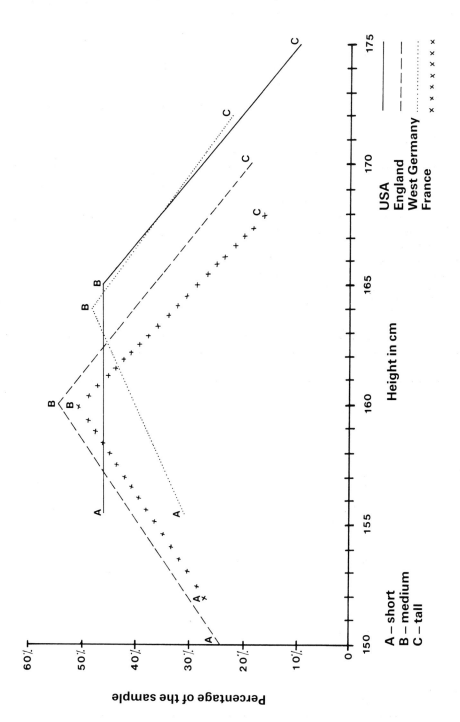

Fig. 2.6. The distribution of height groups.

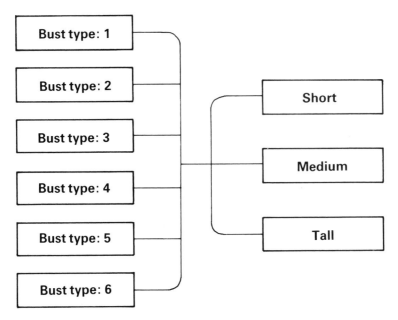

Fig. 2.7. Bust types and height groups.

relationships over the three height groups is shown in Table 2.3.

The distribution in Table 2.3, irrespective of height groups, is shown in Fig. 2.8, and it is of interest to note that the medium bust type represents the largest single category, viz:

USA:	47 % of total
England:	36 % of total
West Germany:	48 % of total
France:	42 % of total

This fact justifies the general approach of the clothing industry, which is to produce one bust type only for each height group. Therefore, the tables showing stature and bust type distributions lead to the following conclusions regarding sizing systems:

(1) It would be economically impossible to produce garments for every size range and bust type and to ensure their correct distribution throughout a given population.
(2) The most practical sizing systems which would suit the largest proportion of the population is that where:
  (a) Three stature groups are used.
  (b) The garment proportions are based on the medium bust category.
  (c) The grading system employed ensures that

these proportions are maintained throughout each size range.

There are also some other pertinent considerations:

• The clothing industry is concerned with mass produced clothing and accepts the fact that garment fittings will differ slightly due to cutting, sewing and pressing inaccuracies.
• Most garments have an ease allowance over and above the body measurements for which the garment is intended. This ease, plus the normal manufacturing tolerances make small size intervals unnecessary.
• Therefore, it could be expected that the best fitting quality of the garment would be shown when there is a perfect relationship between the customer's measurements and proportions and those of the garment. It is quite reasonable, however, that women with slightly larger or smaller bust girths could all wear the same garment without substantially detracting from its overall appearance.
• Garments, like individuals, are not always identical and customers are willing to accept some variations in fitting. Consequently, the range of women with varying bust types that can also be adequately fitted by one bust girth is considerably increased.
• The same system of pattern grading can be applied to any height group because the proportions of the girth measurements are not affected to any appreciable degree by the difference in stature.

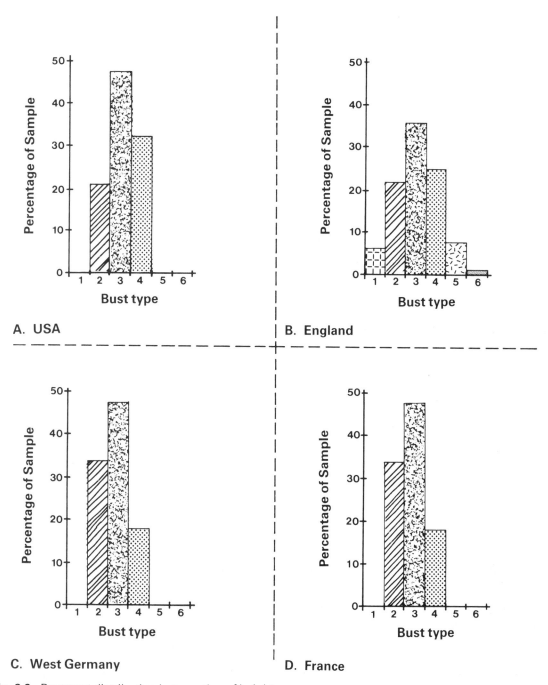

Fig. 2.8. Bust type distribution irrespective of height.

TO SUM UP

From an industrial and commercial point of view, an effective sizing system must cover the largest number of women with the smallest number of sizes. Therefore, some practical compromises are necessary in order to maintain a viable balance between the degree of fitting quality and price levels.

Chapter 3

System Development

The development of the body grade

THE BACK AND FRONT

The finalised size charts of the surveys provided the basic data for developing the body grade and this information was analysed in order to determine the common factors of measurement changes between all of the surveys. The procedure followed was:

(1) The bust girth size interval of each size chart was used as the basis for all comparative calculations. The intervals were 5 cm for the USA and England and 4 cm for West Germany and France. In all cases, the bust, waist and hip girths changed by the same amount.

(2) All of the measurements which related to the body grade were extracted from each chart and the amounts by which they changed in relation to the bust girth interval was calculated. This change was expressed as a percentage of the particular bust girth interval used, as per the following example.

England
Bust girth interval: 5.0 cm
Average across back interval: 1.14 cm
Percentage of change: $\dfrac{1.14\,\text{cm}}{5.0\,\text{cm}} = 22.8\%$

(3) The geometric average of the percentage of change obtained for the same measurement from each chart was then calculated. Where necessary, the results were rounded off or modified according to practical and/or commercial criteria.

Some measurements, such as front neck to bust point and front neck to front waist required a different type

Table 3.1. Analysis of survey measurements

Notation and measurement	Percentage of bust girth size interval					Percentage of body grade
	USA	England	West Germany	France	Average of surveys	Rounded off or modified
A Bust, waist & hip girths	100%	100%	100%	100%	100%	100%
C Bust arc anterior	62.6%	62.6%	—	—	62.6%	62.5%
D Across back	25%	22.8%	25%	27.5%	24.9%	25%
4F Neck base girth	16.9%	15%	17.5%	27.5%	18.68%	25%
G Shoulder length	3.6%	3.9%	2.5%	Static	3.27%	12.5%
I Width of bust prominence	12.6%	17.5%	—	21.5%	16.79%	25%
K Back neck to waist	Dynamic	Static	Static (1983 Dynamic)	Static	According to National size charts	
K Function of armhole depth	12.5%	20%	—	—	15.81%	25%
K Part function of front neck to bust point level	20.5%	23%	24.2%	23.1%	22.66%	25%
L Part function of front neck to bust point level	11%	10.8%	12.4%	—	11.37%	12.5%
M Function of overall front length of waist (L + K)	31.5%	33.8%	36.6%	—	33.96%	37.5%
N Waist to hip	—	8.66%	—	—	—	12.5%

A = Half of size interval.

of calculation because each survey used a different method and datum for obtaining the measurements. In these two instances, the changes were calculated trigometrically and then expressed in percentages. The results of this analysis are shown in Table 3.1 and the increment notation will be used throughout this book.

The system development is divided into two main groups of grades.
Group 1: The Primary and Secondary Girth Grades.
Group 2: The Primary and Secondary Length Grades.

GROUP 1: THE PRIMARY AND SECONDARY DIVISIONS OF GIRTH

Prime divisions of girth
Table 3.2 annotates and describes all of the width divisions and their locations are shown in Fig. 3.1.

Table 3.2

Notation	Girth increments
A	Total pattern grade: from centre front to centre back
B	Total grade of back: from centre back to side seam
C	Total grade of front: from centre front to side seam
D	Across back: from centre back to armhole
E	Side section of front or back
F	Front or back neck width
G	Length of front or back shoulder
H	Width of breast: from centre front to front armhole on bustline
I	Centre front to bust point
J	Bust point to front armhole
I_1	Front side of bust dart
J_1	Armhole side of bust dart

(1) Size intervals may vary from country to country or from size range to size range, but it is widely accepted that the three major girths of bust, waist and hips all change by the same amount. Half of this amount is always equal to the total pattern grade and is notated A. For example, if the size interval was 4 cm, then the total grade of A = 2 cm or 20 mm.
(2) The amount A can be subdivided into three main sections (Fig. 3.1) front, side and back where;
   (a) The back section D, is equivalent to the across back.
   (b) The front section H, is equivalent to the width of the breast.
   (c) The side section 2E, is equivalent to the girth section remaining between the outer limits of D and H and is in effect, also the armhole

width. Thus, at this stage, assuming that the side seam is in the centre of the side section, and that one-half of the side section is equivalent to E then the basic calculation is (Fig. 3.3):

Total grade of back   B = across back plus half of side section
or: B = D + E
Total grade of front   C = width of breast plus half of side section
or: C = H + E
Total pattern grade of   A = B + C

(It should be noted that the actual position of the side seam can vary from garment to garment. Therefore, the total grade increment of 2E would be applied proportionately to the side sections of the front and back.) For the purposes of consistency during this development, it is assumed that the side seam is the centre of the side section.

Side section grade E
(1) The bust arc anterior includes the front side section E, and is equal to 62.5% of A.
(2) Therefore, the remaining girth of the back is equal to: 100% − 62.5% = 37.5%
(3) The across back is equal to 25% of A. Therefore the side section of the back E is equal to: 37.5% − 25% = 12.5%
(4) As the back and front side sections are the same, then the grade for the front side section E is also 12.5%.

To summarise this first stage:
(a) The front grade C is 62.5% of the total width grade.
(b) The back grade B is 37.5% of the total width grade.
(c) The difference between the amounts of these two grades is as a result of the development of the body when the girth measurements increase. This disproportionate growth in relation to an imaginary line drawn vertically through the centre of the side section is shown in Fig. 3.4.
(d) The proportions of the primary width divisions in relation to the total pattern grade of A (100%) have now been established as being:

The back:
Total back grade: B = 37.5%
– Across back   D = 25.0%
– Side section   E = 12.5%
The front:
Total front grade: C = 62.5%

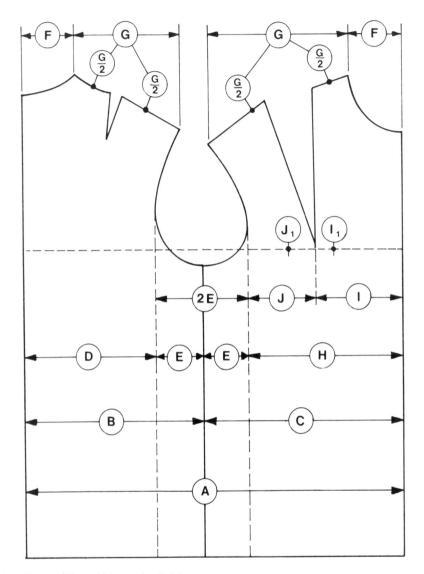

Fig. 3.1. The locations of the width grade divisions.

– Across chest   H = 50.0%
– Side section   E = 12.5%

The secondary divisions of girth

The subdivisions of the girth grade were derived from the following considerations:

(1) What are the subdivisions of the back and front?
(2) What grading increments are applied to these subdivisions?
(3) Which of the subdivision increments are common to both the back and the front?

Subdivisions of the back

The total back width grade B is equal to the across back

grade D, plus the side section grade E. The increment D can be further sub-divided into two sections:

Section 1: From the centre back to a line drawn vertically down from the back neck point.
Section 2: From the back neck point line to a line drawn vertically down from the armhole at the level of the across back line.

Section 1

This section is in effect the width of the back neck base and the average change in neck base girth according to the surveys is 18.6% of the size interval. For practical purposes, this has been increased to 25% due to the following reasons:

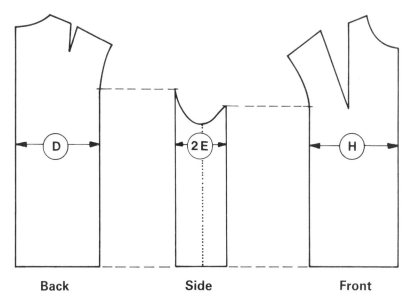

Back   Side   Front

Fig. 3.2. The basic divisions of girth.

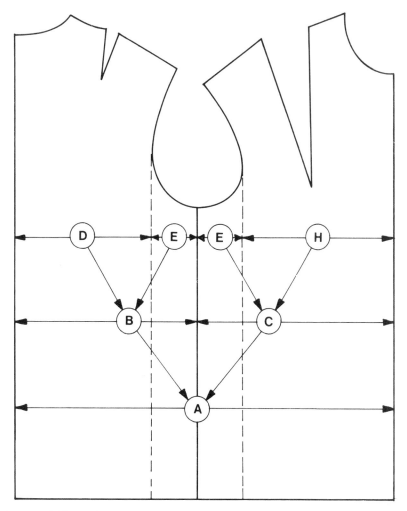

Fig. 3.3. The primary width grades.

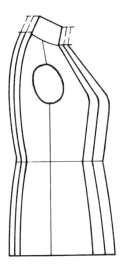

Fig. 3.4. The proportions of growth.

(1) The increase from 18.6% to 25% is equivalent to 2.5 mm for a 4 cm size interval and this amount would have little or no practical relevance on garments which have open types of collars and lapels.
(2) This also holds true for the majority of garments with closed necks. In the event that the neck girth grade requires absolute accuracy, then the adjustments are of a very simple nature.
(3) The calculation of the neck grade is simplified.

For grading purposes, the neck base girth can be considered to be comprised of four width sections, two on the back and two on the front (Fig. 3.5). Therefore, the back neck base width grade on a pattern would be equal to $\frac{1}{4}$ of the total neck grade. This is equivalent to 12.5% of the total width grade and the notation for this increment is F (Fig. 3.6).

Section 2

Having established that one subdivision of D is the increment F, it follows that the remaining subdivision must be graded by an increment which is equal to D − F (Fig. 3.6). This increment would be equivalent to 12.5% of the body grade and would obviously be applied to the shoulder length. However, this calculation (12.5%) is not borne out by the survey's average figure of 9% for the change in shoulder length and as a consequence, some practical aspects must be considered.

(1) For a 4 cm size interval, the difference between 9% and 12% is equal to 0.7 mm in shoulder length.
(2) The most logical method of maintaining the constructional relationship between the across back and back shoulder is to ensure that relative to the centre back, they both change by the same amount (Fig. 3.7). This would also apply to the relationship between the across chest and front shoulder, relative to the centre front.
(3) A pattern graded according to the survey's figure of 9% would require 'cosmetic treatment' in order

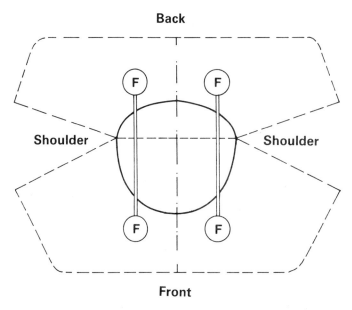

Fig. 3.5. Neck base divisions.

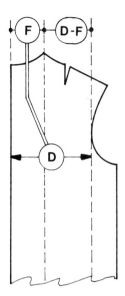

Fig. 3.6. The sub-divisions of increment D.

to retain the correct armhole to shoulder line.
(4) The calculation of the shoulder length grade is simplified.

Therefore, for all practical purposes, the shoulder length grade is equivalent to 12.5% of the body grade, and the notation for this increment is G.

To sum up the subdivisions of the back (Fig. 3.8) where increment G is divided equally on either side of the shoulder dart and notated G/2.

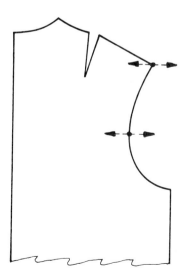

Fig. 3.7. Shoulder point and across-back relationship.

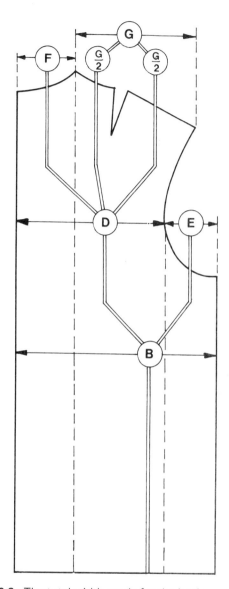

Fig. 3.8. The total width grade for the back.

(1) The total width grade of the back is B and this amount is equal to the total of F + G + E where F + G = D, the across back grade.
(2) F, G and E are each equal to 12.5% of the total width grade.

Subdivisions of the front
It is has been established that the total front width grade C is 62.5% of the total body grade. This amount in part, is comprised of those increments which are common to both the back and the front (Fig. 3.9), and these are:

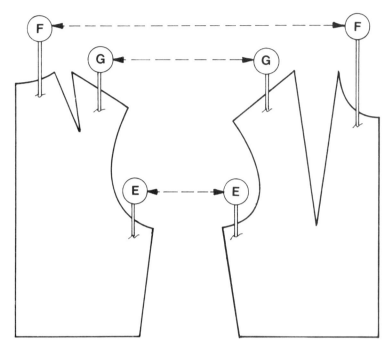

Fig. 3.9. Grading increments common to the back and front.

F Neck base grade: 12.5% of the total body grade.

G Shoulder length grade: 12.5% of the total body grade.

E Side section grade: 12.5% of the total body grade.

Together these increments total 37.5%. Therefore, the additional girth increments required are those that are equal to 62.5% minus 37.5% which is equivalent to 25% of the total body grade.

This amount of 25% is the quantity by which the front width grade of C is greater than the back width grade of B. In order to allocate this amount, the figures given by the surveys for the width of bust prominence (47) must be evaluated according to practical criteria. These figures, as a percentage of the size interval are:

USA: 12.6%
England: 17.5%
France: 21.5%

and they have an average value of 16.8% (no value is given in the West German survey).

As can be seen, these figures are very inconsistent when compared with each other and do not provide an accurate basis for determining the allocation of the amount in question. Therefore, in order to maintain the simplicity of calculation and application, this amount of 25% is allocated equally on either side of the bust point (Fig. 3.10) and the notation is:

I_1 = 12.5%   From nothing at the shoulder, and applied in full from the bust line down, between the centre front and bust point — Section I.

J_1 = 12.5%   From nothing at the shoulder, and applied in full from the bust line

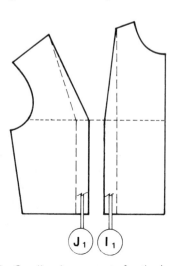

Fig. 3.10. Grading increments for the bust dart.

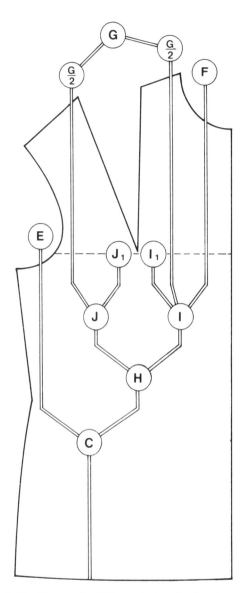

Fig. 3.11. The total width grade for the front.

down, between the bust point and armhole — Section J.

The allocation of grading increments for the front can be summarised as follows, with increment G equally divided between the two parts of the front shoulder and notated G/2 (Fig. 3.11).

C   Total width $= H + E$
H   Width of breast $= C - E$
I   Centre front to bust point $= F + G/2 + I_1$
J   Bust point to armhole $= J_1 + G/2$
E   Side section $= C - H$

The method of determining the primary and secondary grading increments for the width is given in Table 3.3 and the locations of these increments are shown in Fig. 3.12.

Table 3.3. The grades girth

Letter	Section	Percentage of size interval
A	Total pattern grade	100.0%
B	Total back	37.5%
C	Total front	62.5%
D	Across back	25.0%
E	Back & front side sections	12.5%
F	Back & front neck widths	12.5%
G	Back & front shoulder lengths	12.5%
H	Width of breast	50.0%
I	Centre front to bust point	25% + G/2
I_1	Half of bust increment	12.5%
J	Bust point or armhole	12.5% + G/2
J_1	Half of bust increment	12.5%

GROUP 2: THE PRIME AND SECONDARY DIVISIONS OF LENGTH

The prime divisions
This group of divisions is concerned with the changes in length between the girth lines and the garment length itself and the sections involved are:

(1) Back neck line to waist
(2) Front neck point to bust line
(3) Depth of armhole
(4) Armhole base to waistline at side (trunk line)
(5) Waist to hip
(6) Garment length

Neck to waist
According to the size charts issued by the surveys, there are two different methods to consider:

(1) Static neck to waist: when the sizing system is based on three different height groups, then the neck to waist is static for all of the sizes within the particular height group. Table 3.4, taken from the West German survey, is an example of this system.
(2) Dynamic neck to waist: when the sizing system is based on different height groups, but the neck to waist changes from size to size within the group. The USA survey measurement chart (Table 3.5) is an example of this type of system.

There is also also a third system to consider, which

28

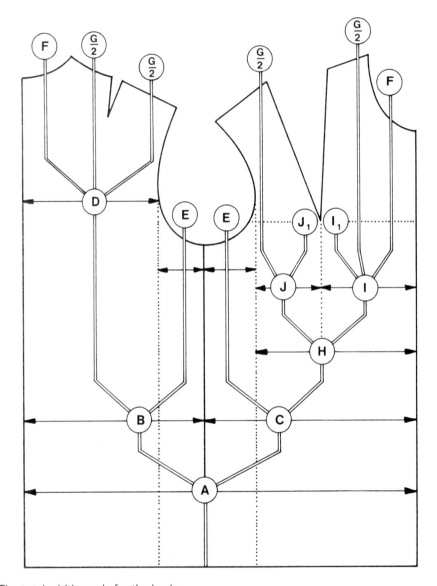

Fig. 3.12. The total width grade for the body.

Table 3.4. West Germany (1973): static within each height group

Height group	Short					Medium					Tall				
Size	18	19	20	21	22	36	38	40	42	44	72	76	80	84	88
Neck to waist	38	38	38	38	38	40	40	40	40	40	42	42	42	42	42

Table 3.5. USA: dynamic within each height group

Height group	Short					Regular					Tall				
Size	8S	10S	12S	14S	16S	30R	32R	34R	36R	38R	10T	12T	14T	16T	18T
Neck to waist	36	36.3	36.9	37.2	37.8	39.4	39.7	40.3	40.6	41.2	41	41.6	41.9	42.5	43.1

although not included in the surveys examined, provides an example of a dynamic neck to waist based on one height group only. The following chart (Table 3.6) is an extract from a survey conducted by the Dutch Clothing Manufacturers Association. These three systems are compared graphically in Fig. 3.13.

The factors which are common to all of these methods are the changes in armhole depth, bust point

Table 3.6. Holland: dynamic for all heights

	One height only								
Size	34	36	38	40	42	44	46	48	50
Neck to waist	38	38.5	39	39.5	40	40.5	41	41.5	42

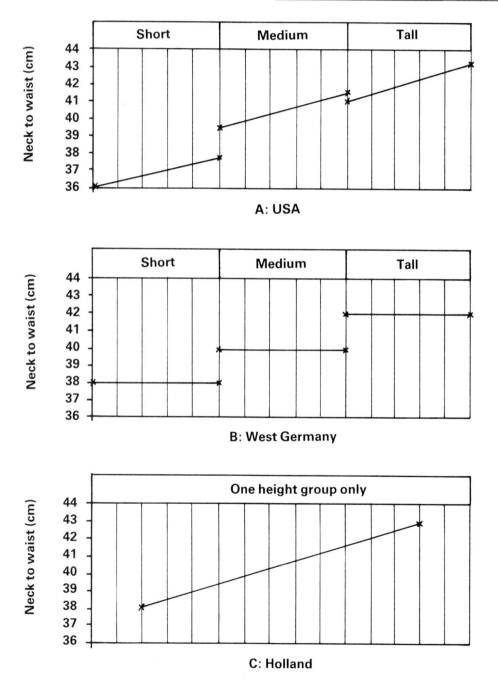

Fig. 3.13. Neck to waist sizing systems compared.

level and the length from the front neck point to the bust line. Each of the surveys had a different method of establishing these increments, but after calculating their values, they showed a marked similarity and the following facts emerged:

(1) For practical purposes, the armhole depth and bust point level change by the same amounts and the notation for this increment is K.
(2) The distance from the bust line to the front neck point changes by an additional amount and the notation for this increment is L.
(3) Thus the total change in length from the front neck point to the bust line is equal to K plus L, which is notated as increment M.

The separate and combined applications of K and L to each of the two neck to waist grading methods produces the following results:

Method 1: The Static Neck to Waist Grade

(1) The back neck to waist length remains unchanged for all sizes within the particular height range.
(2) The length from the front neck point to the bust line changes from size to size by increment L.
(3) The depth of the front and back armhole changes by increment K, from size to size. As this increment is applied between the base of the armhole and the waist line (the trunk line), the length of this section *changes* from size to size.
(4) The length from the front neck point to the waistline changes by K + L, which is increment M.

These applications are shown in Fig. 3.14.

Method 2: The Dynamic Neck to Waist Grade

(1) The back neck to waist length changes from size to size by increment K.

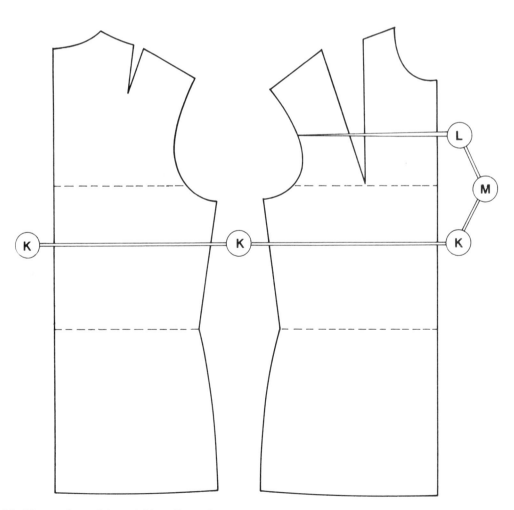

Fig. 3.14. The static neck to waist length grade.

(2) The depth of the front and back armhole changes from size to size by increment K. As this increment is applied through the armhole, the length between the base of the armhole and the waistline remains *static* for all sizes.

(3) The overall length from the front neck point to the front waist changes by increment M (K + L).

(4) The length from the front neck point to the bustline changes by increment M. Thus, the distance from the bustline to the waistline remains *static* for all sizes. The applications of these increments are shown in Fig. 3.15.

With both methods, the armhole depth is changed by increment K and the length from the front neck point to the bustline changes by increment M. The basic difference between the two methods is the application of M to the front. When using Method 1 (static), increment M is applied in two parts — K and L. On the other hand, increment M is applied as a single unit when grading according to Method 2 (dynamic). Example grades using both of these methods are demonstrated in Chapter 5 of this book.

Waist to hip
Generally speaking, this change can be disregarded for the great majority of garments. In the event that a style feature in this area needs to be graded, then the increment is notated N.

Garment length
This is usually according to customers' requirements, but the principles involved are:

(1) Static neck to waist: generally there is no change in length for all of the sizes within a particular height group size range.

(2) Dynamic neck to waist: when the required change

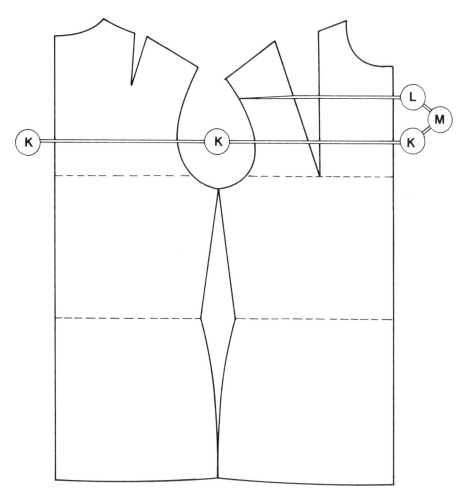

Fig. 3.15. The dynamic neck to waist length grade.

in length is greater than that caused by the application of increment K, then increment O can be applied between the hip line and the hem line of the garment. When using increments N and O, their totals must be offset against the total length grade required.

Table 3.7 summarises the width and length increments for the most generally used size intervals and their applications as shown in Figs 3.16 and 3.17.

The 6 cm size interval is very often used in Europe and Scandinavia for the grading of outsize garments. Due to the outsize figure type (somatotype), the shoulder length grade increment G is smaller than that arrived at by using the standard calculation, i.e. 2.5 mm instead of 3.75 mm. Other increments have been rounded off to simplify their applications.

TO SUM UP

The first part of this chapter has examined how the girth and length grading increments for the body have been determined according to the data provided by the four surveys. The resultant increments and their applications now provide the foundations for deriving the grades of other basic components.

The development of derived grades

The grades for the basic sleeve, collar and facing are all derived from parts of the body grade and as a result, the grading increments developed for the body sections are also applied to these related components. This principle ensures that the system is integrative, and that the changes made to a particular section of the body pattern are accurately transferred to the relevant matching part. The relationships are those between:

> The armhole and sleeve head;
> The neck base and collar length;
> The forepart and facing.

The first component to be examined is the basic one-piece sleeve.

THE BASIC SLEEVE

The grading relationship between the width of the armhole and sleeve head is shown in Fig. 3.18 where increment E is the side section grade for the front and back, whilst increment K is the armhole depth grade. These increments are applied to the sleeve are described below.

Table 3.7. The body grades

Notation	Pattern section	Size interval		
		4.0 cm (1.5 inches)	5.0 cm (2.0 inches)	6.0 cm (2.4 inches)
A	Total pattern grade	20.0	25.0	30.0
B	Total back	7.5	9.0	11.0
C	Total front	12.5	16.0	19.0
D	Across back	5.0	6.0	7.0
E	Back and front side sections	2.5	3.0	4.0
F	Back and front neck widths	2.5	3.0	3.5
G	Back and front shoulder lengths	2.5	3.0	2.5
H	Width of breast	10.0	13.0	15.0
I	Centre front to bust point (on bust line)	6.25	8.0	9.0
I_1	Half of bust increment	2.5	3.5	4.0
J	Bust point to armhole (on bust line)	3.75	5.0	6.0
J_1	Half of bust increment	2.5	3.5	4.0
K	Back neck to waist – armhole Depth – part of bust line height	5.0	6.0	7.0
L	Part of front neck point to bustline	2.5	3.0	3.5
M	Front neck point to bustline (K + L)	7.5	9.0	10.5
N	Waist to hip (when required)	2.5	3.0	3.5
O	Garment length (when required)	As per size chart		

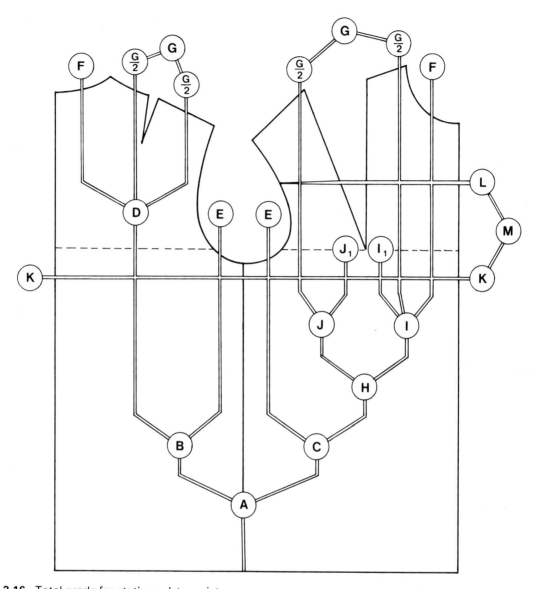

Fig. 3.16. Total grade for static neck to waist.

THE WIDTH GRADE

The sleeve width can be considered to be comprised of two main sections and four subsections, and this division is based on a line drawn vertically down through the true centre of the sleeve. This line marks the division between the front and back sleeve, and when these two main sections are divided in half, then the sub-width sections are:

Section 1: Front undersleeve
Section 2: Front top sleeve

Section 3: Back top sleeve
Section 4: Back undersleeve

The lines dividing sections 1 and 2 of the front sleeve and sections 3 and 4 of the back sleeve effectively divide each half of the sleeve into two sections of equal width (Fig. 3.19a). As this width relationship must be maintained, i.e. between the undersleeve and top sleeve sections of the sleeve half, the same increment is used to grade all four subsections of the sleeve. This is increment E, and therefore the total width grade for the sleeve is 4E, which is equal to 25% of the size interval. Each of the four surveys gives this amount,

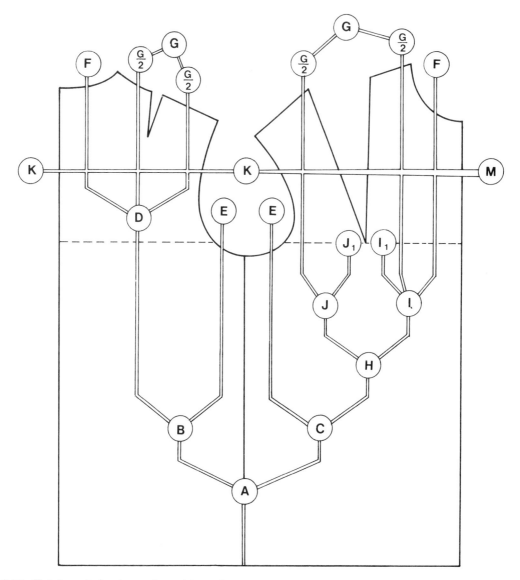

Fig. 3.17. Total grade for dynamic neck to waist.

25%, as the average change in upper arm girth relative to the size interval (Fig. 3.19b).

Where the true centre line of the sleeve is displaced to the front or back, then the proportions of increment E applied to each section are those as determined by the proportions of the side section grades. It has been established that the total width grade of the side section of the body is 2E and if the side seam is in the centre of the side section then the back and front side sections would each be graded by E. In the event that the garment side seam is displaced to the back or front, then there would be two different values for increment E, one for the back sleeve sections and another for those of the front sleeve. For example, if the side seam is displaced to the back and the division of the body side section is 40% back and 60% front, then increment E for the back sleeve sections would be 40% of 2E whilst that for the front sleeve sections is 60% of 2E. Therefore, if the total grade for the body side section is say, 5 mm, then the allocation would be:

E   For the back sleeve sections = 40% of 5 mm = 2 mm

E   For the front sleeve sections = 60% of 5 mm = 3 mm

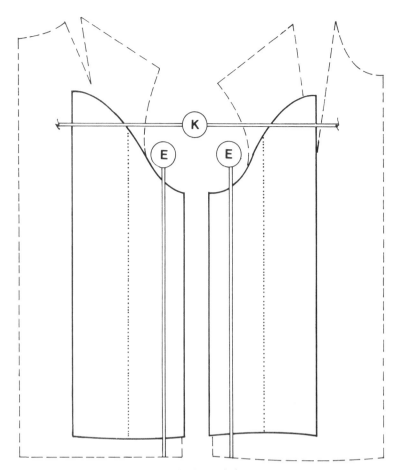

Fig. 3.18. Grading relationship between the armhole and sleeve.

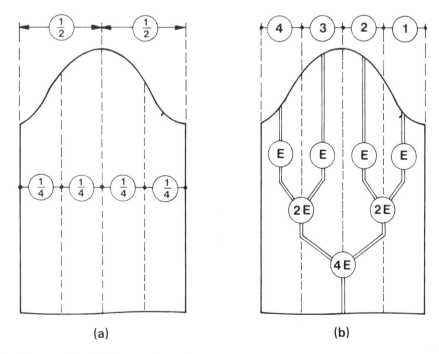

(a)   (b)

Fig. 3.19. The sleeve width divisions and grades.

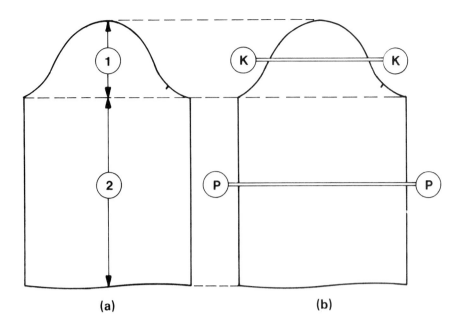

(a)   (b)

Fig. 3.20. The sleeve length divisions and grades.

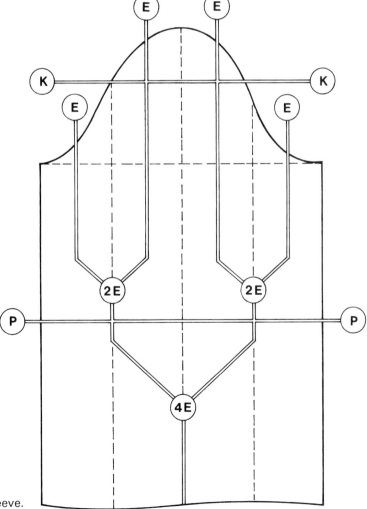

Fig. 3.21. Total grade for straight sleeve.

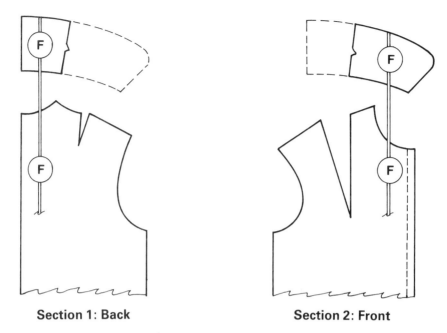

Section 1: Back　　　**Section 2: Front**

Fig. 3.22. The collar length divisions.

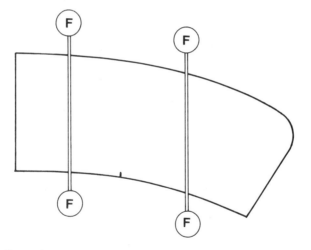

Fig. 3.23. The collar length grade.

The principle involved here is that the total muscle girth grade will always be equal to 4E irrespective of the width relationship between the back and front sections of the sleeve. First and foremost, the value of increment E for each half of the sleeve is determined by the value used to grade the related side section of the body.

THE SLEEVE LENGTH GRADE

Changes in the length of the sleeves occur in two sections (Fig. 3.20a).

Section 1: Between the highest point of the crown to the sleeve head base.
Section 2: Between the sleeve head base to the cuff of the sleeve.

The head height of the sleeve. Section 1, is directly related to the depth of the armhole. Therefore as increment K is used to grade armhole depth, it would also be applied to the head of the sleeve. There are also two other factors which influence the sleeve length grade.

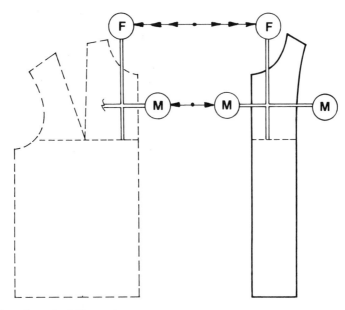

Fig. 3.24. The facing length and width grades.

Static neck to waist grading

Usually the overall sleeve length remains unchanged for all of the sizes within a particular height group. In practice, this means that whatever length change occurs in Section 1 must be counteracted by a corresponding change in Section 2. The guiding principle in this situation is:

(1) If the length of Section 1 is increased, then the length of Section 2 is decreased.
(2) If the length of Section 1 is decreased, then the length of Section 2 is increased.

In both instances, increment P (Fig. 3.20b) which is located on the elbow line of the sleeve, is used to grade Section 2 of the sleeve, and the value of this increment would always be equal to that of increment K. Using the same value for both K and P ensures that the overall sleeve length remains unchanged for one height group.

Dynamic neck to waist grading

The change in the overall length of the sleeve caused through the application of increment K to the sleeve head is generally considered to be an adequate length change from size to size. In the event that the sleeve length change is larger or smaller than increment K, then the difference can be applied through increment P. In this case, the value of increment P would be equal to the overall length change required minus the value of increment K. For example, given that the value of K is 5 mm and the overall sleeve length change is 12 mm,

then the value of P would be 7 mm. Alternatively, if K is equal to 6 mm and the overall length change is 3 mm per size, then the value of P would be 3 mm.

In these two situations, the application of increment P to Section 2 of the sleeve is governed by the following rules:

Rule 1: Where the overall length change is greater than increment K, then when:
Grading up: the length of Section 2 is increased by P.

Rule 2: Where the overall length change is smaller than increment K, then when:
Grading up: the length of Section 2 is decreased by P.
Grading down: the length of Section 2 is increased by P.

The locations and values of the increments used for grading the basic sleeve are shown in Fig. 3.21 and this is the master grade format for all other types of straight sleeves.

THE BASIC COLLAR

The only grade required for the basic collar is a length grade, and the increments are derived from those for the back and front neck base sections. This type of collar can be divided into two sections of length (Fig. 3.22).

Section 1: From the centre back to the point on the neck seam which matches the centre of the shoulder, usually the shoulder seam. The length of this section is directly related to the back neck width, which is graded by increment F. Therefore, this section of the collar is graded by the same increment.

Section 2: This is the length from the shoulder seam to the front edge of the collar. As this length is related to the front neck width, then the same increment F, would apply.

Thus, a basic collar of this type changes in length by 2F for each size, and by doing so, maintains its original relationship with the neck sections of the garment (Fig. 3.23).

THE BASIC FACING

The length and width grades of the facing are derived from those used for the relevant section of the front, namely increments F and M.

Increment F. This is applied to the facing neck width in the same way as the front and it is applied from the neck line down to the bust line. There are no practical reasons to change the width of the facing below this line.

Increment M. This is applied to the length section of the facing between the shoulder line and bust line. During grading, the overall length of the facing should be adjusted by the same amounts as those used for the garment length. The grades for the basic facing are shown in Fig. 3.24.

TO SUM UP

The grading of sleeves, collars and facings is determined by the increments applied to the respective matching parts of the body. Thus the initial calculation of the body grade increments automatically provides the increments for grading the derived components.

Chapter 4

Introduction to Grading

General principles

The approach and working method of the system demonstrated in Chapters 5 and 6 is based on manual grading either with, or without, the use of a mechanical grading machine. In doing so, this book sets out the fundamentals of the craft of grading without which, there can be no genuine understanding of the principles and criteria involved. Whilst computerised grading technology is becoming more and more widely used, the quality of the output of any system is still primarily dictated by the quality of the input. Therefore, knowing what to do, how to define it and how to verify it is a prerequisite for the effective operation of sophisticated technology.

Pattern grading is a technique used to increase or decrease the size of a garment pattern according to the measurements in a given size chart. Both before and during this process, there are some general principles which must be applied in order to achieve the optimum results.

PATTERN AND GRADE DEVELOPMENT

The dynamics of fashion necessitates the continual development of new styles, with each of these styles requiring a different pattern. Whilst the number of style and pattern variations are seemingly endless, all of the patterns have one principle in common, which is that nearly all of the major components are derived from basic block patterns. In other words, there is a direct relationship between a garment pattern and the block pattern which was used as a basis for developing the pattern. This relationship also applies to the grading of garment patterns.

The grading network for a block pattern is also the basic network for the components which have been developed from the block pattern. As a result, the application of the network can be considered to parallel the process of developing a styled component such as the jacket back shown in Fig. 4.1.

Obviously, there are many techniques involved in the grading of garment patterns but they all have one common principle: The Basic Grade.

THE GRADING SYSTEM

The system which is demonstrated in the following chapter does not relate to one particular sizing system, but rather is capable of being applied to any rational size chart for women's outerwear. The principle of the system lies in the method developed in the previous chapter for calculating and allocating the grading increments for a given size interval. This principle provides the necessary accuracy and versatility required for grading patterns according to the considerable variations in customers' requirements. As an example of these variations, the following table shows some of the size intervals used by different countries (Table 4.1).

Today, the clothing industry supplies markets throughout the world and as a result, a rigid grading

Table 4.1.

| Country | Size intervals used | |
	Regular sizes	Outsizes
USA	4 cm	5 cm
England	5 cm	5 cm
West Germany	4 cm	6 cm
France	4 cm	4 cm
Switzerland	4 cm	6 cm
Holland	4 cm	8 cm
Canada	4 cm	5 cm
Australia	5 cm	5 cm

Example size chart no.1
(all measurements in centimetres)

| | Women's sizes | | | | | | | | |
| | Regular range | | | | | Outsize range | | | |
Sizes	A	B	C	D	E	F	G	H	I	J
Bust	80	85	90	95	100	105	110	115	120	125
Waist	60	65	70	75	80	85	90	95	100	105
Hips	85	90	95	100	105	110	115	120	125	130

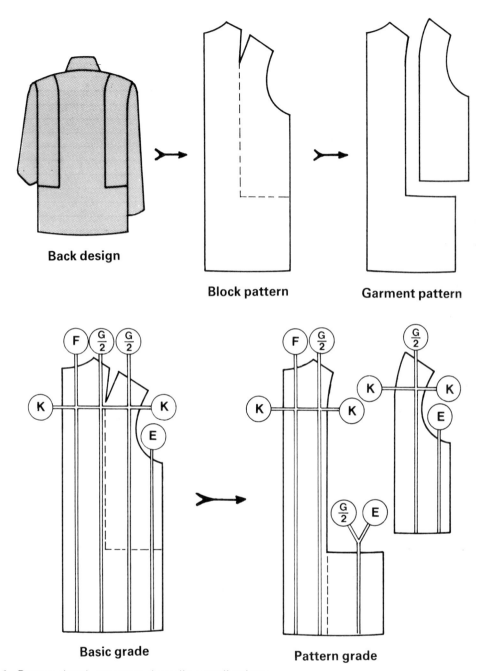

Back design

Block pattern

Garment pattern

Basic grade

Pattern grade

Fig. 4.1. Pattern development and grading applications.

system built around one size chart and one size interval has a very limited value.

SIZE RANGES

This term refers to the differences in the major girth measurements between the smallest and largest size in

the size chart. For example, the following size chart (No. 1) contains a range of women's sizes where the total girth span is 45 cm and shows the typical division of a size range into two sub-groups: regular and outsizes.

This division is dictated by the differences in the figurations and proportions between the two body types and it would be a fallacy to assume that a woman's regular size could be graded through to an outsize. To perform this correctly, a large amount of pattern manipulation would be involved and this is not a function of grading. In practice, a different block-pattern would be used for each sub-size range and two or three sizes would be graded up and down from the central size for the group.

SIZE INTERVALS

A sizing system is nothing more than the artificial division of the population into size groups according to a pre-determined size interval, i.e. the major girth differences between each size.

Apart from convenience, the size of an interval is basically influenced by the magnitude of the garment measurement tolerances. Consequently, it would be pointless to use an interval smaller than the limits of measuring error for a major girth measurement. For example, a size interval of 1 cm would be capable of being measured on a pattern but in practical terms, it would be very difficult to measure it with the same degree of accuracy on a finished garment.

Therefore if we assume that the range of size variations is in the order of plus or minus 2 cm, then the logical size interval would be 4 cm. In practice, intervals smaller than 4 cm would only result in the use of more sizes for the same range.

SIZE CHARTS

There are two types of size charts in general use:

Type 1: Body measurements
This type of chart provides the body measurements for each size and the pattern maker uses these measurements as a basis for constructing a pattern with the requisite amounts of ease.

Type 2: Garment measurements
This chart details the finished measurements specification for each size and is used for pattern grading and quality control purposes.

The standard components of a size chart are shown in Fig. 4.2.

SIZE CHART CONSISTENCY

The size chart is in effect the grading specification for garment patterns and as such, must be capable of being applied in a systematic fashion to all of the sizes being graded. This situation requires that all of the size intervals in the range should be consistent in all aspects. The practical advantages of a consistent size interval is that it enables the grader to work with standard increments for each size, which makes memorisation easier and performance more efficient. Conversely, inconsistent size intervals introduce unnecessary complications, which could lead to

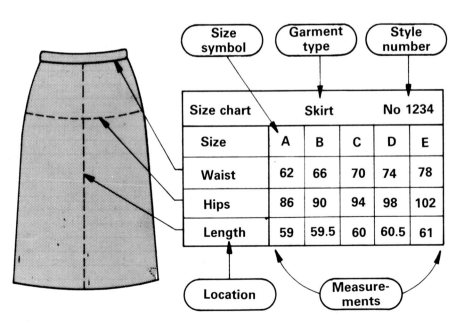

Size chart	Skirt			No 1234	
Size	A	B	C	D	E
Waist	62	66	70	74	78
Hips	86	90	94	98	102
Length	59	59.5	60	60.5	61

Fig. 4.2. The components of a size chart.

possible errors and low performance levels. Therefore, a prior operation in the preparation for grading would involve checking the consistency of the size intervals given in the size chart from which the grader has to follow.

Using the following size chart (No. 2) as an example, the highly important subject of consistency can be developed in more detail.

Example size chart no. 2
(all measurements in centimetres)

Size	A	B	C	D	E	F
Bust girth	84	87	92	97	100	104
Waist girth	62	65	69	72	78	82
Hip girth	94	98	101	106	109	114

On examination of this chart, four factors are readily observable:

(1) There are six sizes in this size range.
(2) There are five intervals between the sizes.
(3) The measurement span for each of the girth measurements is 20 cm.
(4) The size intervals for each girth measurement are inconsistent.

If this size chart was left unaltered, then grading through the sizes would be extremely difficult and involve resorting to all kinds of manipulations in order to achieve the given measurements for each size. Therefore, in order to grade this range of sizes in a systematic fashion, the size intervals inconsistencies would firstly have to be levelled out.

The procedure for levelling is to take the girth measurement span, e.g. 20 cm and divide it by the number of size intervals, in this case five. This would produce a size interval factor of 4 cm and the resultant levelled size chart (No. 3) would be:

Levelled size chart (no. 3)
(all measurements in centimetres)

Size	A	B	C	D	E	F
Bust girth	84	88	92	96	100	104
Waist girth	62	66	70	74	78	82
Hip girth	94	98	102	106	110	114

which now provides for a consistent grade of 4 cm between all of the sizes. However, this consistency has not been achieved without some changes, and the

question is how material are these changes in practical terms?

Firstly, the basic parameters of the original size chart have been left unchanged, i.e. six sizes, five intervals and the girth measurement spans of 20 cm. What has happened is that from the total of 18 given measurements 11 have remained unchanged and seven have changed as follows:

Five: Increased by 1 cm
One: Increased by 2 cm
One: Decreased by 1 cm

It could reasonably be expected that the ease allowances combined with making up tolerances would absorb the differences, although the differences in waist measurements if the garment was close fitting might cause a slight problem. In this situation some common sense must be used in order to decide whether these differences can be safely disregarded or some compromise is necessary. This usually means the 'doctoring' of graded patterns, and in these circumstances the golden rule is to grade to one consistent girth interval, preferably the bust girth, and alter the other measurements accordingly.

From a practical point of view, size interval levelling is a prerequisite of efficient grading and it would pay to remember that there are a multiplicity of size charts in circulation and the most consistent factor about them is their inconsistency.

MEASUREMENTS

The measurements given for a size represent the average measurements of a woman having a particular bust or hip girth, and this combination is denoted by size symbol. These measurements usually refer to main girths, girth divisions and length but do not always provide the detail necessary for accurate grading. Therefore, a grading system must automatically provide efficient and accurate answers not only for the given measurements, but also for those which are not given.

A 'short-cut' grading system which is dedicated to producing patterns in the shortest time possible will never provide a comparable level of fitting quality as that of a system which incorporates the relevant major and minor anthropometric detail in all of its applications.

NOMENCLATURE

A size is a combination of measurements and each combination is designated by a symbol which is a common 'code' between the manufacturer and the consumer. These symbols are alphabetical and/or

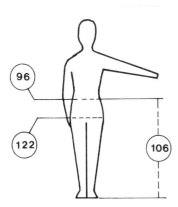

Fig. 4.3. ISO pictogram for ladies' trousers.

numeric, and for the consumer the size symbol provides instant recognition as to whether the garment size is suitable or not.

Over the years, many countries have developed their own systems of size symbols, but for the consumer the situation becomes problematic when faced with foreign size symbols. It is now recognised that in view of the world trade in clothing, an international system of size designation is essential. To this end, the International Standards Organisation (ISO) has issued a draft standard (TC/133) which provides:

(1) Definitions and measurement procedures.
(2) A system of designating the sizes of women's and girls' outwear, other than knitted garments.

In essence, these drafts recognise the fact that the simplest and most effective form of size coding is to provide the garment with a readily understandable label or ticket showing the basic body measurements for which the garment is intended to fit. The recommended symbol is a pictogram (Fig. 4.3), which indicates the position on the body of the relevant measurements. The size designation system is based on body measurements only and finished garment measurements are left to the manufacturer, who is concerned with style, cut and other fashion elements.

At the time of writing, these and other standards concerned with sizing systems are the subject of international discussion, and it is hoped that for the benefit of all concerned, they will be finalised and implemented as soon as possible.

Practical principles

The practise of grading is concerned with producing dimensionally accurate patterns efficiently, and in order to do so, some basic rules must be observed.

AXES

The final result of grading a pattern is, in effect, a reconstructed version of the original pattern in another size. It would therefore follow that this process of reconstruction should be based on the same lines as those which were employed to construct the original pattern.

Nearly every pattern construction system uses, as its basic framework, a rectangle divided in the length and width by lines at right angles to each other (Fig. 4.4). Consequently, the movement of patterns during grading must follow the same network of lines in order to ensure accurate alignment throughout the range of sizes being graded. These construction lines provide the axes for grading and they are determined in the following way:

The X axis: for body and skirt grades, this would be a line on, or parallel to, the centre back or centre front. The X axis for other grades can be established from the true, straight grain direction.
The Y axis: a line on, or parallel to, a major girth line such as the bust, waist or hip.

Irrespective of how the axes are determined, they are always at right angles to each other.

As a result, the preparation for grading would require the marking of grading axes on each pattern, component and the positioning of the pattern in the most convenient position for grading. For most components, a single X axis would be sufficient for the origin of the width grades whilst it might be necessary to have a number of Y axes for the length grades. Usually the original X and Y axes are common to all the sizes graded from one particular component. These principles are shown in Fig. 4.5 where the pattern is positioned for a right-handed grader.

For practical purposes it is more convenient to grade a pattern component when its length is parallel to the edge of the work table and where the pattern is positioned close enough to the grader to ensure a clear slight of all marks, etc. Where there is a fair amount of detailed grading in one area of a component, this area should be closest to the marking hand of the grader so as to eliminate the awkward necessity of working with crossed arms, i.e. one hand securing the pattern whilst the other is marking.

ORIGIN LINES

This refers to the common starting line for all of the sizes to be graded from one component, and there are two methods to choose from:

Method 1: common external line: where one edge of the component, usually parallel to the X axis is

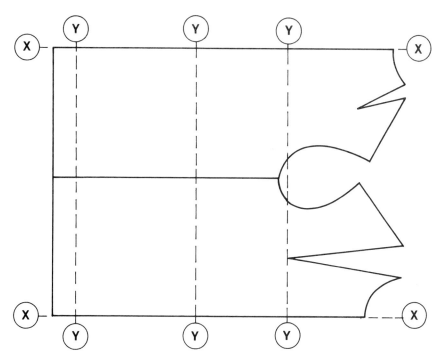

Fig. 4.4. Construction lines and grading axes.

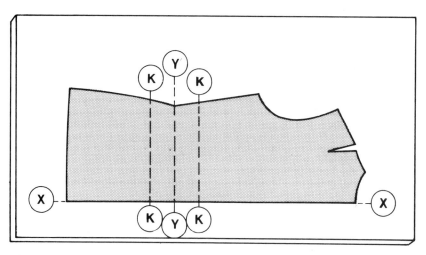

'Y' axis: mark on pattern and paper   'X' axis: mark on paper
'K' axis: mark on paper

Fig. 4.5. The width and length grading axes.

common to all sizes. This is the most generally used method because it enables the grader to move in one direction only for up-grades and in the opposite direction for down-grades.

Method 2: common internal line: where an internal line or location point is common to all sizes. This method is

sometimes used when it is necessary to grade around a special feature in the pattern. Figure 4.6 shows the principles of these two methods. There is no difference in the final results achieved by either of them. It is mainly a question of habit and convenience.

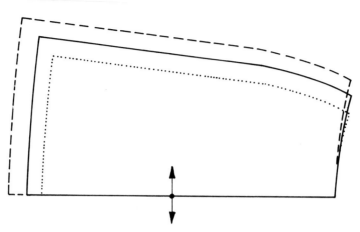

Method 1: common external line

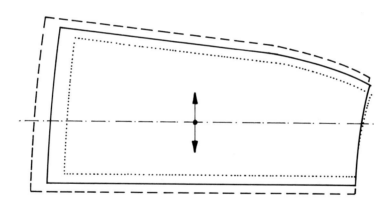

Method 2: common internal line

Fig. 4.6. Origin lines.

INCREMENT NETS FOR MANUAL GRADING

In the following grading examples (Chapter 5), the same routine is followed in each case:

Stage 1: Marking the grading axes on the pattern component.
Stage 2: Marking around the original pattern and transferring the pattern axes to the paper.
Stage 3: Adding other axes as required.
Stage 4: Marking the increment nets from the origin points.

With very few exceptions, all grading increments are measured from the intersection of the base X and Y axes (the origin point) and are marked parallel to the relevant axis. Where one axis is common to all sizes it is preferable to mark the increments for one size on one side of the axis, and those for the other sizes on the opposite side of the axis (Fig. 4.7). Where there are more than two sizes in the same direction having a common axis, it is recommended that fine coloured pencils be used to mark the increments.

As an alternative to wholly manual methods, a mechanical grading machine can be employed. This

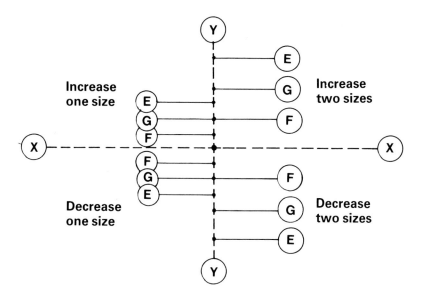

A: Increments on a common 'Y' axis

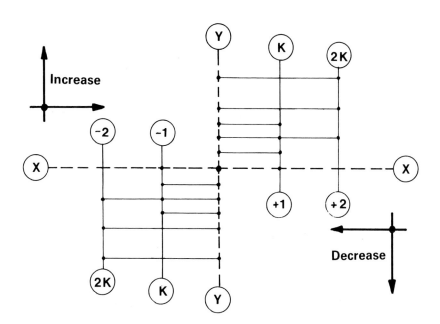

B: Increments on different axes

Fig. 4.7. The marking of grading increments and axes.

machine (Fig. 4.8) is clamped to the edge of the table and the pattern is inserted into the sprung arms and held in position by small pins. Pattern movement is effected by means of two knobs, one for movement along the X axis and the other for the Y axis. The grader controls the amount of movement by means of the calibrations along the track of each axis.

One of the advantages of using a hand operated grading machine is that it eliminates the need to mark axes and increments both on the pattern and paper,

Fig. 4.8. Manually operated grading machine.

and thus reduces preparation time and improves dimensional accuracy. However, the machine is limited to movements along the X and Y axes only, which means that grading elements requiring movements at different angles or the completion of curves must be done manually when all of the X and Y movements for the pattern are completed. The question of whether or not to use a grading machine for a particular component must be evaluated according to the accuracy obtained and the number of elements which can be performed with the machine as against those which would have to be completed manually. With curved and angled pattern sections, there are always the elements of double handling and alignment.

WORKING METHODS

There are no hard and fast rules as to how to actually produce the sets of graded patterns and the choice of working method is an individual question of accuracy and convenience. Some of the most commonly used methods are described below.

NEST OR STACK GRADING

The base pattern is used to grade all the sizes, and each component has a common origin for the sizes graded

from the same component. The actual cutting out can be done in one of two ways:

(1) A number of sheets of paper, equal to the pattern sizes required are stapled together and the components are cut out, starting with the largest size. Apart from not being a particularly accurate method, there are many components which have overlapping external and internal lines and this somewhat reduces the efficacy of this method.
(2) A single sheet of paper is held underneath the grade nest and each individual size is picked off with an awl or tracing wheel. The base size pattern is then used to complete the lines necessary for cutting out.

MARK AND CUT

This is a very commonly used method whereby one size at a time is graded and then cut out. The usual way of working with this method is to start by grading one size up and down from the base pattern and then to cut them out. These patterns are then used for the next size up or down and the process is continued.

VECTOR GRADING (Fig. 4.9)

This is sometimes called the Master Grade Method and is a very widely used variation of the Nest Grade. Using common origin lines, the base pattern is graded to the largest and smallest sizes required for the particular set of patterns. Then the cardinal internal and external points are connected together by vector lines. The distance between the points to which the vectors connect is measured and then divided by the number of size intervals between the largest and smallest size. These divisions are marked on the vectors and are picked off or traced onto individual sheets of paper. The base pattern is then used to connect up the points in order to produce the outline of the component.

NIP SPACINGS

When preparing the original pattern, the pattern maker provides guides for accurate assembly through the provision of nips along the seams to be matched. The distances between these nips is based on the complexity and form of the parts to be matched. In general, the distances between the nips on a long, straight seam or a slightly curved one would be far greater than those, between a sleeve head and the armhole.

In most cases, there is no need during the grading to alter the distances between nips on most assembly seams. Where a nip is used to match two components,

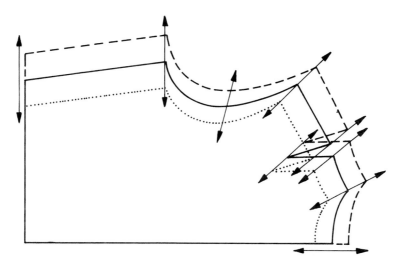

Fig. 4.9. Vector grading method.

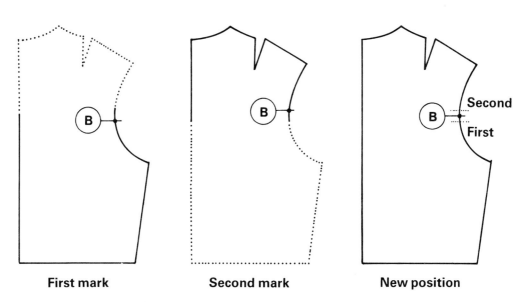

First mark	Second mark	New position

Fig. 4.10. Back armhole nip position.

the lengths of which change during grading, then the system automatically incorporates this change. An example of this function is the relationship between the collar neck seam and that of the back and front neck base sections (Example 1.4, Chapter 5). A very important quality feature of a garment is inset sleeve setting and in order to ensure that the fullness distribution around the armhole is maintained correctly, the following procedure should be observed.

ARMHOLE

Back section (Fig. 4.10)
When completing the across back grade of D, mark nip B when drawing the lower section of the armhole. Perform the armhole depth grade of K and the shoulder length grade of G and mark nip B again.

The new position of nip B is in the centre of the two marks.

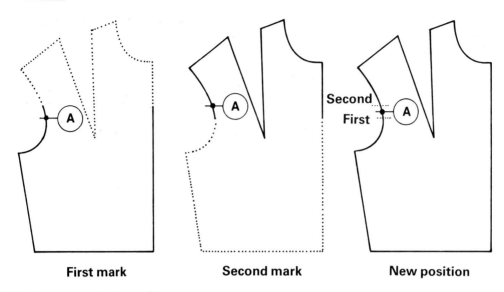

Fig. 4.11. Front armhole nip position.

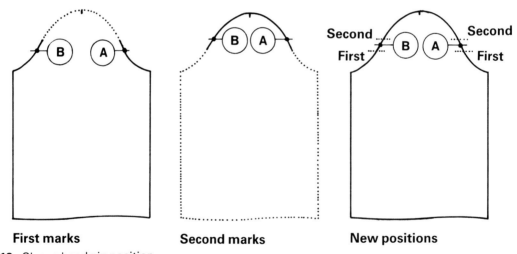

Fig. 4.12. Sleeve head nip position.

Front section (Fig. 4.11)

When completing the across chest grade of H, mark nip A when drawing the lower section of the armhole. After completing the armhole depth and shoulder length grades, mark nip A again.

The new position of nip A is in the centre of the two marks. The new nip position on the back and front armhole sections is always in the centre of the two marks irrespective of whether the pattern is being graded up or down.

SLEEVE

Front and back sections (Fig. 12)

Marks nips A and B when performing the first width grade (E) on the front and back sections of the sleeve, and whilst the sleeve is on the original Y axis.

After the sleeve crown height grade (K) has been performed, the sleeve head pattern is used to blend the back and front sleeve head runs and also to again mark nips A and B. This is done as follows:

Align the centre head nip of the pattern to the new centre head nip and pivot it from this point until the pattern aligns with the line of the lower section of the back sleeve and mark nip B. Repeat the same procedure for the front sleeve and mark nip A. The new positions of nips A and B are in the centre of the two nip positions previously marked.

This simple procedure ensures that the fullness distribution proportions between the armhole and sleeve head is consistent for all the sizes being graded.

TO SUM UP

This introduction to the practical aspects of pattern grading has stressed the basic principle that it pays to invest time in correct and accurate preparation. Unfortunately, there are no short cuts to quality.

PART 2

BASIC GRADING APPLICATIONS

Chapter 5

The Master Grades

The following examples demonstrate the applications of the system to standard types of block patterns. These are the basic patterns from which most outerwear garment patterns are developed and each example provides:

(1) Where necessary, an illustrated introduction to the principles involved in grading the demonstration pattern.
(2) The increments used, and their locations.
(3) The net of grading increments required for one size up and one size down from the base size.
(4) Instructions regarding the common and other axes required in relation to the grading position of the pattern.
(5) Grading instructions accompanied by illustrations showing each successive stage. The line sectors to mark after each move denoted by a thickened line.

(6) An example of the finished grade is shown together with the vectors used for checking accuracy.

The first five groups of examples show the applications the dynamic neck to waist grading method and in group six, the static method is demonstrated.

The first examples demonstrate the basic body and derived grades, and these grades are central to the entire system. All of the other grades for bodies, sleeves, lapels and collars are based on these examples. The transfer of applications from the basic grade to a more complicated one is facilitated by the integrative basis of the system itself. For example, the grading of a Magyar sleeve and gusset involves the use of the same principles as those used for grading a basic one-piece sleeve and the same relationship applies for all of the other grades.

It is recommended that the basic grades are mastered before advancing to the other examples.

The basic whole back

This first grading example utilises the following increments:

B: The total width grade from the centre back to the side seam.
D: Across back. This is equal to increments F plus G.
E: Side section.

F: Neck width.
G: Shoulder length in two sections (G/2 + G/2).
K: Armhole depth.

Fig. 5.1 illustrates the locations of these increments with Fig. 5.2 showing the grading axes and Fig. 5.3 the increment net for this grade.

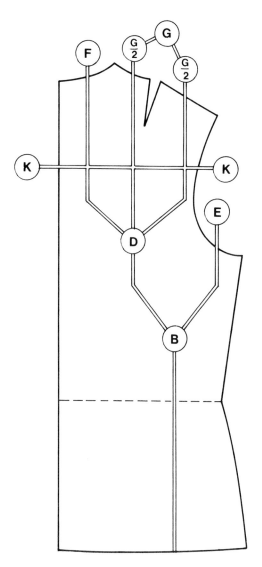

Fig. 5.1. Grading increments for basic whole back.

57

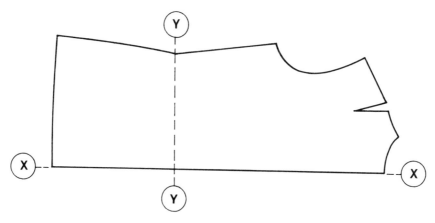

Fig. 5.2. Grading axes.

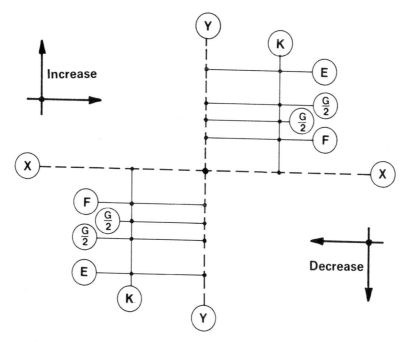

Fig. 5.3. Increment net.

Grading instructions: BASIC WHOLE BACK

Stage 1: align pattern on X and Y axes (Fig. 5.4)
- Move on Y axis to second G/2
- Mark part of armhole.

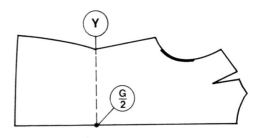

Fig. 5.4.

Stage 2: continue on Y axis to E (Fig. 5.5)
- Mark side seam
- Complete armhole to side seam
- Complete hem.

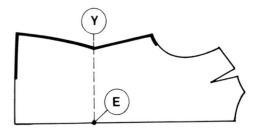

Fig. 5.5.

Stage 3: re-align on X axis and align the Y axis of the pattern to the relevant K line (Fig. 5.6)
- Mark corner of centre back and neck.

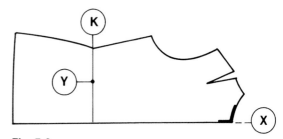

Fig. 5.6.

Stage 4: remain on K line (Fig. 5.7)
- Move on K axis to F
- Complete neckline
- Mark start of shoulder.

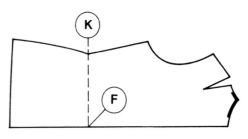

Fig. 5.7.

Stage 5: remain on K line (Fig. 5.8)
- Move to first G/2
- Complete first part of shoulder
- Mark dart
- Mark start of second part of shoulder.

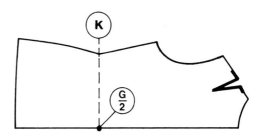

Fig. 5.8.

Stage 6: remain on K axis (Fig. 5.9)
- Move to second G/2
- Complete shoulder
- Complete armhole.

Fig. 5.9.

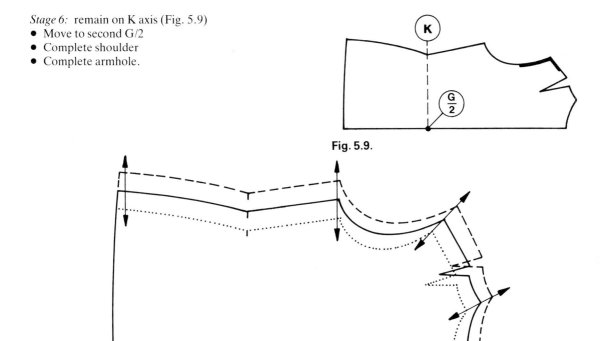

Grade for basic back

The basic front

This is the basic grade for all fronts with bust darts and the example is demonstrated on a standard block front with the bust dart coming from the shoulder. The increments used for this grade are:

C: The total grade from the front edge to the side seam.
E: Side section.
F: Neck width.
G: Shoulder length in two sections (G/2 + G/2).
H: Width of breast.
I: Front edge to bust point on bust line.
I_1: First side of the bust point.
J: Bust point to armhole on bust line.
J_1: Second side of the bust point.
M: Front neck point to bust line. This increment is equal to increments K plus L, and is applied as one unit for the dynamic neck to waist grade.

THE BUST DART GRADE

Apart from changing the bust girth, the bust dart grade also affects two other dimensions:

(1) The vertical length from the front neck point to the bust line. Increment M is used for this purpose.

(2) The depth of the front armhole as measured from the armhole base to the shoulder point. This change in depth is caused by increment K which is the resultant quantity after the application of increment M.

The principles of this particular grade are:

(1) Increment $I = F + G/2 + I_1$ affects the total width on the bust line from the front edge to the bust point. This side of the bust dart receives increment I_1 at the bust point (Fig. 5.10).
(2) The other side of the bust dart receives increment J_1 at the bust point and this point is joined to the intersection of the shoulder and bust dart line at point S (Fig. 5.11). The length of this connecting line A, is changed by increment M so as to equal the change in length of the other side of the bust dart.
(3) The angle of the shoulder line (alpha) relative to the bust dart line remains unchanged irrespective of how much the connecting line A is pivoted around point S.
(4) When J_1 is applied at the bust point and increment M is applied along line A, the result is that the armhole depth is affected by about two-thirds of

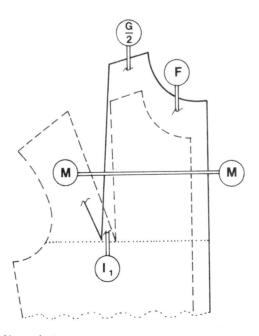

Fig. 5.10. Grade for first side of bust dart.

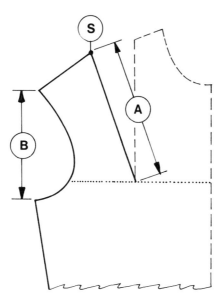

Fig. 5.11. Length A and Depth B.

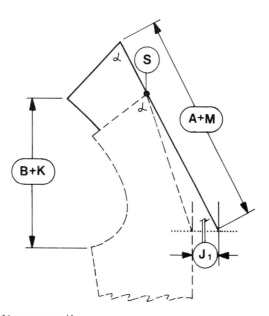

Fig. 5.12. The generation of increment K.

the value of M. (This result can be calculated trigonometrically.)

(5) Thus when M is applied to the length of the bust dart and J_1 at the bust point, increment K is generated automatically (Fig. 5.12).

(6) The resultant quantity for increment K ensures that the depths of the front and back armholes change by the same amount. As increment K is also applied to the sleeve head, the relationships between the components is accurately maintained.

The distances shown in the illustrations accompanying this section have been exaggerated for the purposes of clarity.

Grading instructions: THE BASIC FRONT

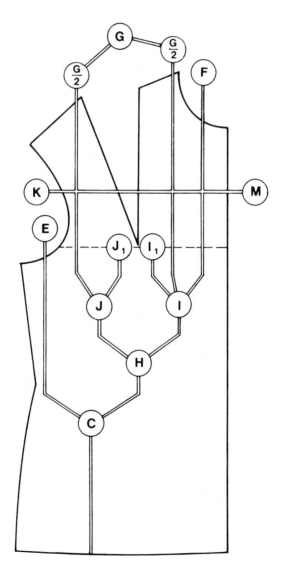

Fig. 5.13. Grading increments for basic front.

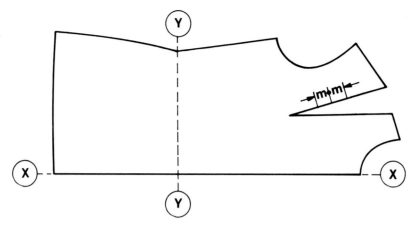

Fig. 5.14. Grading axes.

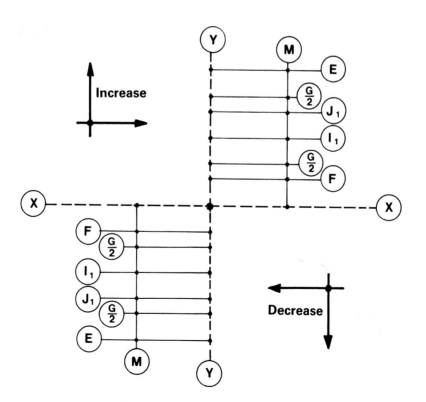

Fig. 5.15. Increment net.

Stage 1: mark central M on bust dart line (Fig. 5.16)
- M to M1 = one size increase
- M to M2 = one size decrease.

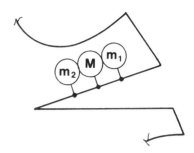

Fig. 5.16.

Stage 2: align pattern on X and Y axes (Fig. 5.17)
- Mark front edge
- Mark hem corner.

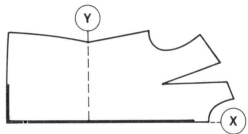

Fig. 5.17.

Stage 3: remain on Y axis (Fig. 5.18)
- Move to I₁, mark new bust point.

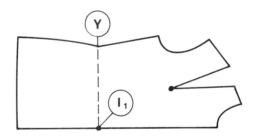

Fig. 5.18.

Stage 4: remain on Y axis (Fig. 5.19)
- Move to J₁, mark point S.

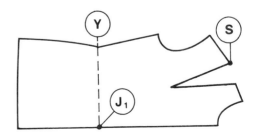

Fig. 5.19.

Stage 5: remain on Y axis (Fig. 5.20)
- Move to second G/2.
- Mark armhole from across chest line to about 3 cm from side seam.

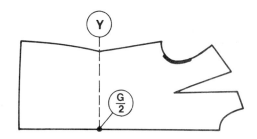

Fig. 5.20.

Stage 6: remain on Y axis (Fig. 5.21)
- Move to E
- Mark side seam
- Complete base of armhole
- Complete hem.

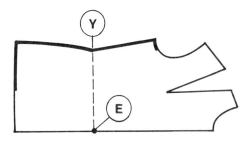

Fig. 5.21.

Stage 7: align Y axis to relevant M line (Fig. 5.22)
- Mark corner of neck and front edge.

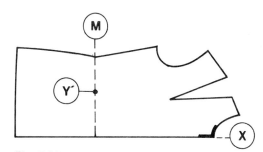

Fig. 5.22.

Stage 8: remain on M line (Fig. 5.23)
- Move to F
- Complete neck
- Mark start of shoulder.

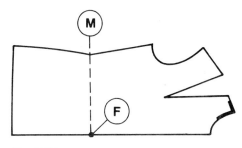

Fig. 5.23.

Stage 9: remain on M line (Fig. 5.24)
- Move to first G/2
- Complete first section of shoulder
- Mark corner of bust dart and shoulder.

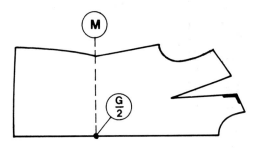

Fig. 5.24.

Stage 10: use the pattern to join shoulder corner (Stage 9) to bust point (Fig. 5.25)

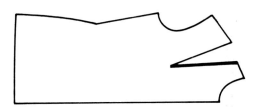

Fig. 5.25.

Stage 11: align pattern from bust (Fig. 5.26) point to point S (marked in Stage 3)
- Join bust point to this point
- Mark central M
- Mark relevant M.

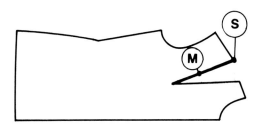

Fig. 5.26.

Stage 12: move pattern along this line and align central M with relevant M (*) (Fig. 5.27)
- * Move towards shoulder to increase
- * Move towards bust point to decrease
- Mark start of shoulder.

Fig. 5.27.

Stage 13: move pattern by distance G/2 parallel to bust
dart line (*) (Fig. 5.28)
* Towards side to increase
* Towards front to decrease
• Complete shoulder and armhole.

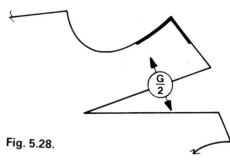

Fig. 5.28.

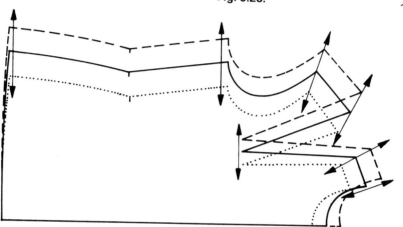

Grade of basic front

The basic sleeve

The one-piece straight sleeve is the first of the basic derived grades where all of the necessary grading increments are obtained from the armhole and side section grade of the body.

When allocating the sleeve width increments, it is essential to maintain two relationships (Fig. 5.29.)

(1) That between the top and bottom halves of the sleeve.
(2) That between the two halves of the front and back sleeves.

This is irrespective of whether the side seam of the garment has been displaced from the centre of the armhole. In these instances, the same allocation of the armhole width grade 2E, on the side sections of the back and front, should be used for the related sleeve sections.

This grade is the key to all of the other sleeve grades demonstrated in this section, and as such should be thoroughly understood.

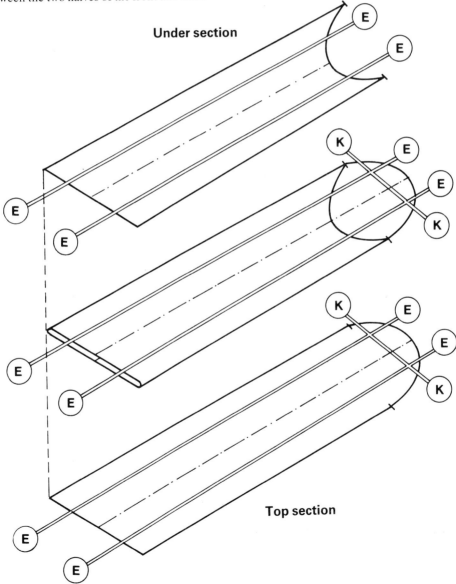

Fig. 5.29. Top and under sleeve relationships.

Grading instructions: BASIC SLEEVE

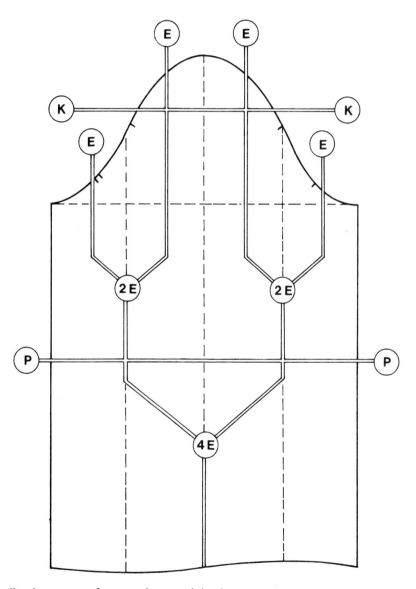

Fig. 5.30. Grading increments for one-piece straight sleeve.

70

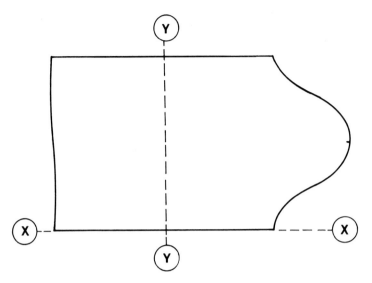

Fig. 5.31. Grading axes.

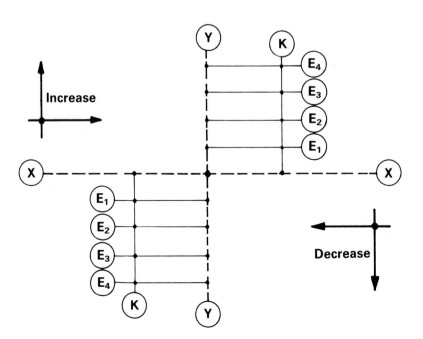

Fig. 5.32. Increment net.

Stage 1: align pattern on X and Y axes (Fig. 5.33)
- Mark front seam
- Mark starts of sleeve head and hem line.

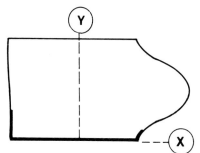

Fig. 5.33.

Stage 2: remain on Y axis (Fig. 5.34)
- Move to E_1
- Mark front section of head
- Mark part of hem.

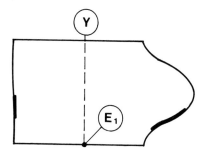

Fig. 5.34.

Stage 3: align Y axis of pattern on relevant K line (Fig. 5.35)
- Move to E_2 mark head section and centre nip
- Mark hem to centre.

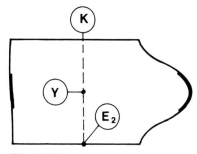

Fig. 5.35.

Stage 4: re-align Y axes of pattern and paper (Fig. 5.36)
- Move to E_3, mark back section of head
- Mark part of hem.

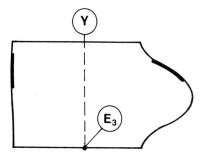

Fig. 5.36.

72

Stage 5: remain on Y axis (Fig. 5.37)
- Move to E_4
- Complete back section
- Mark back seam
- Complete hem.

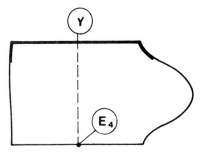

Fig. 5.37.

Stage 6: Use the pattern to (Fig. 5.38)
- Blend head to front section
- Blend head to back section.

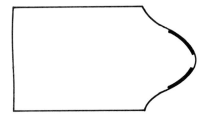

Fig. 5.38.

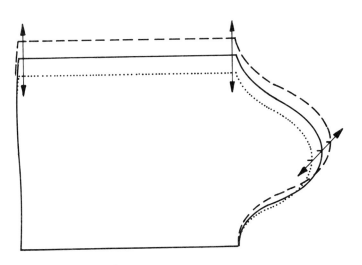

Grade of basic sleeve

The basic collar

The grading increments for this component are derived directly from the back and front neck base sections of the body and they are applied to the collar length as follows:

- Increment F: for the front neck length
- Increment F: for the back neck length

Thus for each size, the length of the basic collar changes by the amount of 2F.

The X axis for this grade comes from the construction systems generally used for this type of collar and this method ensures that the neck seam curvature remains unchanged throughout the grading. This is an important principle because the distance Z (Fig. 5.39) controls the stand and fall of the collar.

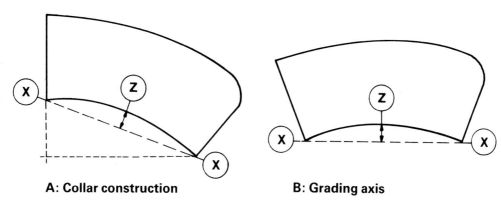

A: Collar construction   **B: Grading axis**

Fig. 5.39. Distance 'Z'.

Grading instructions: THE BASIC COLLAR

Fig. 5.40. Grading increments for basic collar.

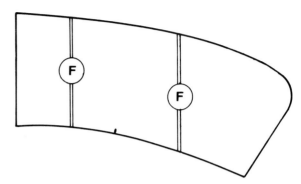

Fig. 5.41. Grading axes.

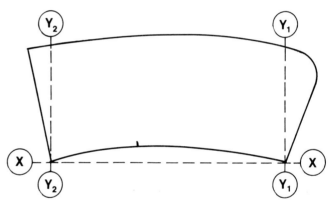

Fig. 5.42. Increment net.

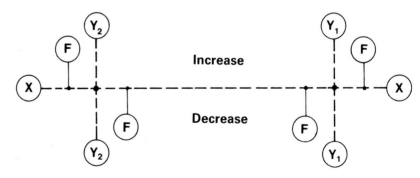

Stage 1: align pattern to (Fig. 5.43)
- X axis
- Y_1 and Y_2 (upper or lower)
- Mark centre sections of neck seam and outside edge
- Mark shoulder seam nip.

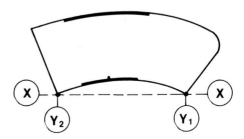

Fig. 5.43.

Stage 2: remain on X axis (Fig. 5.44)
- Move centre back to F
- Mark centre back, part of neck seam and outside edge.

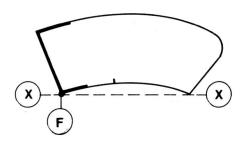

Fig. 5.44.

Stage 3: remain on X axis (Fig. 5.45)
- Move collar front to F
- Mark front, part of neck seam and edge.

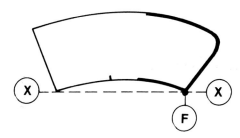

Fig. 5.45.

Stage 4: Use pattern to blend the neck seam and outside edge (Fig. 5.46).

Fig. 5.46.

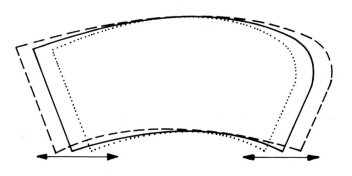

Grade of basic collar

The basic facing grade

The grading increments for this component stem from those used for grading the related sections of the front (Fig. 5.47) and these are:

- Increment F: for the front neck base length.

- Increment M: for the length between the front neck point and bust line.

Below the bust line the facing width remains unchanged for the entire range of sizes being graded.

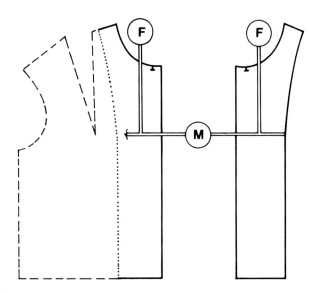

Fig. 5.47. The derived increments.

Grading instructions: THE BASIC FACING

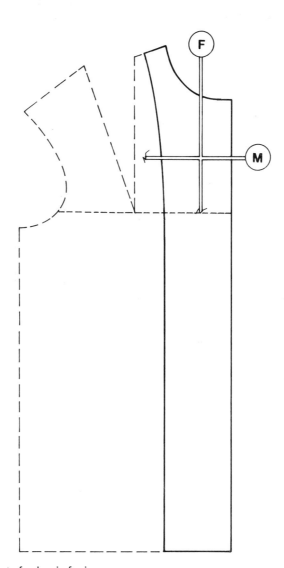

Fig. 5.48. Grading increments for basic facing.

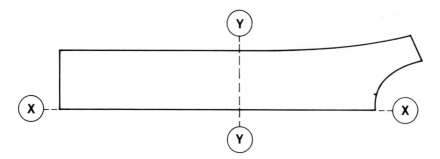

Fig. 5.49. Grading axes.

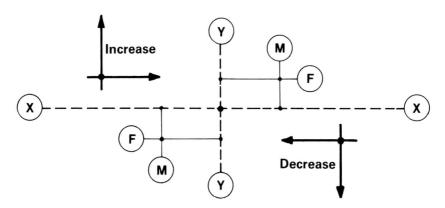

Fig. 5.50. Increment net.

Stage 1: align pattern on X and Y axes (Fig. 5.51)
● Mark front edge and hem
● Mark lower, inside edge to bust line.

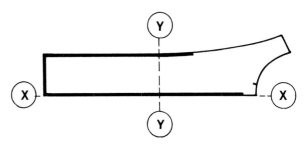

Fig. 5.51.

Stage 2: align Y axis of pattern on relevant M line
(Fig. 5.52)
- Mark corner and nip
- Mark start of neck.

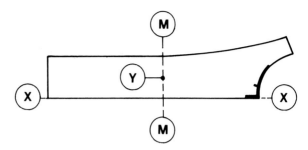

Fig. 5.52.

Stage 3: remain on M line (Fig. 5.53)
- Move to F
- Complete neck
- Mark shoulder section and inside corner.

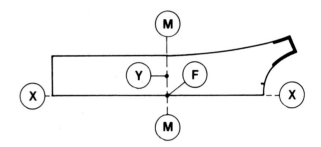

Fig. 5.53.

Stage 4: Use the pattern to blend from shoulder corner
to inside edge at the bust line (Fig. 5.54).

Fig. 5.54.

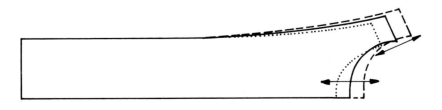

Grade of basic facing

The neck piece

When a neck piece is used for the back neck section only, then the grading increment utilised is increment F. This is the same increment which is used to grade the back neck (Fig. 5.55).

The grade itself consists of applying increment F at the centre back line of the neck piece (Fig. 5.56).

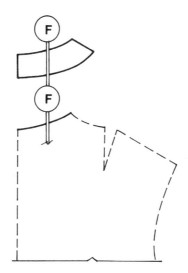

Fig. 5.55. The derived grading increment.

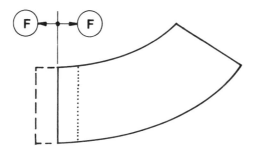

Fig. 5.56. The neck piece grade.

Chapter 6

Displaced Bust Darts

The displacement, or shifting of the bust dart, is relative to the bust dart position used as an origin by the pattern maker. The bust suppression itself can be applied from any line on the periphery of the front pattern or from the junction of two lines, such as the front neck and shoulder. In the following examples, the bust dart has been displaced from its conventional origin on the shoulder line to five other positions:

(1) The waistline
(2) The side seam
(3) The armhole
(4) The neck
(5) The front edge

and these positions are illustrated in Fig. 6.1. All of the grades for this group of fronts are derived directly from that of the basic front, and the increments used are exactly the same in all instances.

The principles of grading displaced bust darts

A technique common to this group of grades is the use of a guide point located on the shoulder line. This point is referred to as 'S' in the grading instructions, and it is marked on the approximate centre of the shoulder line. Point 'S' (Fig. 6.2) is used during grading when pivoting from the bust point, and the reasons underlying its use are explained via the following work-through example of the bust dart width grade:

- The example front has a bust dart from the waist line and point 'S' is marked on the shoulder. The dotted line connects the bust point to 'S' (Fig. 6.3).
- This front is now split into two panels A and B, by cutting along the dotted line between the bust point

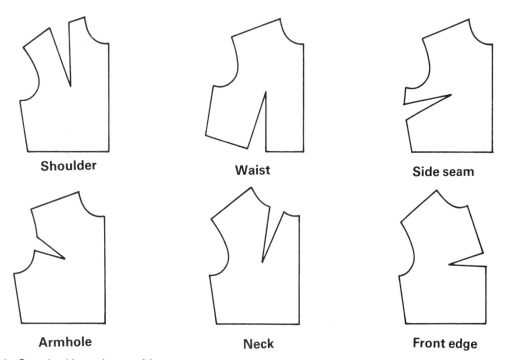

Fig. 6.1. Standard bust dart positions.

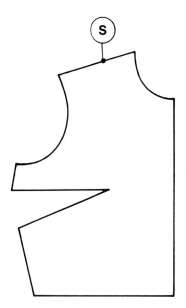

Fig. 6.2. The location of point 'S'.

and 'S'. This point now becomes S_1 and S_2. (Fig. 6.4).

- Panel A is graded up by increment I_1 only, and panel B is graded up by increment J_1 only (Fig. 6.5).
- The two panels are joined together from the two S points to the bust point, and Fig. 6.6 shows the effect which the bust dart width grade has had on this front:

  (1) A triangle has been inserted into the front with

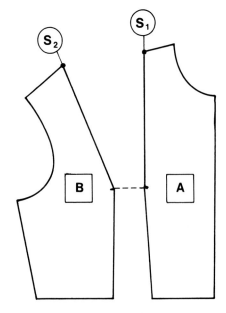

Fig. 6.4. The panels separated.

its base on the bust point line and the apex at point S. The width of the base of the triangle is equal to increment I_1 plus increment J_1.

  (2) Two rectangles have also been inserted into the front from the bust point line down to the waist. The short side of one rectangle is I_1, whilst the other is J_1.

- This is the required result of the bust dart width grade but in practical terms, patterns cannot be cut

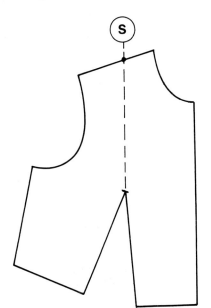

Fig. 6.3. The splitting line.

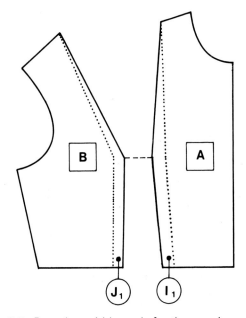

Fig. 6.5. Bust dart width grade for the panels.

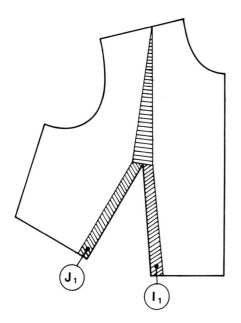

Fig. 6.6. The effects of the bust dart width grade.

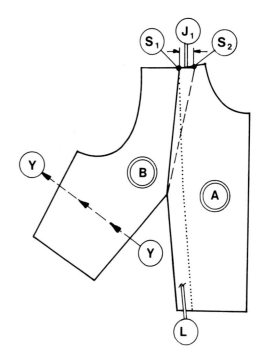

Fig. 6.7. The overlap of points S_1 and S_2.

up, graded and then joined together for each size. Therefore, the grading method must incorporate a simple technique whereby both the triangle and the rectangle can be inserted into the front without the need for scissors and paste.

The key to this technique is the use of the bust point for pivoting and point 'S' as a measure of the amount pivoted. In practice, this works as follows:

- Referring to the previous example, panel A is graded up by increment I_1. Panel B is then joined to it at the bust point, with the 'S' points overlapped at the shoulder by the amount of increment J_1. As a result of being opposite angles, the bust dart angle of panel B is exactly the same as that which would be obtained by inserting the triangle from the bust point line to the shoulder (Fig. 6.7).
- It would therefore follow that if the 'S' points are overlapped when increasing size they would have to be spaced apart when decreasing size (Fig. 6.8).
- When pivoting in either direction, the line of the 'Y' axis remains unchanged in relation to the pattern, but its angle to the 'X' axis changes relative to the amounts by which the 'S' points are overlapped or opened.
- The principles of this technique can be summarised as follows:
  (1) Point 'S' is used to measure the overlap when grading up in size.

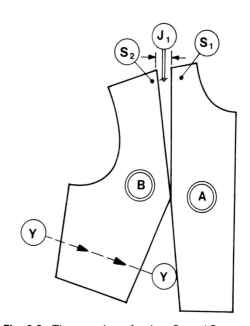

Fig. 6.8. The opening of points S_1 and S_2.

(2) It is used to measure the opening or spacing apart when grading down in size.

These two functions are the basis for grading all of the fronts with displaced bust darts.

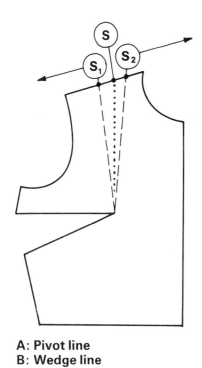

A: Pivot line
B: Wedge line

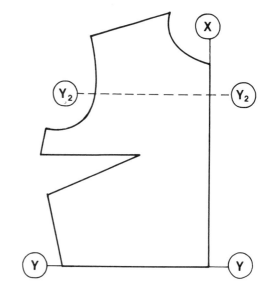

C: New 'Y' axis

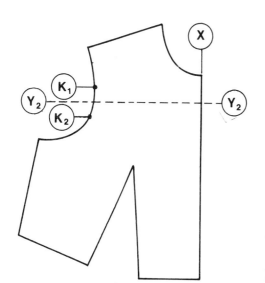

D: 'Y₂' axis
E: 'K' marks

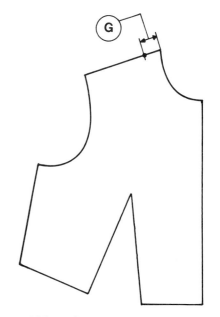

F: 'G' marks

Fig. 6.9. Guide marks.

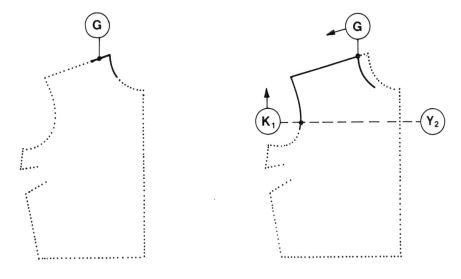

A: Grading up

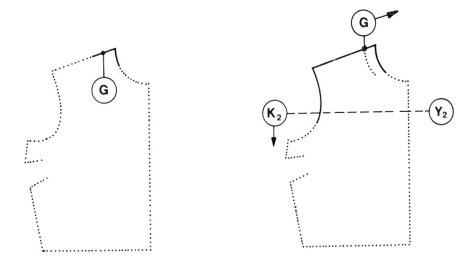

B: Grading down

Fig. 6.10. The use of the 'K' and 'G' points.

GUIDE LINES

When a front pattern is pivoted in either direction, the angle of the X or Y axis changes relative to the amount and direction by which the pattern has been moved. In practice, this means that each size will have a different axis for performing the bust dart width grade. In order to perform this particular grade simply and efficiently on the different types of fronts in this group, some of the following 'guide' lines or points are used and they are shown in Fig. 6.9.

(1) *Pivot line:* this joins the bust point to point 'S'.
(2) *Wedge line:* a line which connects the new bust

86

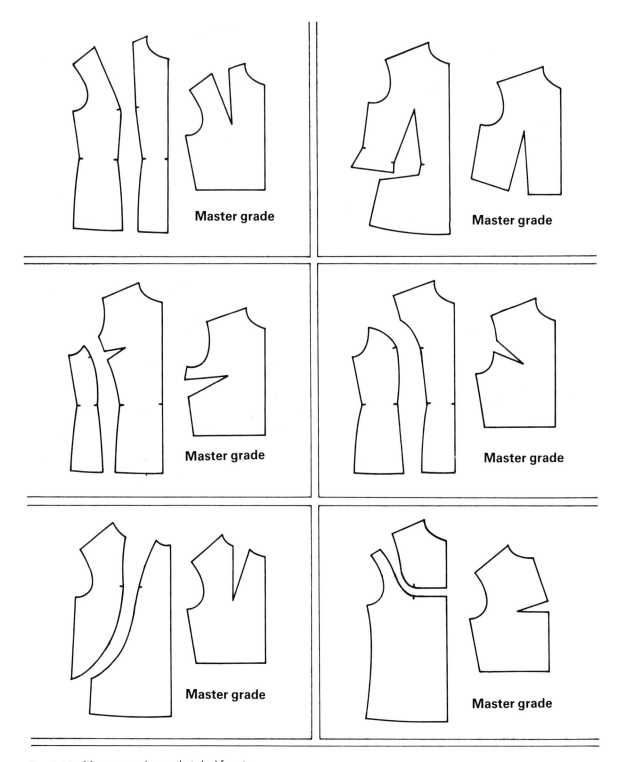

Fig. 6.11. Master grades and styled fronts.

point to the displaced 'S' point.

(3) *New 'Y' axis:* this is marked when called for, after the overlap or opening at the shoulder has been completed.

(4) *Y_2 axis:* this line is marked at the level of the across chest line parallel to the bust line.

(5) *'K' marks:* these are marked on the pattern armhole at the level of the across chest line in the following positions:

To increase size: above the Y_2 axis, i.e. towards the shoulder line.

To decrease size: below the Y_2 axis, i.e. towards the armhole base.

In both cases, the distance of the 'K' marks from the Y_2 axis is equal to the value of the increment used for the grade.

(6) *'G' marks:* this guide point is marked on the shoulder line at the distance of increment 'G' from the front neck point and eliminates the need to measure the shoulder length grade whilst grading. Point 'G' is used in the following way:

Grading up:

(a) Complete the neck grade — mark the start of the shoulder — mark the 'G' point.

(b) Move the pattern along the shoulder line towards the armhole until the neck point matches the 'G' point.

(c) Complete the shoulder length grade by marking the shoulder end point and the start of the armhole.

Grading down:

(a) Complete the neck grade — mark the start of the shoulder.

(b) Move the pattern along the shoulder line towards the neck until the 'G' point matches the neck point.

(c) Complete the shoulder length grade by marking the shoulder end point and the start of the armhole.

(7) *'K' and 'G' Marks:* these two marks are used together (Fig. 6.10) for completing the armhole and shoulder grades. When instructed, use as follows:

Grading up:

(a) Align the neck point of the pattern to the 'G' point on the paper and the Y_2 axis to the relevant 'K' mark on the armhole.

(b) Complete marking the armhole and shoulder.

Grading down:

(a) Align the 'G' point on the pattern to the neck point on the paper and the Y_2 axis to the relevant 'K' mark.

(b) Complete marking the armhole and shoulder. This is a quick and accurate method of pattern movement and apart from being a checking routine, also ensures that the armhole and shoulder runs are maintained.

(8) *Applications:* instructions for the use of these guide lines and points are given in the grading demonstrations of each front.

TO SUM UP

The grading of nearly every styled front which has regular bust suppression is based on the master grade for the dart position which relates to the seam runs. The ability to recognise this relationship and to know how to apply it is an essential element of the grading process. Some typical examples of this principle are shown in Fig. 6.11.

Grading instructions:
FRONT WITH BUST DART FROM WAIST

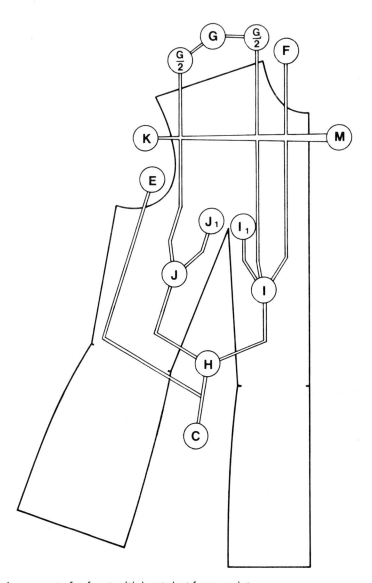

Fig. 6.12. Grading increments for front with bust dart from waist.

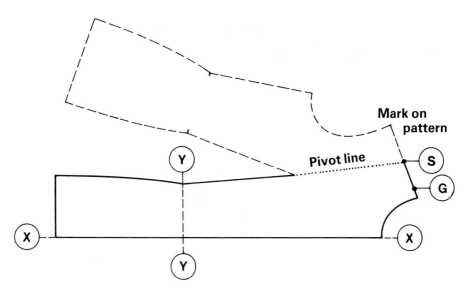

Fig. 6.13. Grading axes for front section.

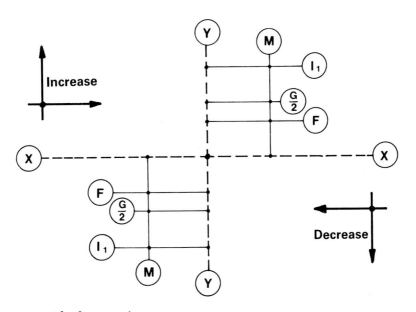

Fig. 6.14. Increment net for front section.

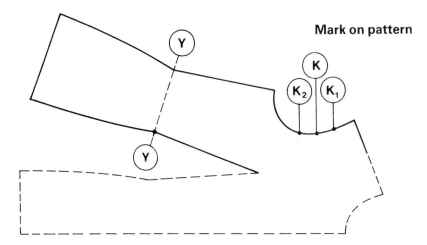

Fig. 6.15. Grading axis for side section.

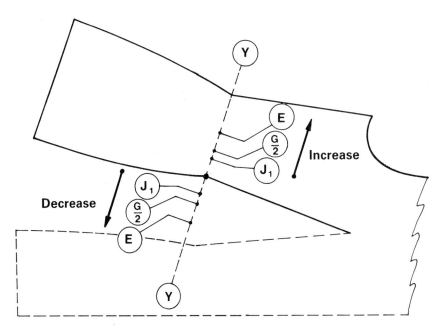

Fig. 6.16. Increment net for side section.

Stage 1: align on X and Y axes (Fig. 6.17)
- Mark part of front and hem.

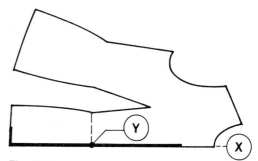

Fig. 6.17.

Stage 2: remain on Y axis (Fig. 6.18)
- Move to first G/2
- Mark point S.

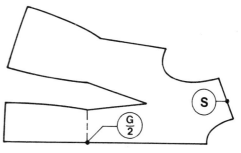

Fig. 6.18.

Stage 3: move to I_1 (Fig. 6.19)
- Mark first panel line
- Complete panel hem.

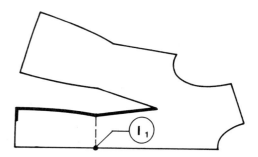

Fig. 6.19.

Stage 4: mark overlap or opening of J_1 from point S (Fig. 6.20)
- On the paper, join this point to new bust point
- This line is now the wedge line.

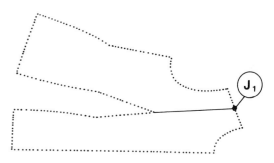

Fig. 6.20.

Stage 5: align pivot line on pattern to wedge line on paper (Fig. 6.21)
- Mark bust panel line
- Mark part of panel hem
- Mark new Y axis
- Mark increments $J_1 - G/2 - E$ on new Y_1 axis.

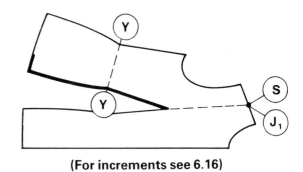

(For increments see 6.16)

Fig. 6.21.

Stage 6: align pattern on new Y axis (Fig. 6.22)
- Move to G/2
- Mark part of armhole
- Mark K increments.

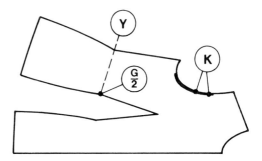

Fig. 6.22.

Stage 7: remain on new Y axis (Fig. 6.23)
- Move to E
- Mark armhole and side seam
- Complete hem.

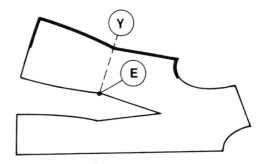

Fig. 6.23.

Stage 8: align pattern on X axis (Fig. 6.24)
- Align Y axis to relevant M line
- Mark front corner and start of neck.

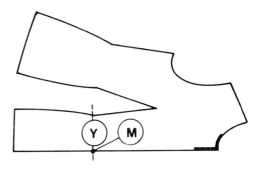

Fig. 6.24.

Stage 9: remain on Y–M axis (Fig. 6.25)
- Move to F
- Complete neck
- Mark start of shoulder.

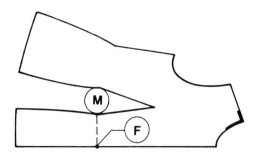

Fig. 6.25.

Stage 10: use pattern to (Fig. 6.26)
- Mark relevant G on shoulder line
- Align pattern to G point and relevant K point at armhole.

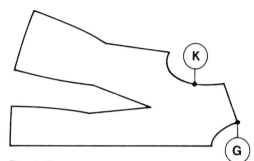

Fig. 6.26.

Stage 12: use the pattern to complete the shoulder and armhole (Fig. 6.27).

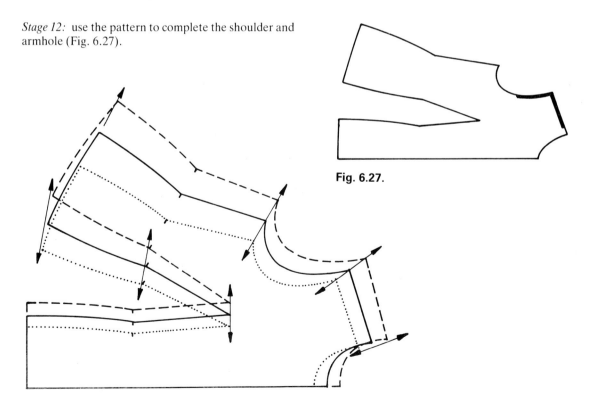

Fig. 6.27.

Grade of front with bust dart from waist

Grading instructions:
FRONT WITH BUST DART FROM SIDE SEAM

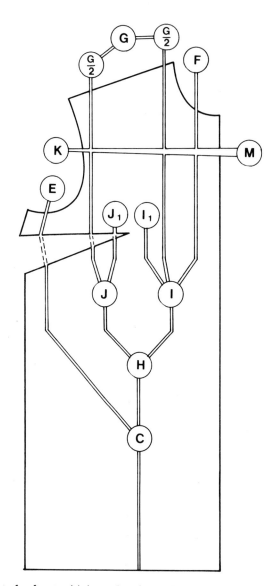

Fig. 6.28. Grading increments for front with bust dart from side seam.

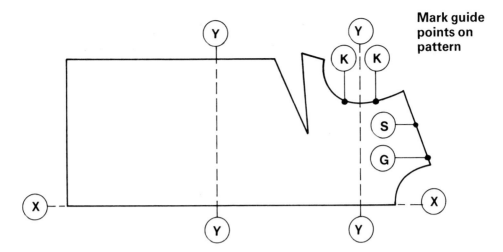

Fig. 6.29. Grading axes.

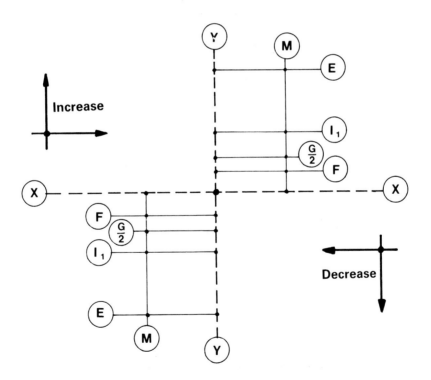

Fig. 6.30. Increment net.

96

Stage 1: align pattern on X and Y axes (Fig. 6.31)
● Mark part of front and hem.

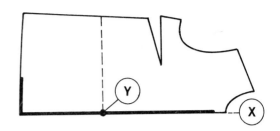

Fig. 6.31.

Stage 2: move to first G/2 (Fig. 6.32)
● Mark S point.

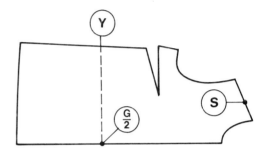

Fig. 6.32.

Stage 3: remain on Y axis (Fig. 6.33)
● Move to I_1
● Mark bust point.

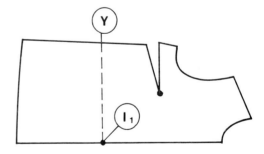

Fig. 6.33.

Stage 4: remain on Y axis (Fig. 6.34)
● Move to E
● Mark lower corner of bust dart
● Complete side seam
● Complete hem.

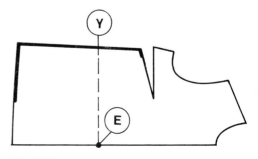

Fig. 6.34.

Stage 5: mark overlap or opening of J_1 from S point (Fig. 6.35)
- On the paper, join new bust point to J_1 point.

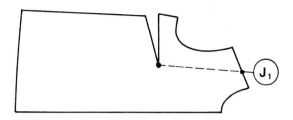

Fig. 6.35.

Stage 6: align pivot line of pattern to wedge line on paper (Fig. 6.36)
- Mark axis Y_2–Y_2.

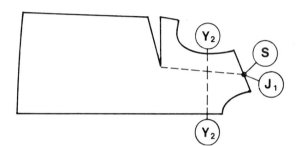

Fig. 6.36.

Stage 7: mark increments J_1 − G/2 − E (Fig. 6.37)
- Towards armhole to increase
- Towards front edge to decrease.

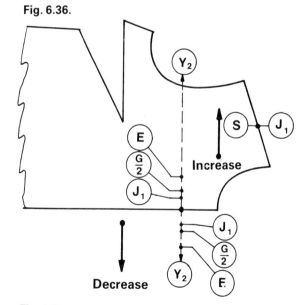

Fig. 6.37.

Stage 8: align pattern to Y_2 axis (Fig. 6.38)
- Move to second G/2
- Mark part of armhole
- Mark relevant K point.

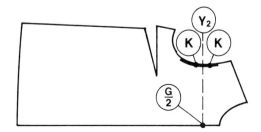

Fig. 6.38.

Stage 9: remain on Y_2 axis (Fig. 6.39)
- Move to E
- Complete armhole
- Complete small section of side seam
- Mark top corner of dart.

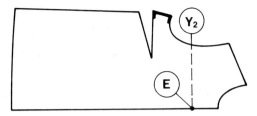

Fig. 6.39.

Stage 10: (Fig. 6.40):
- Align pattern to X axis
- Align Y axis of pattern to relevant M line
- Mark front corner and start of neck.

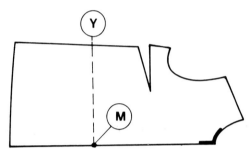

Fig. 6.40.

Stage 11: remain on M line (Fig. 6.41)
- Move to F
- Complete neck
- Mark start of shoulder
- Mark G point.

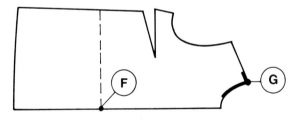

Fig. 6.41.

Stage 12: using pattern (Fig. 6.42)
- Align to K and G points
- Complete shoulder and armhole
- Complete bust dart.

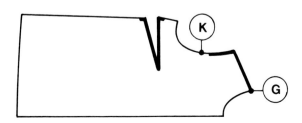

Fig. 6.42.

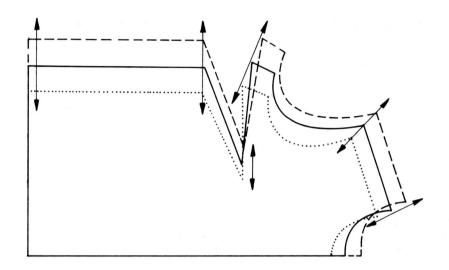

Grade of front with bust dart from side seam.

Grading instructions:
FRONT WITH BUST DART FROM ARMHOLE

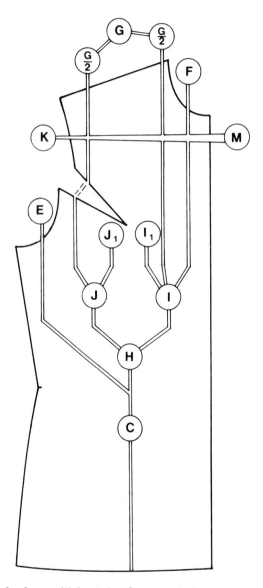

Fig. 6.43. Grading increments for front with bust dart from armhole.

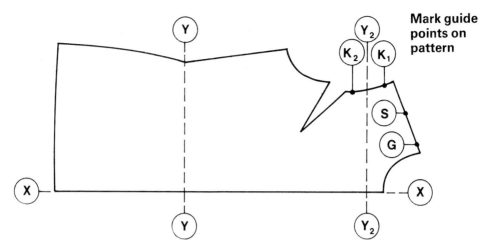

Fig. 6.44. Grading axes.

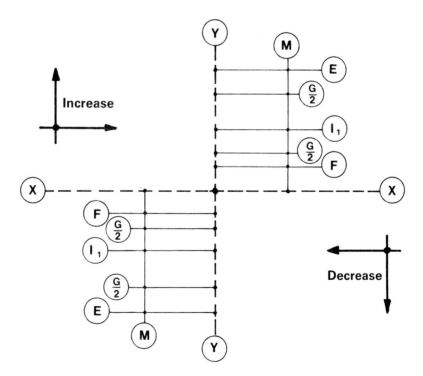

Fig. 6.45. Increment net.

Stage 1: align on X and Y axes (Fig. 6.46)
- Mark part of front and hem.

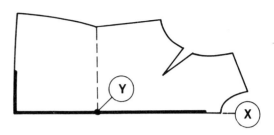

Fig. 6.46.

Stage 2: remain on Y axis (Fig. 6.47)
- Move to first G/2
- Mark point S.

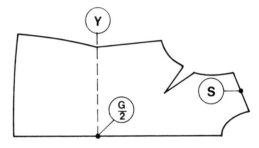

Fig. 6.47.

Stage 3: remain on Y axis (Fig. 6.48)
- Move to I_1
- Mark bust point.

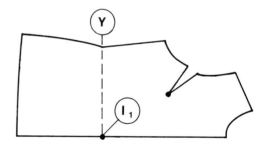

Fig. 6.48.

Stage 4: remain on Y axis (Fig. 6.49)
- Mark lower corner of bust dart
- Mark part of armhole.

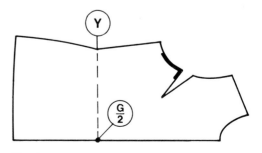

Fig. 6.49.

Stage 5: remain on Y axis (Fig. 6.50)
- Move to E
- Complete armhole
- Complete side seam and hem.

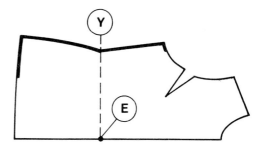

Fig. 6.50.

Stage 6: mark overlap or opening of J_1 from S point (Fig. 6.51)
- On paper, join new bust point to J_1
- This is the wedge line.

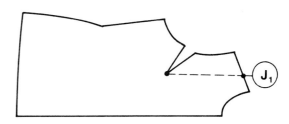

Fig. 6.51.

Stage 7: align pivot line of pattern to wedge line on paper (Fig. 6.52)
- Mark axis Y_2–Y_2.

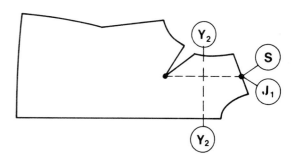

Fig. 6.52.

Stage 8: mark increments J_1 and $G/2$ on Y_2 axis (Fig. 6.53)
- Mark towards armhole to increase
- Mark towards front to decrease.

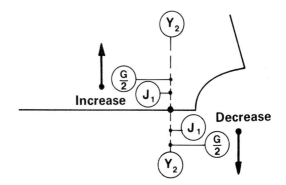

Fig. 6.53.

Stage 9: align pattern on Y_2 axis (Fig. 6.54)
- Move to G/2
- Mark to top corner of dart
- Mark part of armhole
- Mark relevant K point.

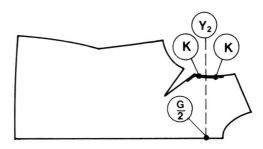

Fig. 6.54.

Stage 10: align pattern on original X axis (Fig. 6.55)
- Align Y axis on relevant M line
- Mark front corner and part of neck.

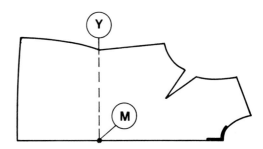

Fig. 6.55.

Stage 11: remain on M line (Fig. 6.56)
- Move to F
- Complete neck
- Mark start of shoulder
- Mark G point.

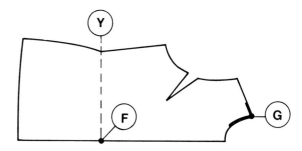

Fig. 6.56.

Stage 12: use pattern to (Fig. 6.57)
- Align to relevant K and G points
- Complete part of armhole and shoulder
- Complete bust dart.

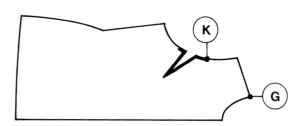

Fig. 6.57.

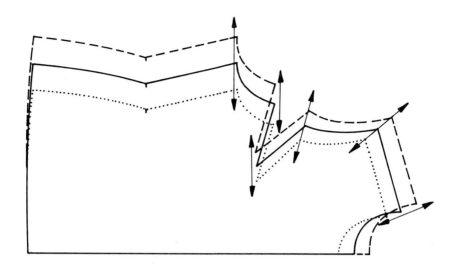

Grade of front with bust dart from armhole

Grading instructions:
FRONT WITH BUST DART FROM THE NECK

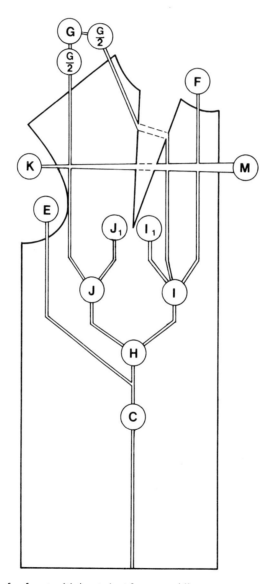

Fig. 6.58. Grading increments for front with bust dart from neckline.

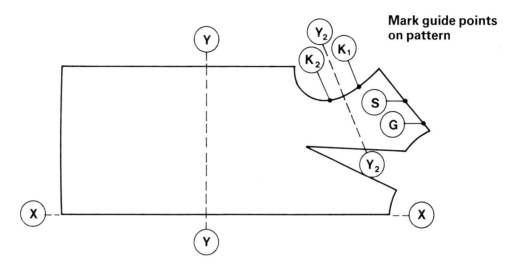

Fig. 6.59. Grading axes.

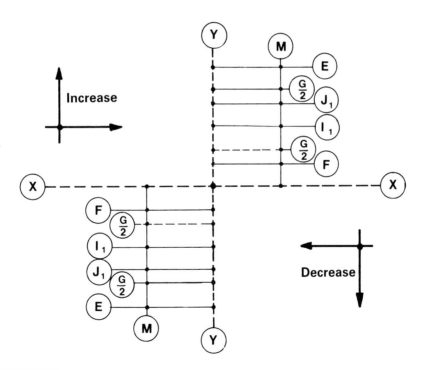

Fig. 6.60. Increment net.

Stage 1: align on X and Y axes (Fig. 6.61)
- Mark part of front and hem.

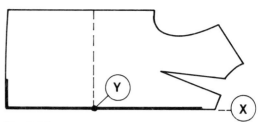

Fig. 6.61.

Stage 2: remain on Y axis (Fig. 6.62)
- Move to I_1
- Mark new bust point.

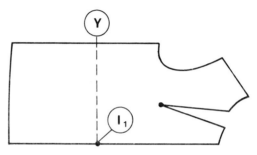

Fig. 6.62.

Stage 3: remain on Y axis (Fig. 6.63)
- Move to J_1
- Mark point S at shoulder.

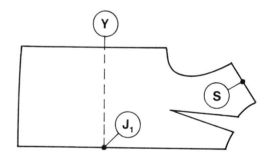

Fig. 6.63.

Stage 4: remain on Y axis (Fig. 6.64)
- Move to second G/2
- Mark part of armhole
- Mark relevant K point.

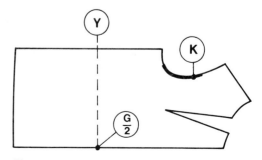

Fig. 6.64.

Stage 5: remain on Y axis (Fig. 6.65)
- Move to E
- Complete armhole
- Complete side seam and hem.

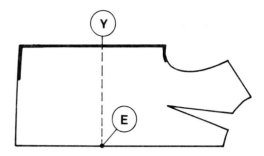

Fig. 6.65.

Stage 6: align pattern on X axis (Fig. 6.66)
- Align Y axis on relevant M line
- Mark front corner and start of neck.

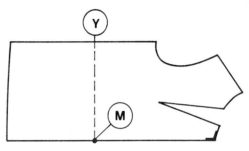

Fig. 6.66.

Stage 7: remain on M line (Fig. 6.67)
- Move to F
- Complete first part of neck
- Mark corner of bust dart
- Joint this corner to new bust point.

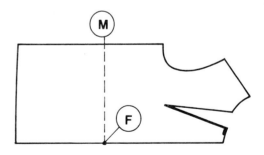

Fig. 6.67.

Stage 8: join new bust point to point S (Fig. 6.68)
- Align pivot line of pattern to wedge line on paper
- Mark intersection of the shoulder on this line.

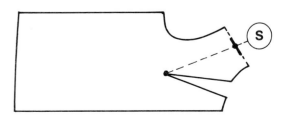

Fig. 6.68.

Stage 9: mark increment M along the line of this intersection (Fig. 6.69)
- Mark M higher than this point to increase size.
- Mark M lower than this point to decrease size.

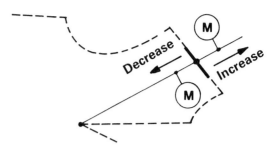

Fig. 6.69.

Stage 10: align pivot line to wedge line (Fig. 6.70)
- Move along this line to relevant M point
- Mark Y_2
- Mark increment G/2 from intersection of Y_2 axis and armhole side of bust dart.

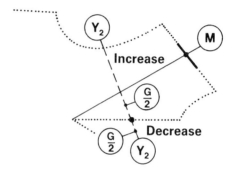

Fig. 6.70.

Stage 11: remain on Y_2 axis (Fig. 6.71)
- Move to G/2
- Mark armhole and part of shoulder
- Mark G point on shoulder.

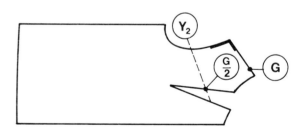

Fig. 6.71.

Stage 12: use pattern to (Fig. 6.72)
- Align K and G points
- Complete shoulder
- Complete neck
- Complete bust dart (The distance from the neck point to the upper corner of the bust dart is the same for all sizes.)

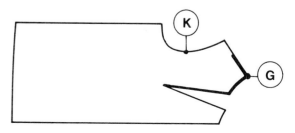

Fig. 6.72.

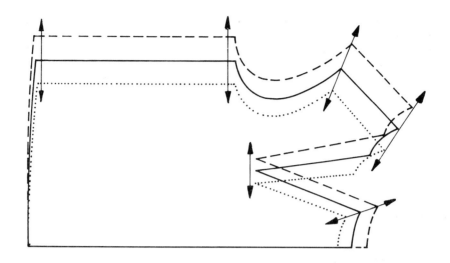

Grade for front with bust dart from neck

Grading instructions:
FRONT WITH DART FROM FRONT EDGE

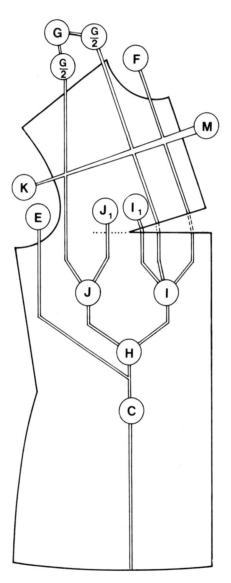

Fig. 6.73. Grading increments for front with bust dart from front edge.

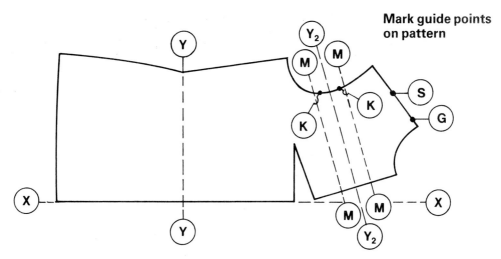

Fig. 6.74. Grading axes.

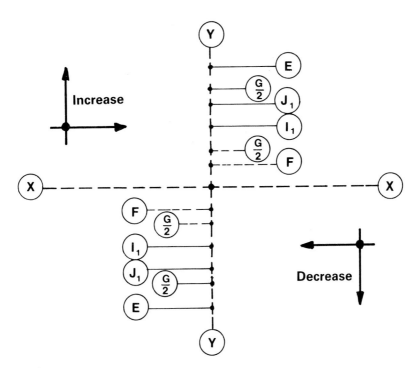

Fig. 6.75. Increment net.

114

Stage 1: align to X and Y axes (Fig. 6.76)
- Mark front up to dart
- Mark corner of dart
- Mark part of hem.

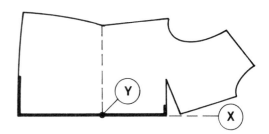

Fig. 6.76.

Stage 2: remain on Y axis (Fig. 6.77)
- Move to I_1
- Mark new bust point.

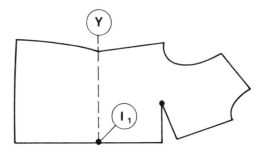

Fig. 6.77.

Stage 3: remain on Y axis (Fig. 6.78)
- Move to J_1
- Mark S point
- Mark central part of shoulder line.

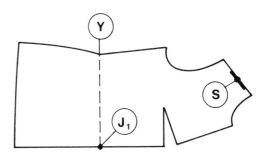

Fig. 6.78.

Stage 4: remain on Y axis (Fig. 6.79)
- Move to second G/2
- Mark part of armhole
- Mark K point.

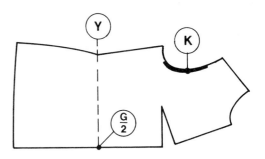

Fig. 6.79.

Stage 5: remain on Y axis (Fig. 6.80)
- Move to E
- Complete lower part of armhole
- Complete side seam and hem.

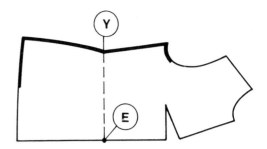

Fig. 6.80.

Stage 6: mark increment J_1 for wedge line (Fig. 6.81)
- Mark towards armhole to increase size
- Mark towards front to decrease size.

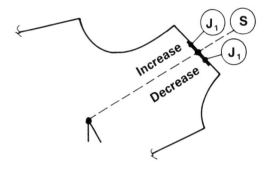

Fig. 6.81.

Stage 7: align pivot line of pattern with wedge line on paper (Fig. 6.82)
- Mark Y_2.

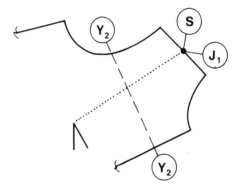

Fig. 6.82.

Stage 8: mark increments $I_1 - G/2 - F$ on Y_2 axis (Fig. 6.83)
- Towards armhole to increase size.
- Towards front edge to decrease size.

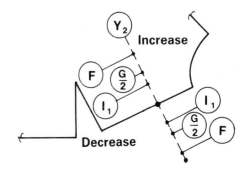

Fig. 6.83.

Stage 9: remain on Y$_2$ axis (Fig. 6.84)
- Mark corner of dart
- Mark part of front edge.

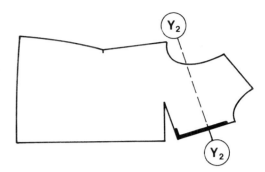

Fig. 6.84.

Stage 10: mark M line as a new axis (Fig. 6.85)
- Align Y$_2$ to M line
- Mark front corner and start of neck.

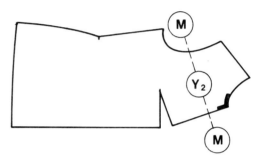

Fig. 6.85.

Stage 11: remain on M line (Fig. 6.86)
- Move to F
- Complete neck
- Mark start of shoulder
- Mark G point.

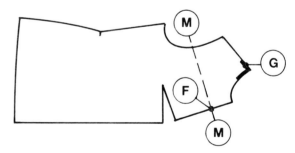

Fig. 6.86.

Stage 12: align pattern to K and G points (Fig. 6.87)
- Complete armhole and shoulder
- Complete bust dart.

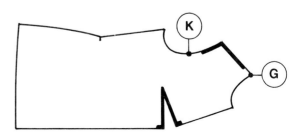

Fig. 6.87.

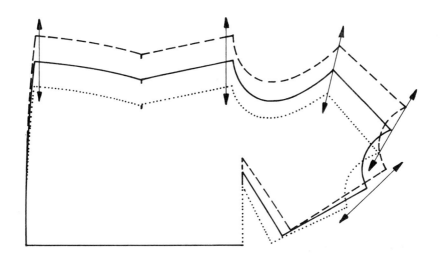

Grade for front with bust dart from front edge

The 'no' bust dart front

A women's garment without bust suppression is technically wrong from the onset and the grading of the front will only compound the basic fault. Some fronts without regular bust suppression can be shaped and manipulated to provide for the bust prominence but to do this involves a great deal of work which is not viable for mass produced clothes.

The best which can be done in grading this type of front is to compromise between the fitting quality required and the fitting quality which can be achieved. The main problem of course, is how to introduce the bust dart width grade of increments I_1 and J_1 without having a dart to the bust point or a seam located on or near the bust prominence. The practical answer is to ignore these two increments as individual elements, but to use their combined value in the width of breast grade, which is increment H. The run of the front armhole line in relation to the shoulder will also change slightly but this can be compensated for by a little 'cosmetic' treatment after the patterns have been graded.

Finally, it should be accepted that a garment having this type of front was presumably designed with full awareness of its inferior fitting qualities. Therefore, the old adage about sows ears and silk purses holds true for the grading.

Grading instructions:
THE 'NO' BUST DART FRONT

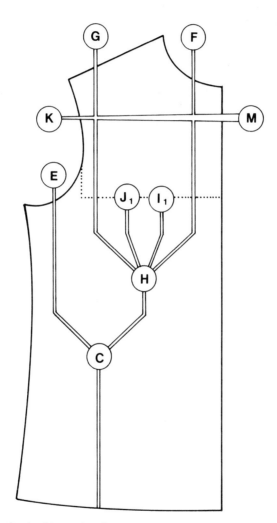

Fig. 6.88. Grading increments for 'no' bust dart front.

Mark axis Y₁–Y₁ on pattern

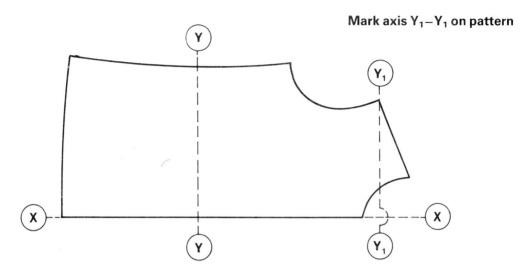

Fig. 6.89. Grading axes.

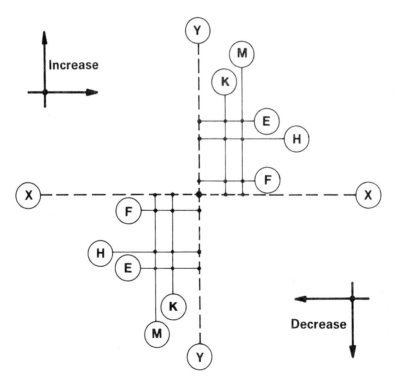

Fig. 6.90. Increment net.

Stage 1: align pattern on X and Y axis (Fig. 6.91)
- Mark part of front edge
- Mark part of hem.

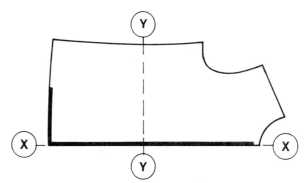

Fig. 6.91.

Stage 2: remain on Y axis (Fig. 6.92)
- Move to H
- Mark lower section of armhole.

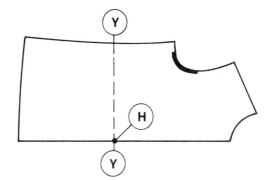

Fig. 6.92.

Stage 3: remain on Y axis (Fig. 6.93)
- Move to E
- Complete armhole
- Mark side seam
- Complete hem.

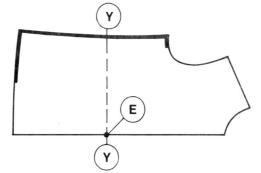

Fig. 6.93.

Stage 4: align Y axis of pattern to relevant K line (Fig. 6.94)
- Align front edge to X axis
- Mark guide line Y_1-Y_1.

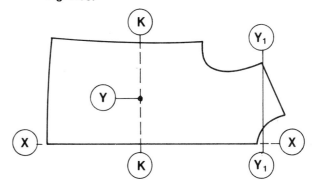

Fig. 6.94.

122

Stage 5: remain on X axis (Fig. 6.95)
- Align Y axis of pattern to relevant K line
- Complete front edge
- Mark start of neck.

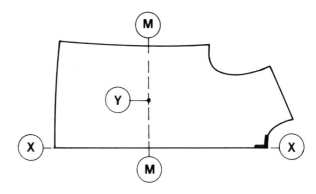

Fig. 6.95.

Stage 6: remain on M line (Fig. 6.96)
- Move to F
- Complete neck
- Mark start of shoulder.

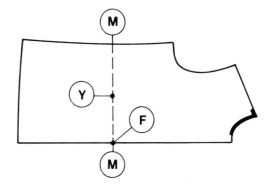

Fig. 6.96.

Stage 7: use a ruler to measure the length of the new shoulder from the new neck point to the line drawn in Stage 4 (Fig. 6.97)
- Mark the new shoulder length on this line.

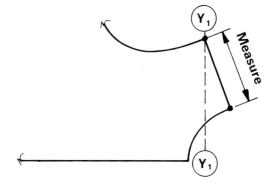

Fig. 6.97.

Stage 8: join new neck point to new shoulder point (Fig. 6.98)
- Mark start of armhole
- Use the pattern to blend the armhole.

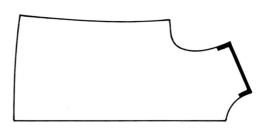

Fig. 6.98.

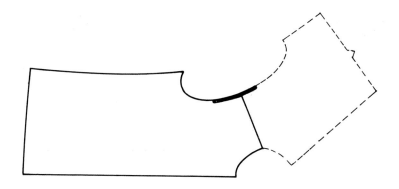

Checking the armhole run after grading

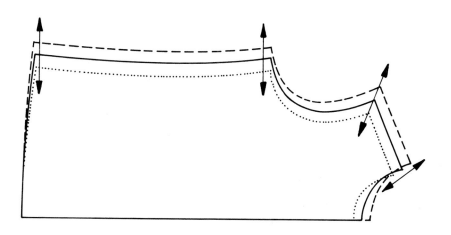

Grade of 'no' bust dart front

Chapter 7

Collars and Lapels

The principles of collar and lapel grading

INTRODUCTION

There are three basic methods of grading collars and lapels, and each one of them should be evaluated in relation to the forms and components being graded, the sizing system being used and the maintenance of design proportions.

METHOD 1

Apart from changes in collar and lapel lengths, necessitated by the front length and neck length grades, the actual design proportions of the collar and lapel remain unchanged for all of the sizes graded. This is the simplest way to grade but it fails to maintain the proportions of a feature which is an integral part of the garment's design.

Consider these aspects:

(1) During grading, the widths and lengths of the upper section of the garment change by a noticeable degree over two or three sizes.
(2) Therefore, if a design feature was, say, a narrow lapel and the width was left unchanged during grading, then the following would result:
   • Proportionate to a large size, the lapel would appear narrower and longer.
   • Proportionate to a small size, the lapel would appear wider and shorter.

This method is one of those used when there are technical restrictions on how the collar and lapel should be graded. Apart from these special circumstances, the following method provides the optimum mixture between practicality and the grading of design proportions.

METHOD 2

This second method takes into account that the lapel and collar proportions are a design feature and their widths and lengths are set against a framework which is bounded by the upper section of the body. This frame is comprised of the shoulder line, the width of breast line, the crease row of the lapel and the position of the first button.

Figure 7.1a defines the boundaries of the frame whilst Fig. 7.1b shows how the proportions of the frame change during grading (in Fig. 7.1b), the grade has been centralised).

It would therefore follow that where possible, the design proportions of the lapel and collar, in relation to upper body framework, should be maintained during grading.

METHOD 3

This is a method employed when there are specific restrictions on the grading of the length and/or width of the lapel and collar. The grading instructions for the 'shawl' collar on p. 138, demonstrates a restriction in width due to the following reasons: any widening or narrowing of the front section of the lapel would automatically require the continuation of this change to the back section in order to preserve the line of the collar. If done, this would have the effect of widening or narrowing the collar relative to the crease line from the centre back to the first buttonhole, with the result that the entire collar construction would require altering for every size.

As this type of pattern manipulation is difficult to incorporate into grading, in most cases, this type of lapel and collar is best left at the same width for all sizes.

The two-way collar and lapel demonstrated on p. 143 is also a restricted grade due to the fact that the collar is designed to be worn open or closed. As the collar length must match the neck girth, increment F is used for a neck grade only, whilst the lapel is changed only in the length by increment M.

GRADING

The four main increments used for grading collars and lapels are derived from the body grade, and they are:

Increment F: the back and front neck grades.
Increment K: the neck to waist grade for the front and back.
Increment L: the front neck point length grade.

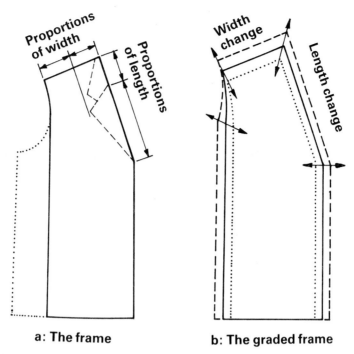

a: The frame **b: The graded frame**

Fig. 7.1. The frame of the collar and lapel.

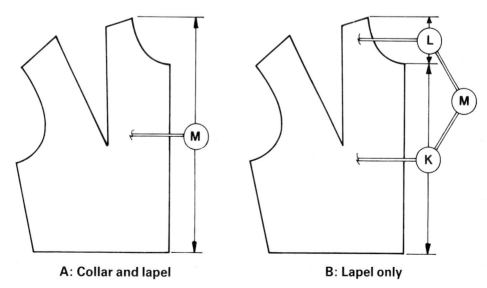

A: Collar and lapel **B: Lapel only**

Fig. 7.2. The applications of increments 'K' – 'L' and 'M'.

Increment M: the total front length grade, which is equivalent to K + L.

APPLICATIONS

The above increments are applied as follows:
(1) Increment F: for grading the back and front sections of collar and/or to grade the width of a lapel.
(2) Increment K: this is used in conjunction with increment L to grade the length proportions of the collar and lapel (Fig. 7.2a).
(3) Increment M: this increment is used as a single grading unit when there are restrictions regarding the lapel length grade (Fig. 7.2b).

DEMONSTRATION

Only those operations specifically concerned with grading the lapel and collar are shown in the following examples. These operations can easily be incorporated into the grading of fronts, usually by the addition of increment K between the original Y axis and the M lines. An example of lapel grading for the static neck-to-waist method is shown p. 228.

Lapels and collars come in a great variety of shapes and proportions but they will not present any problems as long as the foregoing principles are observed.

Grading instructions: THE TAILORED LAPEL

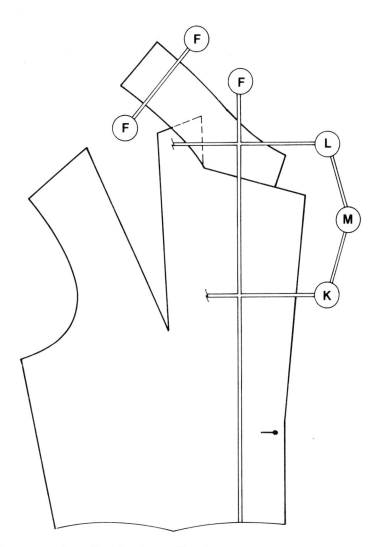

Fig. 7.3. Grading increments for tailored collar and lapel.

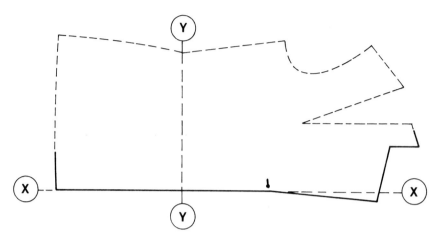

Fig. 7.4. Grading axes.

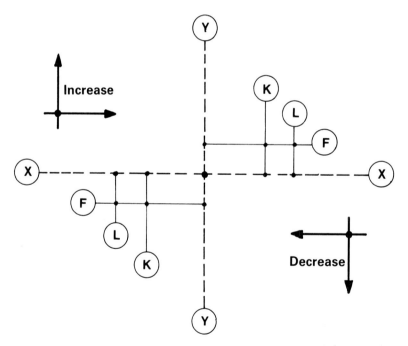

Fig. 7.5. Increment net.

Stage 1: align pattern to X and Y axes (Fig. 7.6)
- Mark front edge and start of lapel
- Mark part of hem.

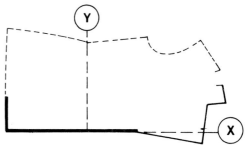

Fig. 7.6.

Stage 2: align Y axis of pattern to relevant K line (Fig. 7.7)
- Mark corner of lapel up to step nip.

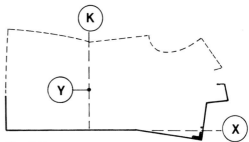

Fig. 7.7.

Stage 3: remain on K line (Fig. 7.8)
- Move to F
- Mark corner and start of neck.

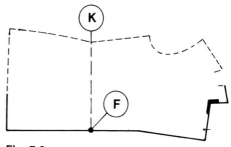

Fig. 7.8.

Stage 4: remain on increment F (Fig. 7.9)
- Align Y axis of pattern to L line
- Complete neck
- Mark start of shoulder.

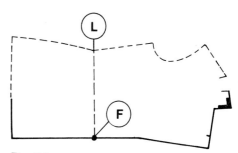

Fig. 7.9.

Stage 5: join lapel corner to neck (Fig. 7.10)
- Blend lapel corner to break point.

Fig. 7.10.

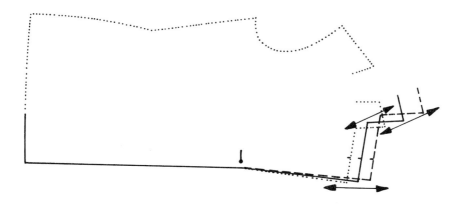

Grade for tailored lapel

Grading instructions: THE TAILORED COLLAR

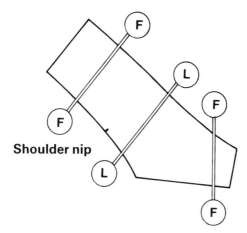

Fig. 7.11. Grading increments for the tailored collar.

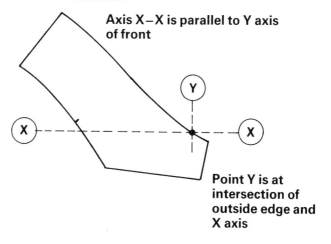

Fig. 7.12. Grading axes.

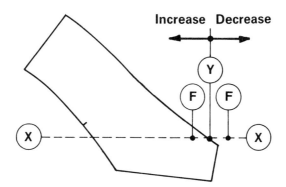

Fig. 7.13. The increment net.

Stage 1: align pattern on X and Y axes (Fig. 7.14)
● Mark collar end and corners.

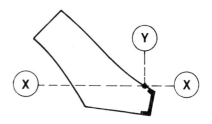

Fig. 7.14.

Stage 2: move on X axis and line up point Y with relevant F (Fig. 7.15)
● Mark gorge corner
● Extent neck seam and part of outside edge
● Lightly mark centre back seam.

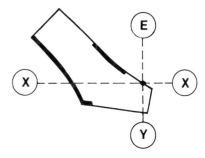

Fig. 7.15.

Stage 3: mark the following increments in the relevant direction from the centre back seam (Fig. 7.16)
● L_1 and F_1 to increase.
● L_2 and F_2 to decrease.

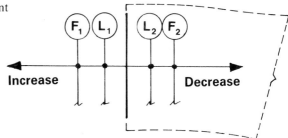

Fig. 7.16.

Stage 4: using the straight section of the neck seam as a guide (Fig. 7.17)
● Move the centre back to L_1 to increase
● Move the centre back to L_2 to decrease
● Mark shoulder nip.

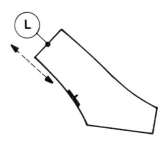

Fig. 7.17.

Stage 5: to change back neck length (Fig. 7.18)
- Move the centre back to F_1 to increase
- Move the centre back to F_2 to decrease
- Mark centre back and seam corners.

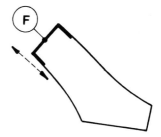

Fig. 7.18.

Stage 6: use pattern to connect gorge corner to step corner (Fig. 7.19)
- Blend outside edge of collar.

Fig. 7.19.

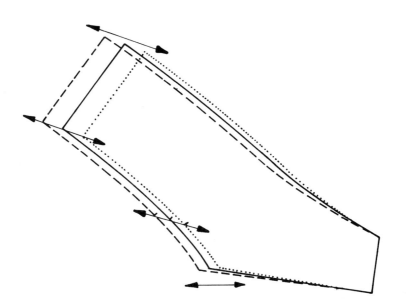

Grade for tailored collar

Grading instructions: THE ONE-PIECE COLLAR AND LAPEL

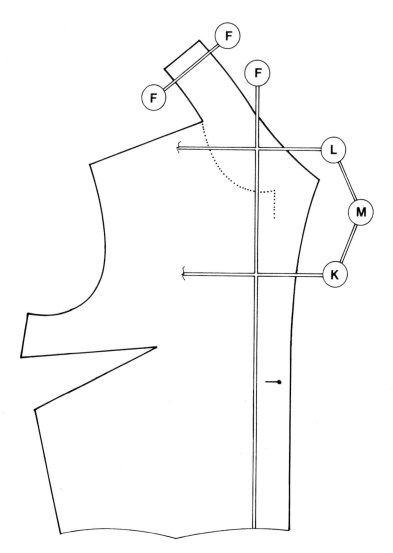

Fig. 7.20. Grading increments for the one-piece collar and lapel.

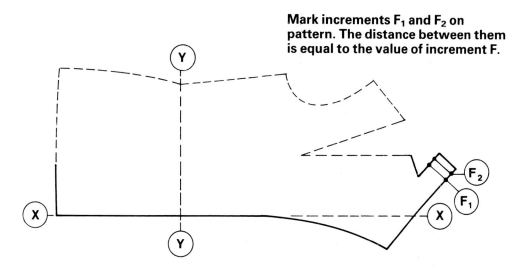

Mark increments F₁ and F₂ on pattern. The distance between them is equal to the value of increment F.

Fig. 7.21. Grading axes.

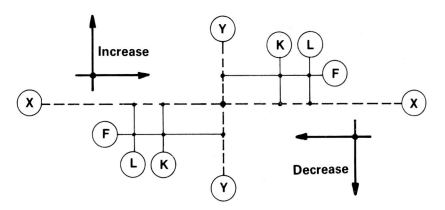

Fig. 7.22. Increment net.

Stage 1: align pattern on X and Y axes (Fig. 7.23)
- Mark front edge and start of lapel.

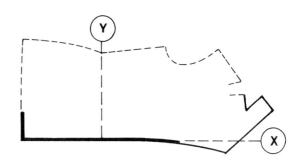

Fig. 7.23.

Stage 2: align Y axis of pattern to K line (Fig. 7.24)
- Mark corner to lapel.

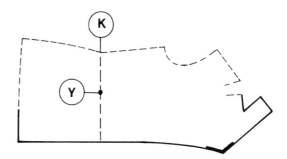

Fig. 7.24.

Stage 3: align Y axis of pattern to L (Fig. 7.25)
- Move to F
- Extend mark to F increments at back neck section
- Mark part of outside edge.
- Mark F_2 to increase
- Mark F_1 to decrease

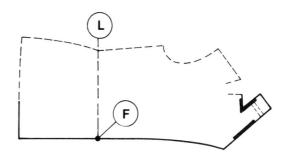

Fig. 7.25.

Stage 4: use back neck seam of collar as guide
(Fig. 7.26)
- Move to F_1 to F_2 to increase
- Move F_2 to F_1 to decrease
- Mark centre back seam and corners.

Fig. 7.26.

Stage 5: use pattern to blend (Fig. 7.27)
- Collar edge
- Lapel corner to break point.

Fig. 7.27.

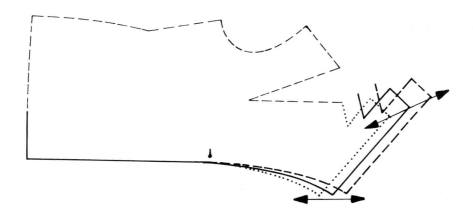

Grade for one-piece collar and lapel

Grading instructions: THE LAPEL SECTION OF THE SHAWL COLLAR

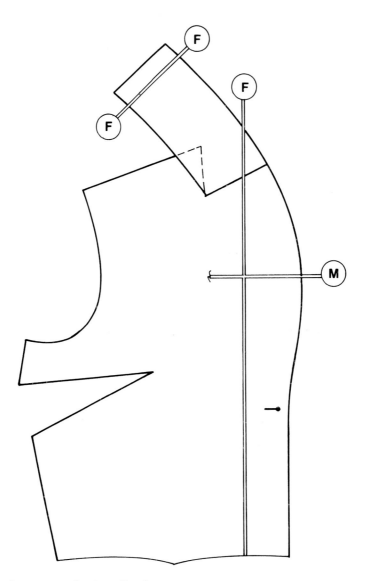

Fig. 7.28. Grading increments for the roll collar.

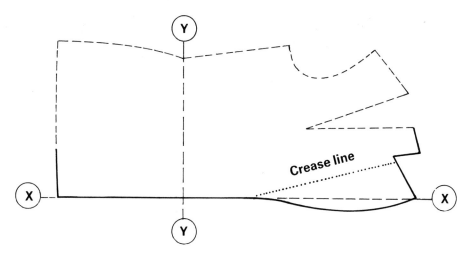

Fig. 7.29. Grading axes.

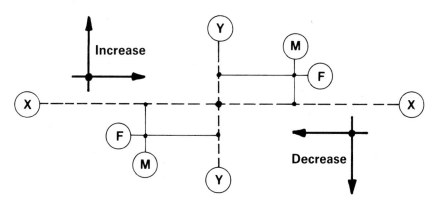

Fig. 7.30. Increment net.

Stage 1: align pattern to X and Y axes (Fig. 7.31)
- Mark front edge and start of lapel.

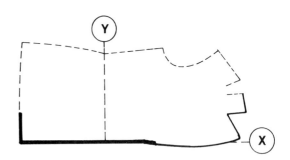

Fig. 7.31.

Stage 2: align Y axis to M line (Fig. 7.32)
- Move to F
- Mark corner
- Mark neck to shoulder
- Mark new crease row.

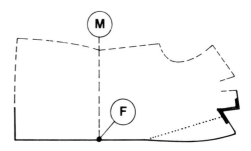

Fig. 7.32.

Stage 3: align crease row of pattern to new crease row from under-collar seam to first buttonhole (Fig. 7.33)
- Mark under-collar seam
- Mark corner of lapel section.

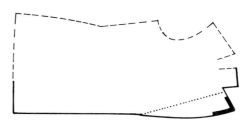

Fig. 7.33.

Stage 4: use pattern to blend lapel to break point (Fig. 7.34).

Fig. 7.34.

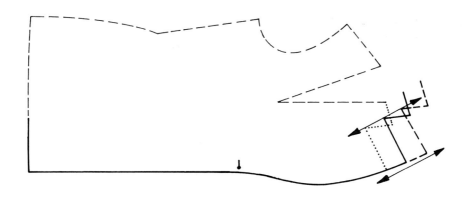

Grade of lapel section

Grading instructions: THE UNDER-COLLAR SECTION OF THE SHAWL COLLAR

Add or subtract increment F at centre back of collar
(Fig. 7.35)

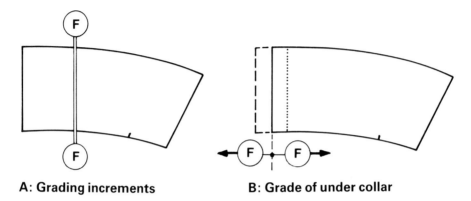

A: Grading increments   **B: Grade of under collar**

Fig. 7.35. The under-collar grade.

Grading instructions: THE TWO-WAY LAPEL

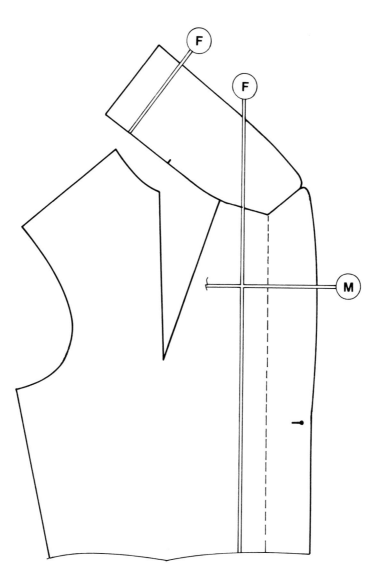

Fig. 7.36. Grading increments for two-way collar and lapel.

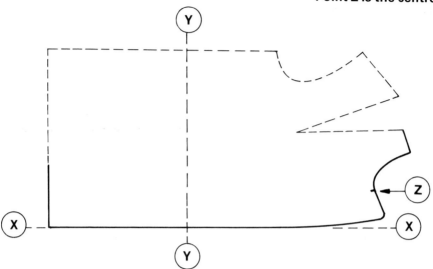

Point Z is the centre front

Fig. 7.37. Grading axes.

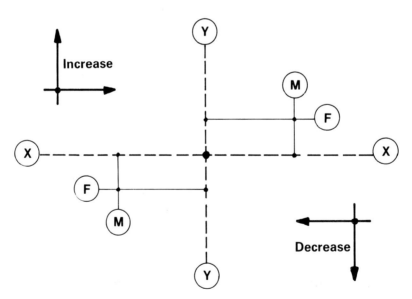

Fig. 7.38. Increment net.

Stage 1: align pattern to X and Y axes (Fig. 7.39)
● Mark front edge and start of lapel.

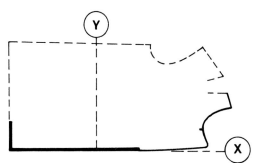

Fig. 7.39.

Stage 2: remain on X axis (Fig. 7.40)
● Align Y axis of pattern with relevant M line
● Mark lapel corner and step
● Mark start of neck.

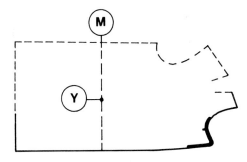

Fig. 7.40.

Stage 3: remain on M axis (Fig. 7.41)
● Move to F
● Complete neck
● Mark start of shoulder.

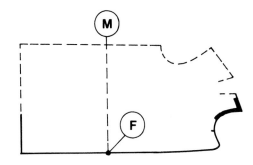

Fig. 7.41.

Stage 4: use pattern to blend lapel to breakpoint
(Fig. 7.42)

Fig. 7.42.

Grading instructions: THE TWO-WAY COLLAR

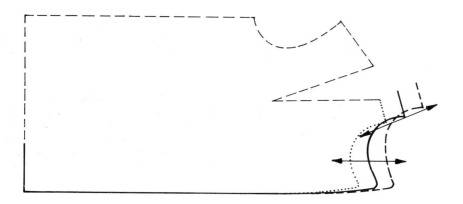

Grade for two-way lapel

Moving on X axis (Fig. 7.43):
• Add or subtract F between shoulder seam nip and front corner
• Add or subtract F between shoulder seam nip and centre back.

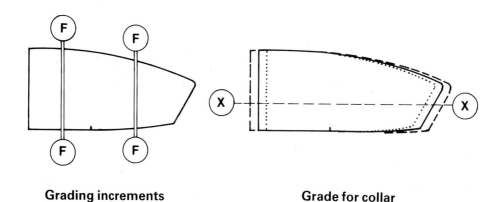

Grading increments   **Grade for collar**

Fig. 7.43. The collar grade.

Chapter 8

Inset Sleeves

The principles of grading shaped sleeves

These are a category of sleeves which are set into a regular armhole as against those sleeves which are wholly or partially attached to the body, or those which have a part of the body attached to them.

SLEEVE TYPES

There are a number of standard variations of inset sleeves and as far as grading is concerned, they can be divided into two main categories:

Type 1: Sleeves which receive the same girth grades at the muscle and the cuff, for example, straight or flared sleeves. With these types of sleeves, both of these girth grades are in total, 4E (Fig. 8.1A).

Type 2: Sleeves which are partially fitted at the cuff, and as a consequence, the muscle and cuff girths have to be graded by different amounts.

There is not a great deal of information forthcoming from the surveys regarding wrist girths, and whatever information is provided is very contradictory. Therefore, in view of the necessity to maintain an aesthetic silhouette to the back sleeve section, the wrist girth will be changed by 2E per size interval (Fig. 8.1B).

INCREMENTS

These are derived from the body and armhole grades:

Increment E: Used in multiples for the muscle and cuff width grades on straight sleeves. Increment E is also used for the muscle section of fitted sleeves.

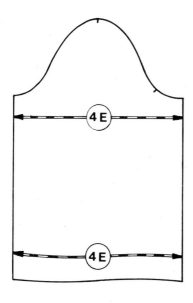

A: Type 1

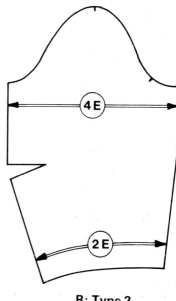

B: Type 2

Fig. 8.1. The muscle and cuff grades.

Increment E/2: This is equivalent to one-half of E and is employed singly or in multiples as part of the total width grade for the cuff for fitted sleeves.

Increment K: The crown height grade.

Increment P: Applied at the elbow line level for changing the overall length of the sleeves.

APPLICATIONS

For tailored sleeves, the total cuff girth grade of 2E is applied in equal halves to the cuffs of the top and under sleeves. However, a sleeve which is partially fitted at the cuff through the use of a cuff or elbow dart requires a slightly more detailed treatment due to the construction of the sleeve itself.

A darted sleeve is basically constructed from a straight sleeve by reducing the cuff girth at the back section of the cuff. Half of the required cuff girth is measured on the cuff line from the front fold line of the sleeve and this point is joined to the elbow line on the back fold line of the sleeve. The resultant dart can be displaced to the elbow line or left at the cuff.

This manipulation has two effects:

(1) *Centre lines:* the centre line of the sleeve remains in the same position from the sleeve head to the elbow line, but changes its run from this point to the cuff line (Fig. 8.2). This change is created

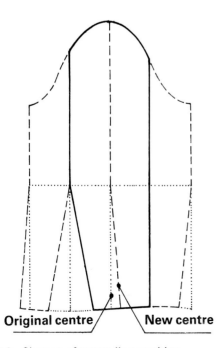

Original centre / **New centre**

Fig. 8.2. Change of centre line position.

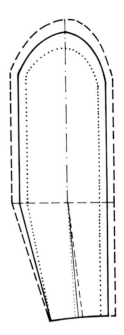

Fig. 8.3. Influence of width grade on dart depth.

by the narrower cuff girth, and ensures that a harmonious line is generated if the sleeve is split. As a result, this change of centre at the cuff has produced four cuff sections and the grading of this section must accurately maintain these divisions.

(2) *Darts:* a result of grading the muscle and elbow girths by 4E and the cuff girth by 2E is that the dart becomes larger when increasing size and smaller when decreasing. This is because the elbow girth is being graded at twice the incremental rate than that of the cuff. This effect is shown in Fig. 8.3 where the three graded sleeves have a common origin point on the back sleeve cuff.

GENERAL POINTERS FOR GRADING

TAILORED SLEEVE (p. 150)

If the top and under sleeve patterns have turn-ups allowed, align the pattern to the X–X axis according to the nett length, i.e. without the turn-up (Fig. 8.4). The turn-up will automatically be graded together with the sleeve but the gross length corner, i.e. the corner formed by the edge of the turn-up and the fore-arm seam should not be used as a location point.

DARTED SLEEVE (p. 156 and p. 161)

The X–X axis used in demonstrating the grading of these sleeves is the original centre line from the sleeve

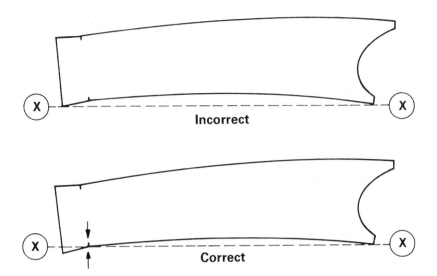

Fig. 8.4. Alignment to the X axis.

crown to the cuff. For these examples, the common origin line method is used, and this entails grading the sleeve in two stages; first the front section and then the back section.

SPLIT SLEEVE (p. 166)

Follow the same grading process for the back and front sleeves. Do not mark the curved section at the sleeve head until the Y axis of the pattern is aligned with the K line on the paper. This ensures that the curve

produced by the sleeve head dart remains the same shape and length for all sizes.

TO SUM UP

The methods of grading 'Grown-On' sleeves in Chapter 9 are based on the master grades demonstrated in the following pages. Transferring techniques from one type of sleeve to another can be simply effected by observing the principles developed in this group of grades.

Grading instructions: THE TAILORED TOP SLEEVE

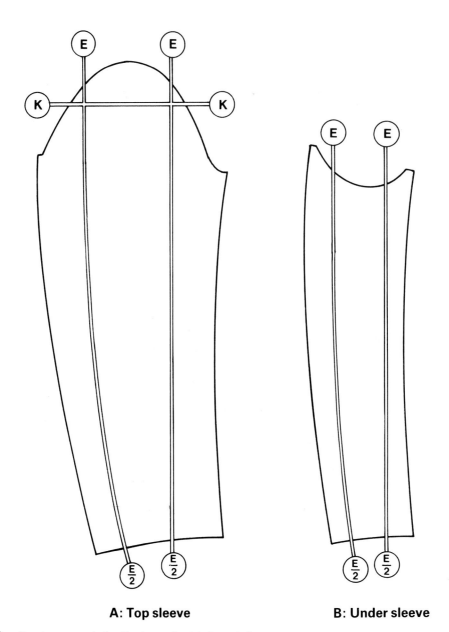

A: Top sleeve   **B: Under sleeve**

Fig. 8.5. Grading increments for the two-piece tailored sleeve.

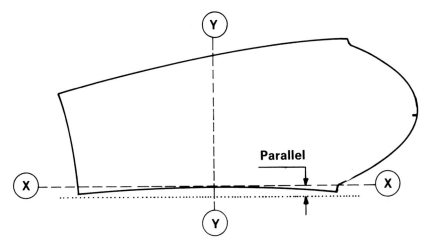

Fig. 8.6. Grading axes.

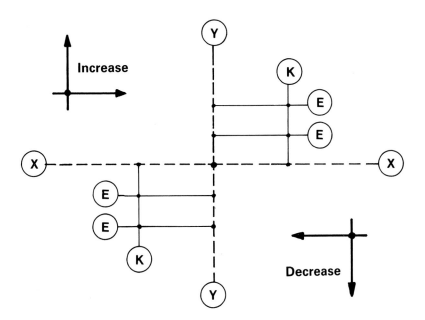

Fig. 8.7. Increment net.

Stage 1: align pattern to X and Y axes (Fig. 8.8)
- Mark fore-arm seam
- Mark beginning of front sleeve head section
- Mark part of cuff.

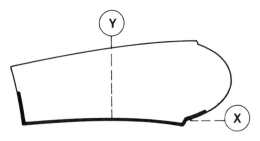

Fig. 8.8.

Stage 2: on Y axis, move to first E (Fig. 8.9)
- Mark corner of cuff and hind-arm seam
- Complete cuff.

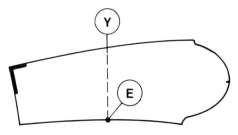

Fig. 8.9.

Stage 3: remain on Y axis (Fig. 8.10)
- Move to second E
- Mark top section of hind-arm seam
- Mark beginning of back sleeve head section.

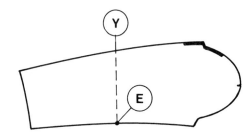

Fig. 8.10.

Stage 4: align pattern to K line and first E (Fig. 8.11)
- Mark crown and centre nip.

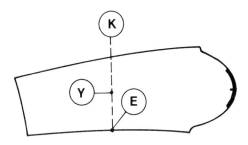

Fig. 8.11.

Stage 5: use pattern to (Fig. 8.12)
- Blend head
- Blend hind-arm seam from head to cuff.

Fig. 8.12.

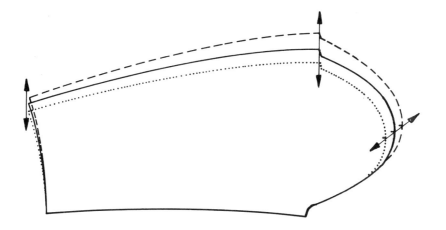

Grade of top sleeve

Grading instructions: THE TAILORED UNDER SLEEVE

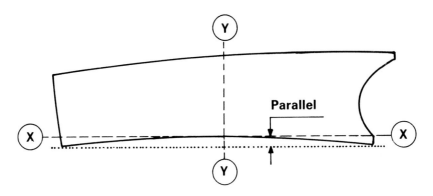

Fig. 8.13. Grading axes.

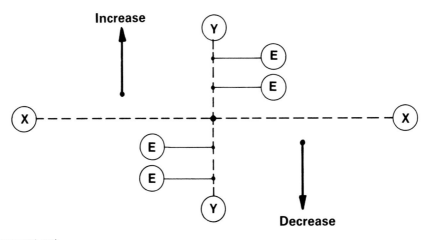

Fig. 8.14. Increment net.

Stage 1: align pattern to X and Y axes (Fig. 8.15)
- Mark fore-arm seam
- Mark part of underseam section
- Mark part of cuff.

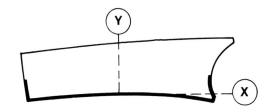

Fig. 8.15.

Stage 2: remain on Y axis (Fig. 8.16)
- Move to first E
- Complete cuff
- Mark start of hind-arm seam at cuff
- Mark centre nip at underseam section.

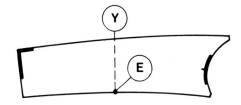

Fig. 8.16.

Stage 3: remain on Y axis (Fig. 8.17)
- Move to second E
- Complete underseam section
- Mark top section of hind-arm seam.

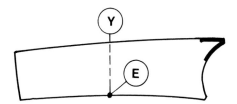

Fig. 8.17.

Stage 4: use the pattern to blend the hind-arm seam from the top to the cuff (Fig. 8.18).

Fig. 8.18.

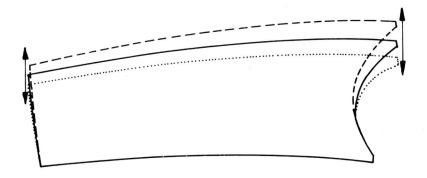

Grade of under sleeve

Grading instructions: INSET SLEEVE WITH ELBOW DART

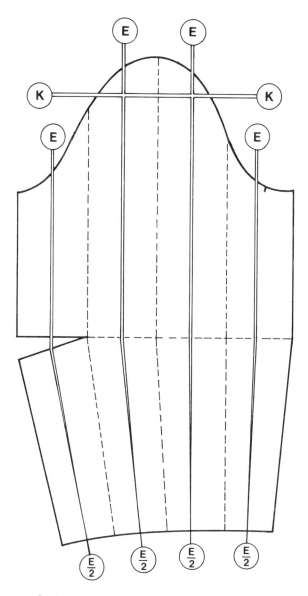

Fig. 8.19. Grading increments for inset sleeve with elbow dart.

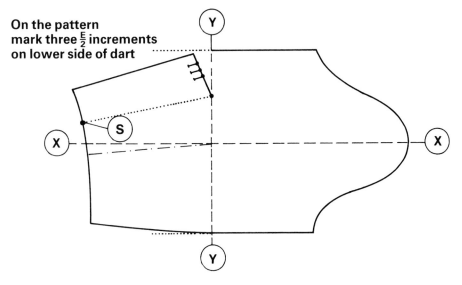

Fig. 8.20. Grading axes.

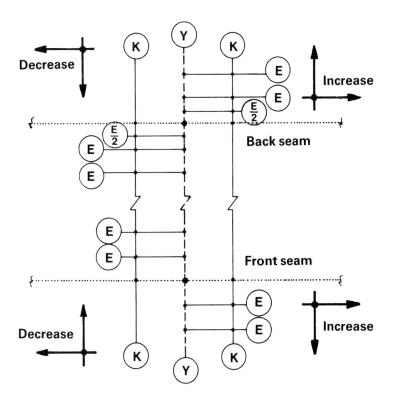

Fig. 8.21. Increment net.

Stage 1: front sleeve section (Fig. 8.22)
- Align pattern on X and Y axes
- Move to first E
- Mark front section of sleeve head
- Mark front cuff corner.

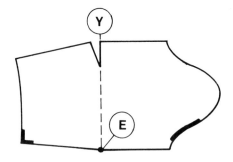

Fig. 8.22.

Stage 2: move to second E (Fig. 8.23)
- Complete under section of sleeve head
- Mark front underseam from undersection to elbow line
- Join underseam from elbow line to cuff corner.

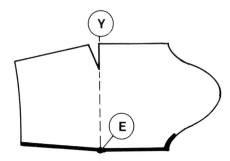

Fig. 8.23.

Stage 3: Align X axes of pattern and paper (Fig. 8.24)
- Align Y axis of pattern to relevant K line
- Mark crown of sleeve and centre nip.

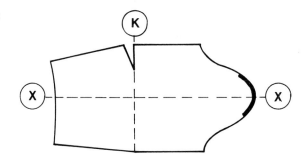

Fig. 8.24.

Stage 4: back sleeve section (Fig. 8.25)
- Return to Y axis
- Move to E/2 of this section
- Mark point S.

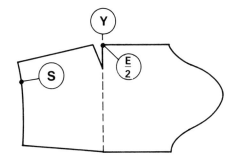

Fig. 8.25.

Stage 5: move to the first E of this section (Fig. 8.26)
- Mark dart apex
- Mark lower section of back sleeve head.

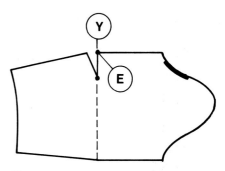

Fig. 8.26.

Stage 6: move to second E in this section (Fig. 8.27)
- Mark top section of underseam to elbow line
- Complete under section of back sleeve head.

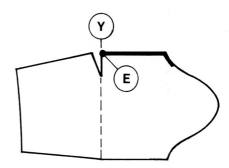

Fig. 8.27.

Stage 7: join the new dart apex to point S (Fig. 8.28)
- Align same line on pattern to this line with the dart apexes matching.

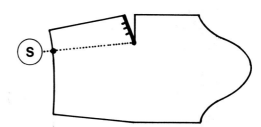

Fig. 8.28.

Stage 8: using new dart line as a guide (Fig. 8.29)
- Move to first E/2 on this line
- Mark underseam cuff corner.

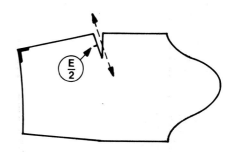

Fig. 8.29.

Stage 9: remain on the dart line (Fig. 8.30)
- Move to second E/2
- Mark corner of dart and lower section of underseam.

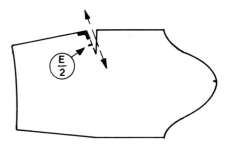

Fig. 8.30.

Stage 10: use pattern to (Fig. 8.31)
- Blend sleeve head
- Complete lower section of back underseam
- Blend cuff line.

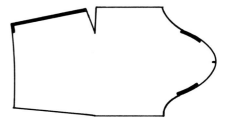

Fig. 8.31.

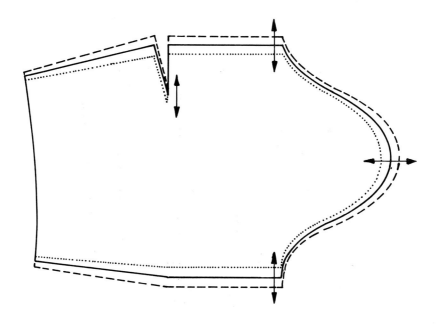

Grade of inset sleeve with elbow dart

Grading instructions:
INSET SLEEVE WITH CUFF DART

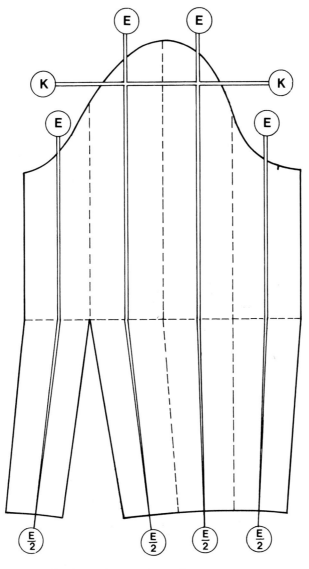

Fig. 8.32. Grading increments for inset sleeve with cuff dart.

162

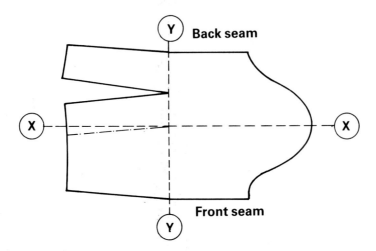

Fig. 8.33. Grading axes.

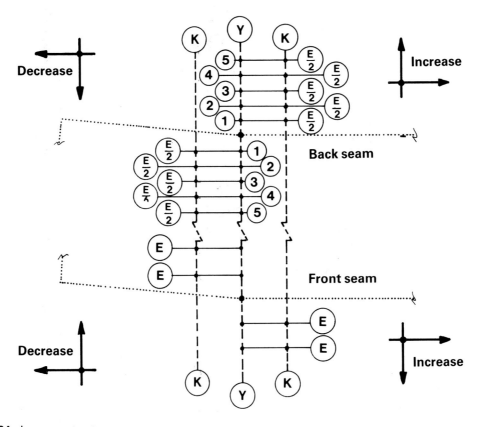

Fig. 8.34. Increment nets.

FRONT SLEEVE SECTION

Stage 1: align on X and Y axes (Fig. 8.35)
- Move to first E
- Mark part of front section of sleeve head
- Mark corner of lower underseam and cuff.

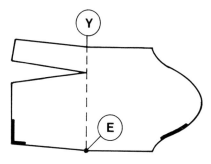

Fig. 8.35.

Stage 2: move to second E (Fig. 8.36)
- Complete undersection of sleeve head
- Mark top section of underseam to elbowline.

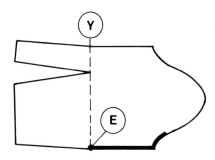

Fig. 8.36.

Stage 3: remain on second E (Fig. 8.37)
- Align Y axis of pattern to relevant K line
- Mark sleeve crown and centre nip.

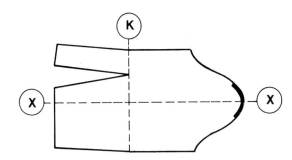

Fig. 8.37.

BACK SLEEVE SECTION

Stage 4: align pattern to Y axis (Fig. 8.38)
- Move to first E/2
- Mark first corner of cuff and dart.

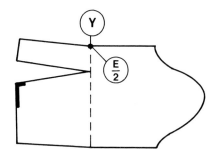

Fig. 8.38.

Stage 5: remain on Y axis (Fig. 8.39)
- Move to second E/2
- Mark new apex of dart
- Mark part of back section of sleeve head.

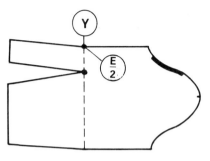

Fig. 8.39.

Stage 6: remain on Y axis (Fig. 8.40)
- Move to third E/2
- Mark second corner of cuff and dart.

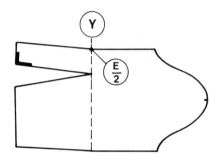

Fig. 8.40.

Stage 7: remain on Y axis (Fig. 8.41)
- Move to fourth E/2
- Complete undersection of sleeve head
- Mark top section of underseam to elbow line.

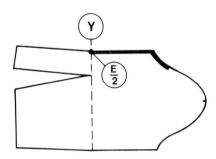

Fig. 8.41.

Stage 8: remain on Y axis (Fig. 8.42)
- Move to fifth E/2
- Mark corner of cuff and underseam.

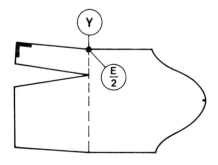

Fig. 8.42.

Stage 9: use pattern to (Fig. 8.43)
- Join underseams from the elbow line to cuff
- Blend cuff
- Blend sleeve head
- Complete dart.

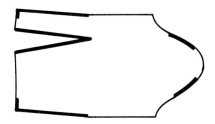

Fig. 8.43.

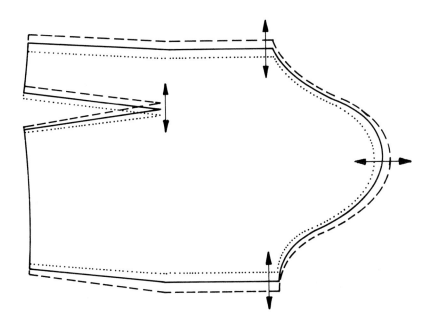

Grade for inset sleeve with cuff dart

Grading instructions: THE SPLIT SLEEVE

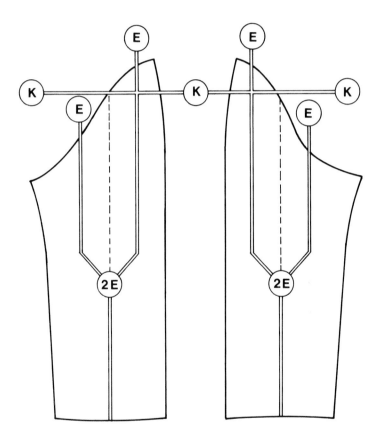

**Both halves are graded
by exactly the same method**

Fig. 8.44. Grading increments for split inset sleeve.

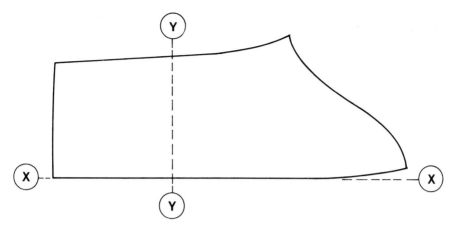

Fig. 8.45. Grading axes for both half sleeves.

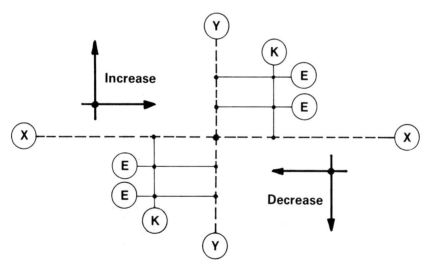

Fig. 8.46. Increment net for both half sleeves.

Stage 1: align pattern on X and Y axes (Fig. 8.47)
- Mark part of centre seam
- Mark part of cuff.

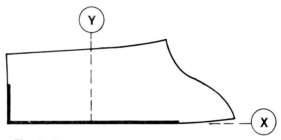

Fig. 8.47.

Stage 2: remain on Y axis (Fig. 8.48)
- Move to first E
- Mark section of sleeve head.

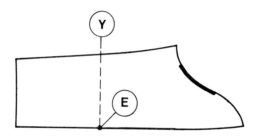

Fig. 8.48.

Stage 3: remain on Y axis (Fig. 8.49)
- Move to second E
- Complete underseam
- Mark underarm seam
- Complete cuff.

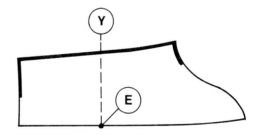

Fig. 8.49.

Stage 4: align pattern to X axis (Fig. 8.50)
- Align Y axis of pattern to relevant K line
- Complete upper section of centre seam
- Mark crown of sleeve.

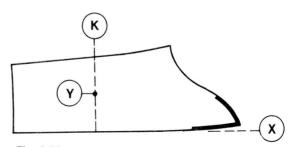

Fig. 8.50.

Stage 5: use pattern to blend sleeve head (Fig. 8.51).

Fig. 8.51.

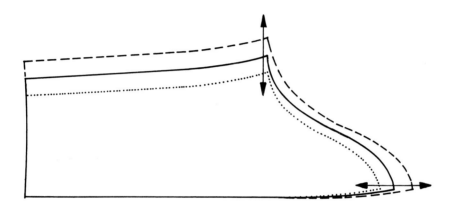

Grade of inset split sleeve (half only)

Chapter 9

'Grown-On' Sleeves

The principles and elements of grading this group of sleeves are exactly the same as those employed for grading the basic body and sleeve (Chapter 5). So far, the body and sleeve have been treated as separate components, but now they are wholly attached to the body like the kimono and magyar, or part of the body is joined to the sleeve as is the case with the full or semi-raglan.

Whatever the individual styling of these bodies and sleeves, the guiding principle for grading them is to apply the basic grade for a sleeve to the sleeve section and that for basic body to the body section.

In the examples for the kimono and Magyar sleeves, the demonstrations commence at that stage of the body grade where the sleeve grade becomes operative. The raglan grade is demonstrated in its entirety because the technique involved is slightly different from that of the regular basic grades.

The Kimono Sleeve

The kimono, a garment worn by Japanese men and women, is an example of a sleeve which is completely 'grown-on' to the body with each half of the sleeve being combined with the back and front respectively.

This is a restricted grade because the relationship of the side seam and underarm seam line, and the angle of the sleeve to the body remain unchanged during grading. Consequently, the width grade of 2E is applied at the overarm seam only. The other increment used is K, which is the sleeve head grade.

The grade for the kimono commences from the two points where the sleeve is attached to the body (Fig. 9.1.)

(1) At the side seam
(2) At the junction of the shoulder and armhole.

Therefore, it is necessary to complete the width grade to the side seam and to finish the shoulder grade (the application of increment G or the second G/2) in order to establish the shoulder point. The width grade axis for both sleeves is Z – Z and this is marked at right-angles to the centre of each sleeve section.

The grading instructions start from the stage where the side seam and shoulder point positions have been

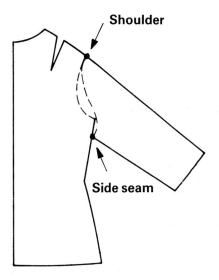

Fig. 9.1. Attachment points to the body.

determined. As the grades for the back and front sleeve sections are exactly the same, only one sleeve grade is demonstrated.

Grading instructions: THE KIMONO SLEEVE

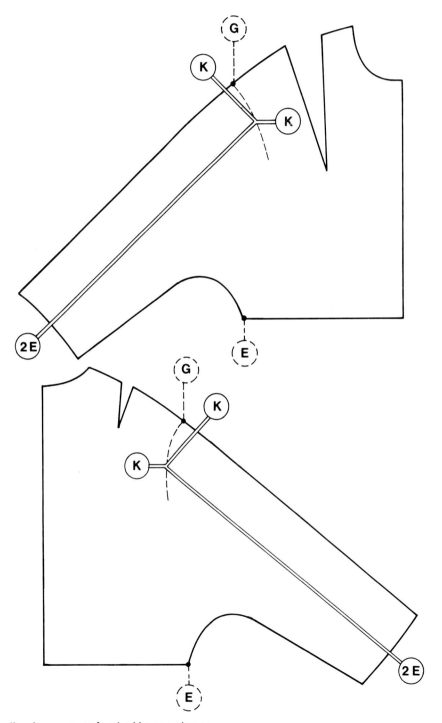

Fig. 9.2. Grading increments for the kimono sleeve.

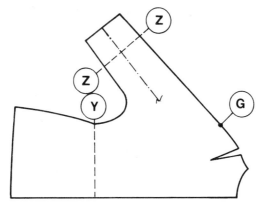

Fig. 9.3. Grading axes for body and sleeve.

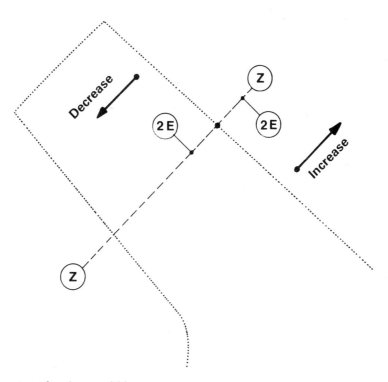

Fig. 9.4. Increment net for sleeve width.

Stage 1: complete width grade t. E (Fig. 9.5)
● Mark side seam, underarm seam and part of cuff.

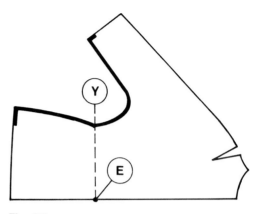

Fig. 9.5.

Stage 2: mark part of overarm seam (Fig. 9.6)
● Mark Z – Z axis.

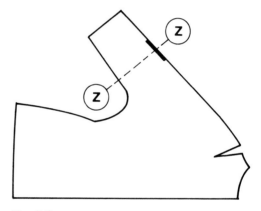

Fig. 9.6.

Stage 3: mark the 2E increment in the direction
required. This is measured from the intersection of axis
Z – Z and the overarm seam (Fig. 9.7).

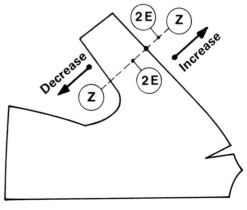

Fig. 9.7.

Stage 4: complete upper section grade to establish
shoulder point G (Fig. 9.8)

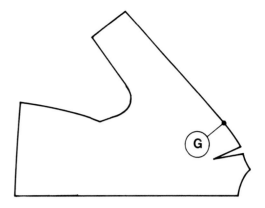

Fig. 9.8.

Stage 5: align sleeve on Z – Z axis (Fig. 9.9)
- Move to E2
- Mark part of overarm seam
- Complete cuff

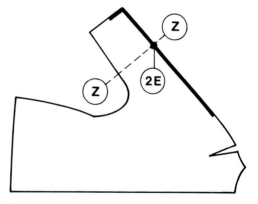

Fig. 9.9.

Stage 6: use pattern to blend the overarm seam to point
G (the overarm length from the shoulder point to cuff
will change in length by the amount of increment K)
(Fig. 9.10).

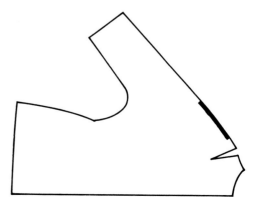

Fig. 9.10.

176

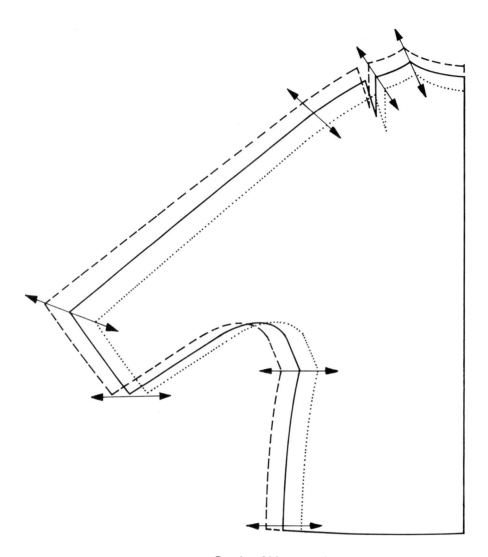

Grade of kimono sleeve

Introduction to the full raglan cut

This cut is named after Lord Raglan who was the British Commander during the Crimean War (1854–1856), and it was designed primarily for ease and comfort in wear. The raglan has an armhole line extending from the neck to a regular or deepened armhole with the body sections of the front and back joined to the head and crown of each of the sleeve halves.

For grading purposes, the section of the body which is attached to the sleeve must be graded according to the body grade and use the same axes whilst the sleeve section is graded by the regular method. The

demonstration grades for the body and sleeve are divided into two sections each having two units:

Section 1: the back and back sleeve
Section 2: the front and front sleeve

Section 1

THE BACK AND BACK SLEEVE

This grade is straightforward and the grading

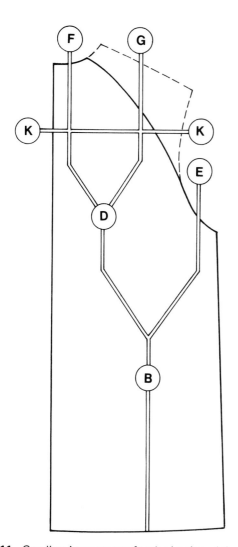
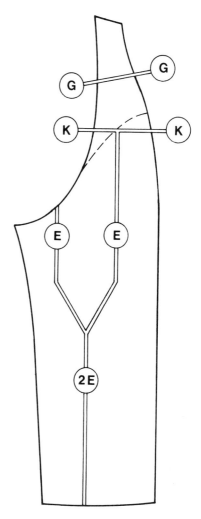

Fig. 9.11. Grading increments for the back and the back sleeve.

relationship between the back and sleeve is shown in Fig. 9.11. For the back, the across-back grade D is used in the same manner as for a regular back. The axis Z – Z which is used for grading the shoulder section of the sleeve horn is parallel to the Y axis used to grade the body. This ensures that the related sections are graded through the same angles.

Grading instructions: THE FULL RAGLAN BACK

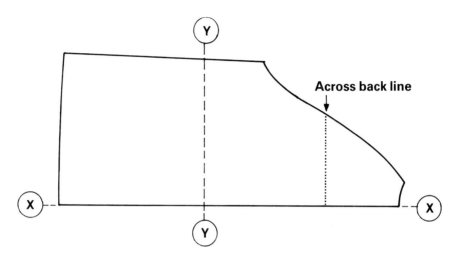

Fig. 9.12. Grading axes for back.

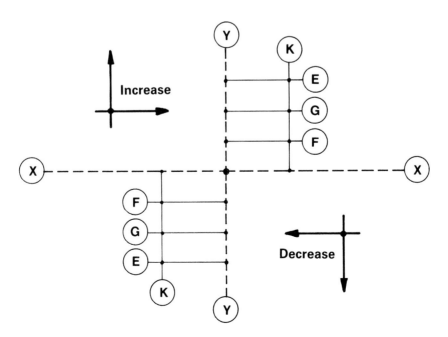

Fig. 9.13. Increment net for back.

Stage 1: align pattern to X and Y axes (Fig. 9.14)
- Mark centre back
- Mark start of hem.

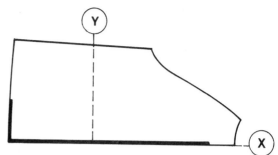

Fig. 9.14.

Stage 2: move on Y axis to G (Fig. 9.15)
- Mark armhole section of either side of across back line.

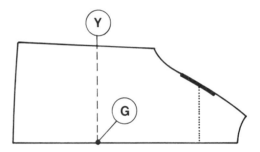

Fig. 9.15.

Stage 3: remain on Y axis (Fig. 9.16)
- Move to E
- Complete lower part of armhole
- Mark side seam
- Complete hem.

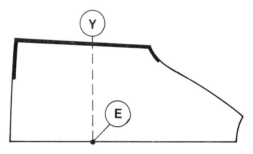

Fig. 9.16.

Stage 4: align Y of pattern to K relevant line (Fig. 9.17)
- Mark start of neck.

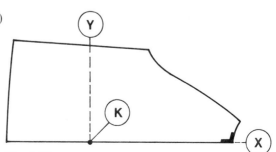

Fig. 9.17.

Stage 5: remain on K line (Fig. 9.18)
- Move to F
- Complete neck
- Mark start of raglan line.

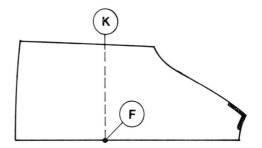

Fig. 9.18.

Stage 6: use pattern to blend raglan line (Fig. 9.19).

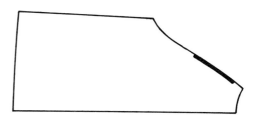

Fig. 9.19.

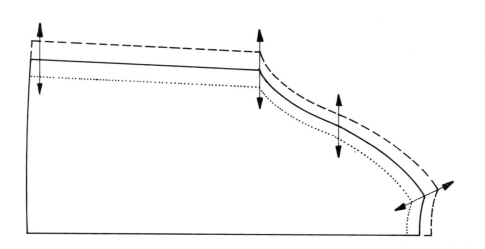

Grade of full raglan back

Grading instructions:
THE FULL RAGLAN BACK SLEEVE

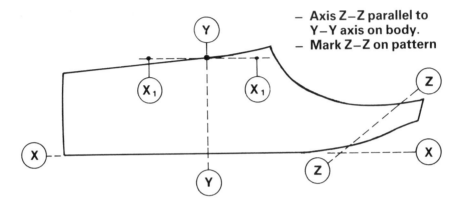

— Axis Z–Z parallel to
  Y–Y axis on body.
— Mark Z–Z on pattern

Fig. 9.20. Grading axes for back sleeve.

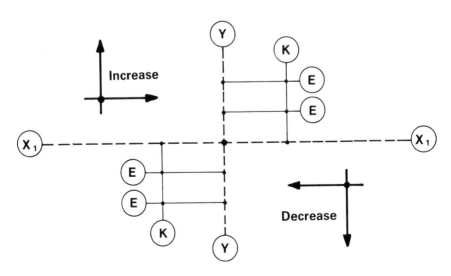

Fig. 9.21. Increment net for back sleeve.

Stage 1: align pattern to X and Y axes (Fig. 9.22)
- Mark part of overarm seam to start of shoulder line curve
- Mark part of cuff.

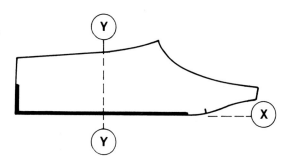

Fig. 9.22.

Stage 2: remain on Y axis (Fig. 9.23)
- Move to first E
- Mark central section of sleeve line.

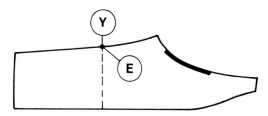

Fig. 9.23.

Stage 3: remain on Y axis (Fig. 9.24)
- Move to second E
- Complete lower section of sleeve
- Mark underarm seam
- Complete cuff.

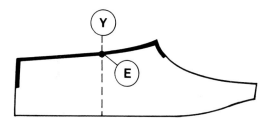

Fig. 9.24.

Stage 4: align Y axis of pattern to K relevant line (Fig. 9.25)
- Mark part of shoulder curve section
- Mark part of body line
- Mark Z – Z axis.

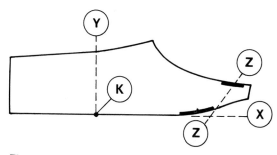

Fig. 9.25.

Stage 5: mark increment G from intersection of body line and axis Z – Z (Fig. 9.26).

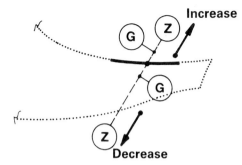

Fig. 9.26.

Stage 6: move along Z – Z axis to G (Fig. 9.27).
- Mark part of horn
- Mark neck section
- Mark start of body line.

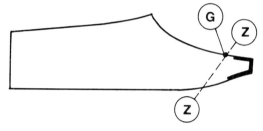

Fig. 9.27.

Stage 7: use pattern to blend the shoulder and body lines (Fig. 9.28)

Fig. 9.28.

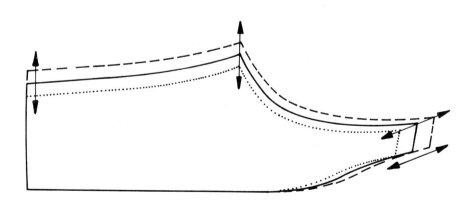

Grade of full raglan back sleeve

Section 2

THE FRONT AND FRONT SLEEVE (Fig. 9.29)

There is no fixed rule for the position and run of the raglan body line on the front. This is an internal line which is style dependent and this situation influences two factors:

(1) The bust dart grade
(2) The technique required to grade a bust dart, the length and position of which, can vary from style to style.

Firstly, the bust dart grade itself.

The effect of the bust dart width grade is the introduction of a triangle into the body from nothing at point S on the shoulder line to increments I_1 and J_1 on the bust line. The raglan body line can cross this triangle at any level between the bust point and shoulder lines which effectively divides this triangle into two sections:

(a) The section belonging to the body
(b) That belonging to the sleeve.

Thus, the sleeve section of the triangle extends from point S on the shoulder to the sleeve seam and the base

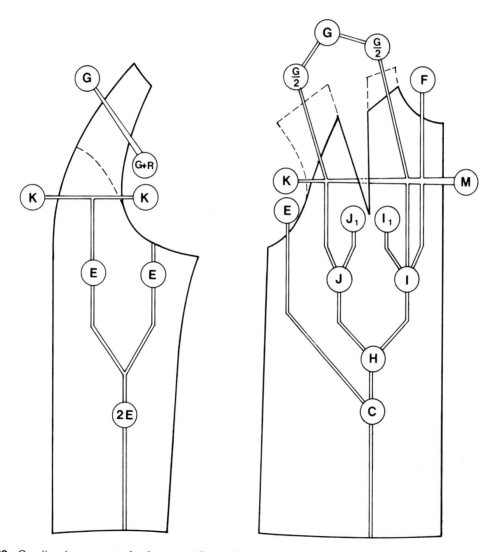

Fig. 9.29. Grading increments for front and front sleeve.

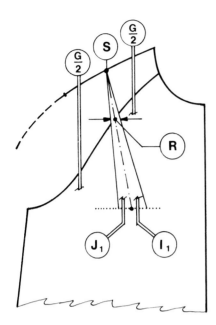

Fig. 9.30. Increment 'R'.

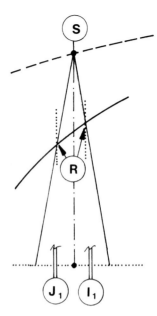

Fig. 9.31. The value of increment 'R'.

length of this section is equivalent to the distance between the intersections of the body line and the sides of the triangle. This distance is notated increment R and its location, in relation to the bust grade triangle, is shown in Fig. 9.30.

The front sleeve
The method of determining the value of increment R for the front sleeve grade is as follows:

(1) Draw a triangle with a base equal to $I_1 + J_1$ and the height equivalent to the distance from the centre of the front shoulder (point S) to the bust point.
(2) Align the bust point of the pattern to the centre of the triangle's base and draw that nett section of the body line which is directly above the bust point.
(3) The distance between the two points on the sides of the triangle which are intersected by the raglan line is increment R for that particular pattern (Fig. 9.31). The application of increment R to the front sleeve grade is described on p. 193.

The front
All of the bust dart width grades use the pivot principle between the bust point and point S on the shoulder. However, as there is no shoulder line on the raglan front, a grading aid is required in order to bring the front into the regular grading framework. This grading aid is prepared as follows (Fig. 9.32):

(1) Mark point S on the shoulder line of the front sleeve pattern.

(2) Staple or pin a piece of pattern paper about 3 cm wide onto the body line at the approximate central position of the line for a bust dart from the shoulder.
(3) Align the nett line of the body and sleeve together from the neck and mark a small section of the shoulder and point S on the grading aid.
(4) Cut the grading aid along the marked shoulder line retaining the point S mark.

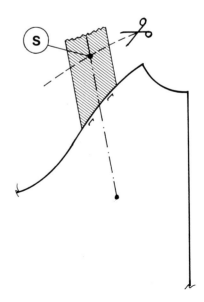

Fig. 9.32. Grading aid for raglan front.

The grading aid is in lieu of a regular shoulder line and can be used for the grades of any type of bust dart or bust panel, and its application is demonstrated on pp. 189 and 190. Where the bust dart has been displaced from the shoulder position, mark the pattern to be graded with a pivot line from the bust point to where point S would be located if there was a conventional front shoulder line.

Grading instructions: THE FULL RAGLAN FRONT

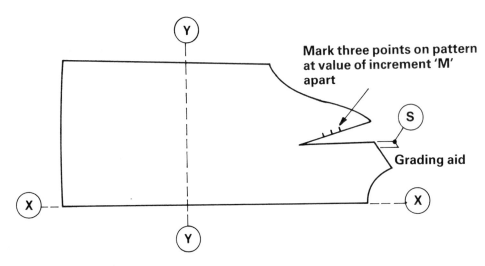

Fig. 9.33. Grading axes for front.

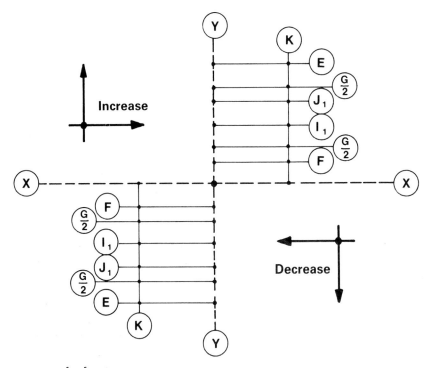

Fig. 9.34. Increment net for front.

Stage 1: prepare grading aid (Fig. 9.35)
- Align pattern on X and Y axes
- Mark front edge
- Mark start of hem.

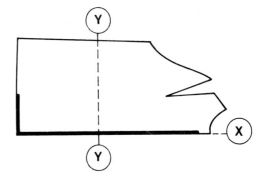

Fig. 9.35.

Stage 2: remain on Y axis (Fig. 9.36)
- Move to I_1
- Mark new bust point
- Move to J_1
- Use grading aid to mark point J_1 at shoulder line level.

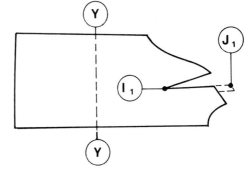

Fig. 9.36.

Stage 3: remain on Y axis (Fig. 9.37)
- Move to second $G/2$
- Mark lower section of armhole.

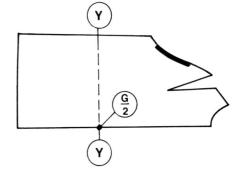

Fig. 9.37.

Stage 4: remain on Y axis (Fig. 9.38)
- Move to E
- Complete lower section of armhole
- Mark side seam
- Complete hem.

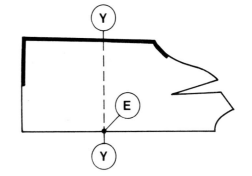

Fig. 9.38.

Stage 5: align Y of pattern to relevant M line (Fig. 9.39)
- Complete front edge
- Mark start of neck

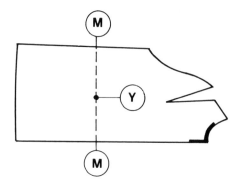

Fig. 9.39.

Stage 6: remain on M line (Fig. 9.40)
- Move to F
- Complete neck
- Mark start of body line.

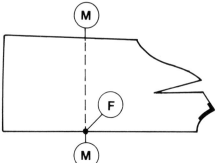

Fig. 9.40.

Stage 7: remain on M line (Fig. 9.41)
- Move to first G/2
- Using grading aid to mark point S.

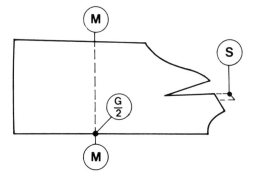

Fig. 9.41.

Stage 8: connect point S to the new bust point (Fig. 9.42)
- Complete first section of body line
- Complete first side of bust dart from body line to bust point.

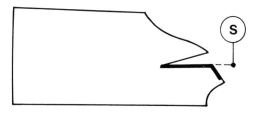

Fig. 9.42.

Stage 9: connect J₁ point to new bust point (Fig. 9.43)
- Align pivot line of pattern on this line from the new bust point to point S
- Mark second side of bust dart and M point
- Mark start of body line.

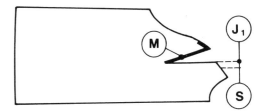

Fig. 9.43.

Stage 10: move pattern by distance G/2 parallel to bust dart line (Fig. 9.44)
- Towards side to increase
- Towards front to decrease
- Complete armhole.

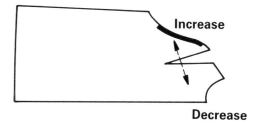

Fig. 9.44.

Stage 11: use pattern to blend body line (Fig. 9.45).

Fig. 9.45.

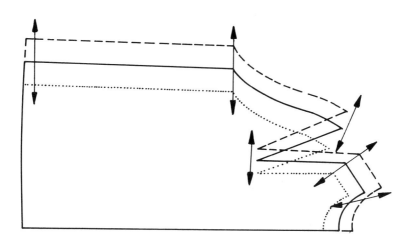

Grade of full raglan front

Grading instructions:
THE FULL RAGLAN FRONT SLEEVE

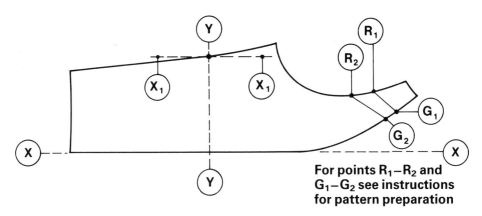

For points R_1-R_2 and G_1-G_2 see instructions for pattern preparation

Fig. 9.46. Grading axes for front sleeve.

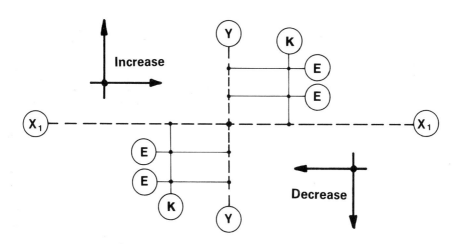

Fig. 9.47. Increment net for front sleeve.

Part 1: Pattern preparation

THE SHOULDER LENGTH GRADE (Fig. 9.48)

- Mark Z – Z axis parallel to Y axis of front
- Mark guide line $Z_1 - Z_1$ at right angles to Z – Z axis. Start guide line at mid-shoulder point and extend body line
- Mark half the value of increment G on either side of the $Z_1 - Z_1$ line at its intersection with the shoulder line. This provides G_1 and G_2
- Continue points G_1 and G_2 to the body line, keeping them parallel to $Z_1 - Z_1$.

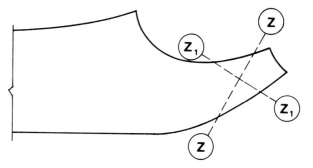

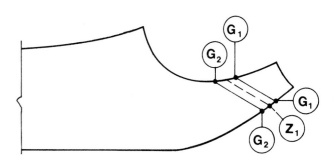

Fig. 9.48. Shoulder length grade 'G'.

APPLYING INCREMENT R (Fig. 9.49)

- Determine the value for increment R
- Mark half this value from G_1 to establish point R_1
- Mark half of this value from G_2 to establish point R_2
- Join points G_1 and R_1
- Join points G_2 and R_2

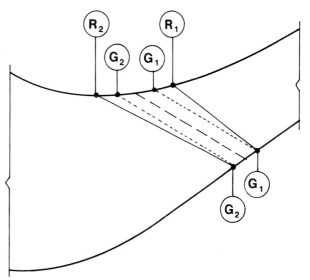

Fig. 9.49. Applying increment 'R'.

Grading instructions:
THE FULL RAGLAN FRONT SLEEVE

Stage 1: align pattern to X and Y axes (Fig. 9.50)
- Mark part of overarm seam to start of shoulder curve
- Mark start of cuff.

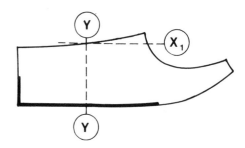

Fig. 9.50.

Stage 2: remain on Y axis (Fig. 9.51)
- Move to first E
- Mark lower section of sleeve line.

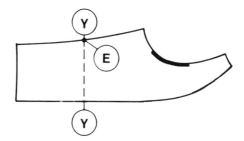

Fig. 9.51.

Stage 3: remain on Y axis (Fig. 9.52)
- Move to second E
- Complete lower section of sleeve
- Mark underseam
- Complete cuff.

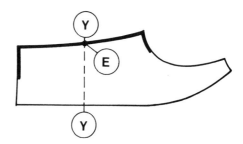

Fig. 9.52.

Stage 4: align on Y axis of pattern to relevant K line (Fig. 9.53)
- Mark part of horn from below shoulder nip to the centre of the shoulder.

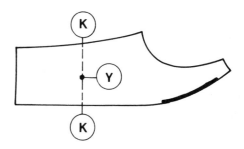

Fig. 9.53.

Stage 5: remain on K line (Fig. 9.54)
- Mark line $R_1 - G_1$ to increase
- Mark line $R_2 - G_2$ to decrease.

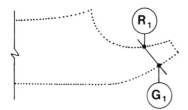
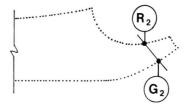

Fig. 9.54.

Stage 6A: to increase (Fig. 9.55)
- Align point G_2 to point G_1 on shoulder line
- Align point R_2 to line $G_1 - R_1$
- Mark sleeve horn.

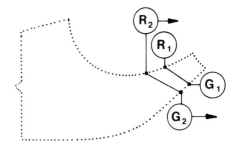

Fig. 9.55.

Stage 6B: to decrease (Fig. 9.56)
- Align point G_1 to point G_2 on shoulder line
- Align point R_1 to line $G_2 - R_2$
- Mark sleeve horn.

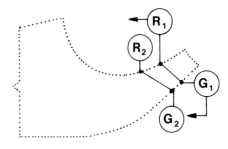

Fig. 9.56.

Stage 7: use pattern to blend body line run and shoulder line (Fig. 9.57).

Fig. 9.57.

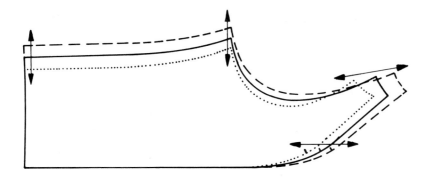

Grade for full raglan front sleeve

Introduction to magyar sleeves

This sleeve is cut in one with the body of the garment but unlike the Kimono, provision is made for lift and ease in wear by the insertion of a single or double wedge (gusset) under the arm at the side seam. The magyar sleeve can be 'grown-on' to the front or the back, or to both, and the basic difference between a full and half-Magyar is in the type of gusset used. This subject is examined on p. 204.

The grade for the back and front magyar sleeves commences from the two points where the sleeve is attached to the body and they are shown in Fig. 9.58. These points are:

(1) The shoulder point and the sleeve crown
(2) The intersection of the sleeve underseam and the armhole. This point is usually the apex of the dart into which the gusset is inserted.

The sleeve grade is carried out as from the following stages:

Front
Width — On Y axis, from the second G/2 increment, i.e. before E is applied.
Length — On M line, when the shoulder point has been established through the application of the second E/2 increment.

Back
Width — On Y axis, when the across-back grade of D has been completed, i.e. before increment E is applied.
Length — On K line, when the shoulder point has been established via F and G.

As the grades for the back and front sleeve are exactly alike, the example demonstrates one sleeve only.

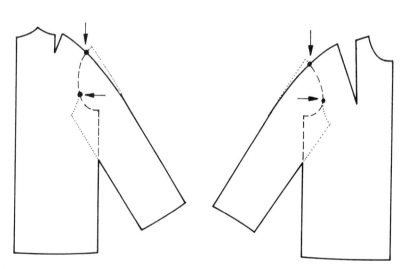

Fig. 9.58. The body and sleeve connections.

Grading instructions: THE MAGYAR SLEEVE

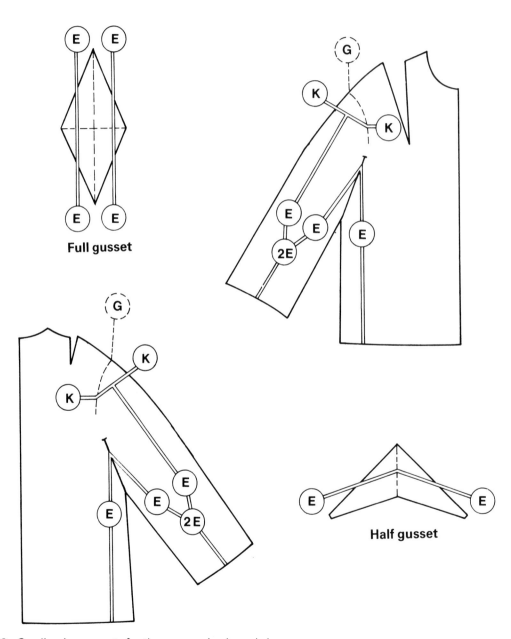

Fig. 9.59. Grading increments for the magyar body and sleeve.

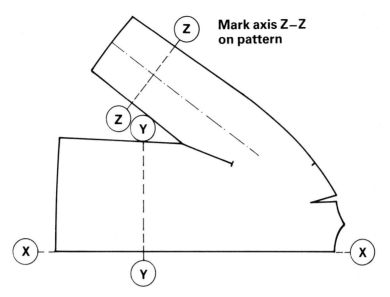

Fig. 9.60. Grading axes for magyar back.

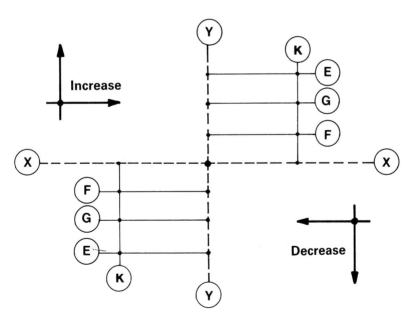

Fig. 9.61. Increment net for magyar back.

Stage 1: align pattern to X and Y axes (Fig. 9.62)
- Mark part of centre back
- Mark part of hem.

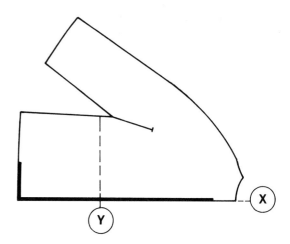

Fig. 9.62.

Stage 2: remain on Y axis (Fig. 9.63)
- Move to G
- Mark gusset line
- Mark Z – Z axis (each size will have its own axis)
- Mark parts of the over and under seams on either side of Z – Z axis
- Mark part of cuff.

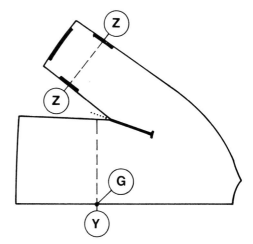

Fig. 9.63.

Stage 3: remain on Y axis (Fig. 9.64)
- Move to E
- Mark side seam
- Complete hem.

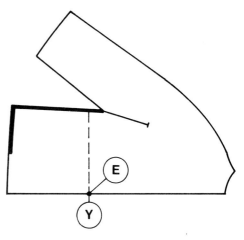

Fig. 9.64.

Stage 4: align Y axis to relevant K line (Fig. 9.65)
- Mark corner of centre back and start of neck.

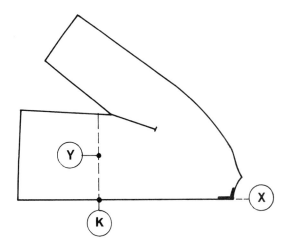

Fig. 9.65.

Stage 5: remain on K line (Fig. 9.66)
- Move to F
- Complete neck
- Mark start of shoulder.

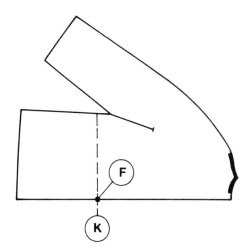

Fig. 9.66.

Stage 6: remain on K line (Fig. 9.67)
- Move to G
- Complete shoulder line.

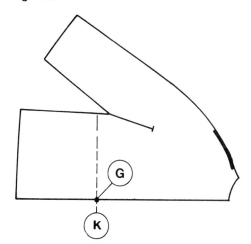

Fig. 9.67.

Stage 7: mark increments E from seams on axis Z – Z
(Fig. 9.68)
● Outside of seams to increase
● Inside of seams to decrease.

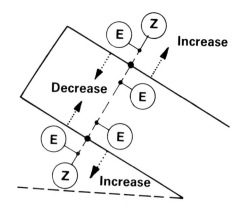

Fig. 9.68.

Stage 8: align pattern to Z – Z axis (Fig. 9.69)
● Move to E on over-arm seam
● Mark part of cuff and start of seam.

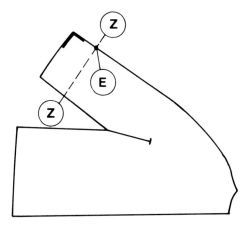

Fig. 9.69.

Stage 9: remain on Z – Z axis (Fig. 9.70)
● Move to E on under-arm seam
● Mark under-arm seam
● Complete cuff.

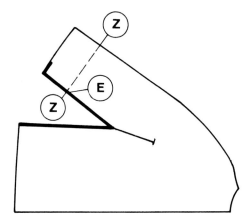

Fig. 9.70.

Stage 10: use the pattern to blend the over-arm seam from cuff to shoulder (Fig. 9.71)

- The length of this seam from the shoulder point to the cuff changes by increment K for each size graded.

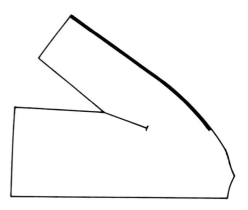

Fig. 9.71.

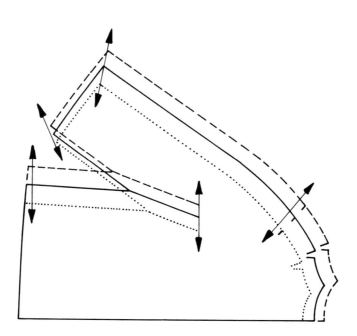

Grade of magyar sleeve

Gussets for magyar sleeves

THE FULL GUSSET

Where both the back and front have a magyar sleeve, the gusset most generally used is the full, or diamond shaped gusset. This gusset is made up from four sections which come from the overlap of the sleeve and body on the back and front (Fig. 9.72). Two of these parts come from the side sections of the body, and the other two are the related sections of the sleeve. Increment E is used to grade all of these parts.

The grade itself requires two applications of increment E on the lateral centre of the gusset (Fig. 9.73) and this measurement is continued around the gusset, parallel to all four sides. This grade (Fig. 9.74)

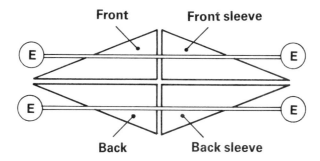

Fig. 9.72. The components of a full gusset.

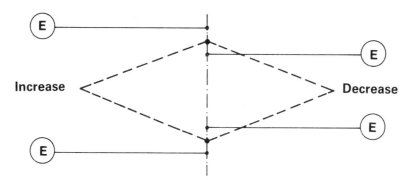

Fig. 9.73. Increment net for full gusset.

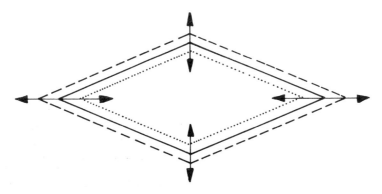

Fig. 9.74. Grade of full gusset.

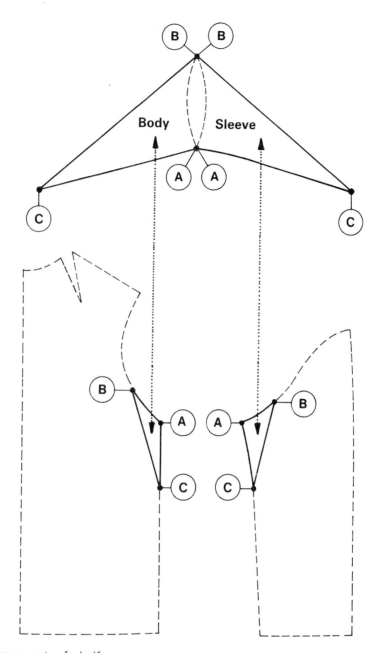

Fig. 9.75. The components of a half gusset.

will lengthen or shorten the gusset by exactly the same amount as that by which the length of the gusset dart changes during the body grade.

THE HALF GUSSET

The components are derived from the overlap of the sleeve and body and the shape of the gusset is

determined by that of the parts removed from the sleeve and the side (Fig. 9.75). These components are joined together at the underarm and overlap points and both of them are graded by increment E (Fig. 9.76).

The application of increment E has the effect of overlapping or opening the intersection of the side seam of the body and the underarm of the sleeve (Fig. 9.77). Consequently, the gusset has to be opened at this point when increasing size and closed when

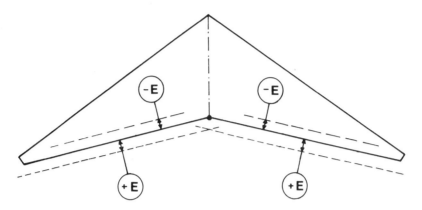

Fig. 9.76. The application of increment 'E'.

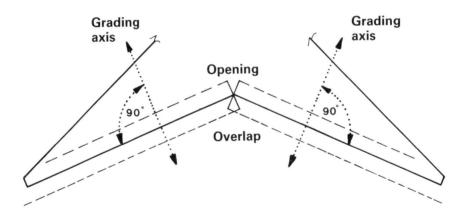

Fig. 9.77. Overlap of opening at the intersection.

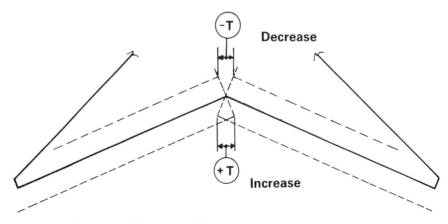

Fig. 9.78. Establishing the value of increment 'T'.

decreasing. The increment used is notated T and its value can only be determined by using the method shown in Fig. 9.78. The reason why there is no fixed rule for calculating this increment is that the angles of gussets are not all the same and that increment E varies according to the size interval being graded.

During the grade, the apex of the gusset, 'A' is used as a pivot point for the opening or closing of the seams intersection. This pivoting action will result in different Z – Z axes for each size being graded.

Grading instructions: THE HALF GUSSET

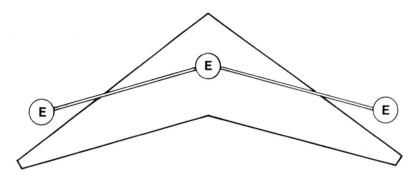

Fig. 9.79. Grading increments.

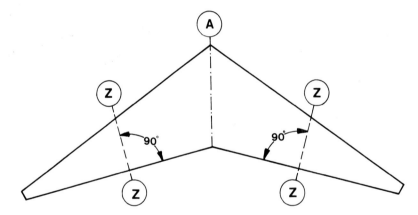

Fig. 9.80. Grading axes.

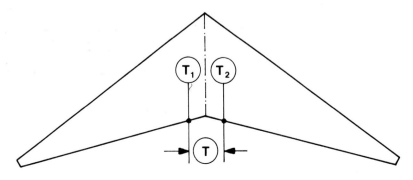

Fig. 9.81. The application of increment 'T'.

Stage 1: mark around base size gusset (Fig. 9.82)
- Mark T_1 and T_2 at distance T apart
- Point A_1 is the lower corner of the gusset.

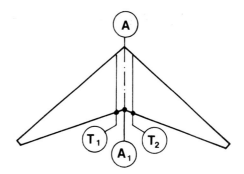

Fig. 9.82.

Stage 2: to increase (opening of A_1)
- (a) Pivot from A so that A_1 touches T_1
- (b) Mark top edge of gusset
- (c) Mark part of bottom edge
- (d) Mark Z – Z axis
- Pivot from A so that A_1 touches T_2
  Repeat stages (b), (c) and (d) on second side of the gusset. (Fig. 9.83)

Stage 3: to decrease (overlap at A_1)
- (a) Pivot from A so that A_1 touches T_2
- (b) Mark top edge of gusset
- (c) Mark part of bottom edge
- (d) Mark Z – Z axis
- Pivot from A so that A_1 touches T_1
  Repeat stages (b), (c) and (d) on second side of the gusset. (Fig. 9.83)

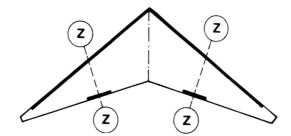

Fig. 9.83.

Stage 4: mark increment E on both sides of the gusset (Fig. 9.84)
- Measure the increments from the intersection of the Z – Z axis and the lower edge of the gusset.

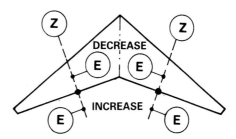

Fig. 9.84.

Stage 5: align one side of the gusset to the new Z – Z axis (Fig. 9.85)
- Move to E
- Mark the lower edge of one side
- Repeat for other side.

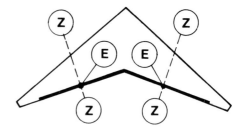

Fig. 9.85.

Stage 6: move lower side of the gusset along the lower graded line until the width between the upper and lower side at the end is the same as that of the base pattern (Fig. 9.86).
- Repeat for other side.

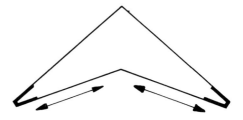

Fig. 9.86.

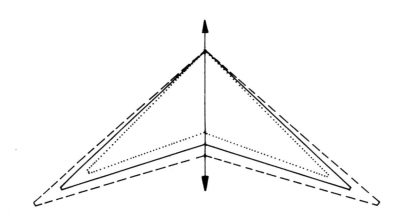

Grade for half gusset.

Chapter 10

The Static Neck-To-Waist Grade

Introduction to the 'one-length' system

The results of grading by this method are that the three following length measurements remain unchanged for all of the sizes within one height category, i.e. short, regular and tall.

(a) The back neck-to-waist
(b) Garment length
(c) Sleeve length

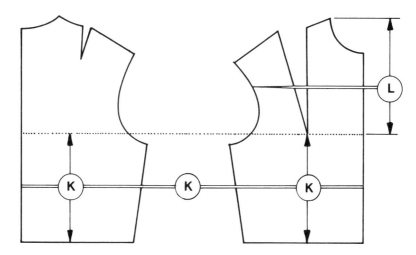

Fig. 10.1. The application of increments 'K' and 'L'.

The grade itself is very similar to the regular grade but with two main differences (Fig. 10.1):

(1) Increment K is applied between the bust and waist lines of the front and back. This has the effect of raising or lowering the armhole and bust point whilst retaining a static neck-to-waist measurement.
(2) Increment L is applied to the front only, from the bust point to the front neck point. Thus the overall length of the front, from the neck point to the waist, changes by increment L for each size whilst the shoulder to bust point changes by L + K, which is equal to M in the regular grade (Fig. 10.2). Increment L will automatically be eliminated at the front armhole due to the triangulation of the armhole side of the bust dart through the application of increment J_1.

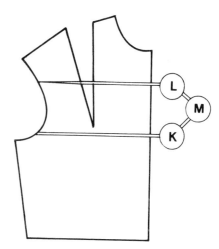

Fig. 10.2. The two components of increment 'M'.

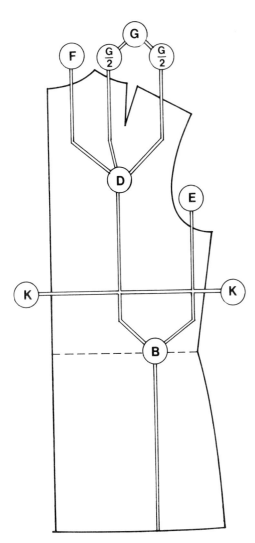

Fig. 10.3 Grading increments for back static neck-to-waist grade.

There is also a slight difference in the grading axes used for the length grades for the back and front.

THE BACK (Fig. 10.3)

The length grade is increment K and applied in the reverse way to that of the regular grade.

(1) When increasing size, the armhole base is lowered by the movement of Y to K in the −X direction.
(2) When decreasing size, the armhole base is raised by the movement of Y to K in the +X direction.

THE FRONT (Fig. 10.4)

The two increments used are the L and K, and they are applied in opposing directions as follows:

(1) When increasing size:
  (a) The armhole base and bust point are lowered by the movement of Y to K in the −X direction.
  (b) The additional change in length between the bust point and shoulder is effected by the movement of Y to L in the +X direction.
(2) When decreasing size:
  (a) The armhole base and bust point are raised by the movement of Y to K in the +X direction.

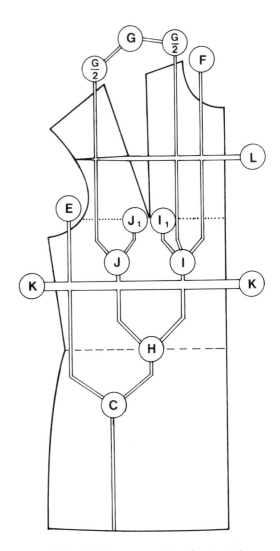

Fig. 10.4. Grading increments for front static neck-to-waist grade.

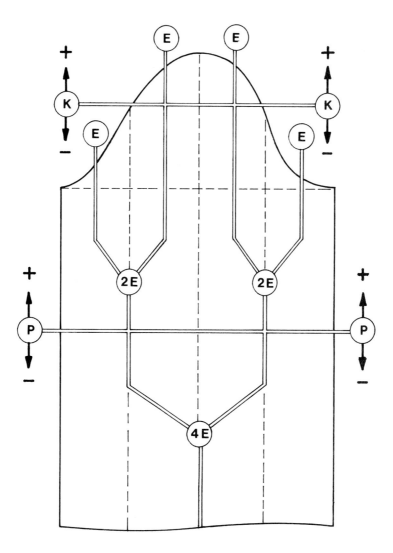

Increments K and P have the same value

Fig. 10.5. Grading increments for one piece sleeve static neck-to-waist grade.

(b) The additional decrease of length between the bust point and neck point is caused by the movement of Y to L in the −X direction.

move up or down according to the K increment applied at the sleeve head.

THE SLEEVE (Fig. 10.5)

In the sleeve grade, the change in length caused by applying increment K across the sleeve head is counteracted by the increment P, which in all cases has the same value of increment K. When grading sleeves with elbow or cuff darts, the apex of the dart should

THE LAPEL AND COLLAR (Fig. 10.6)

Unlike the regular grade, the lapel length receives increment L only and there is no grade required for the front neck length. Thus the collar grade is simplified because it now has only two grading movements instead of three.

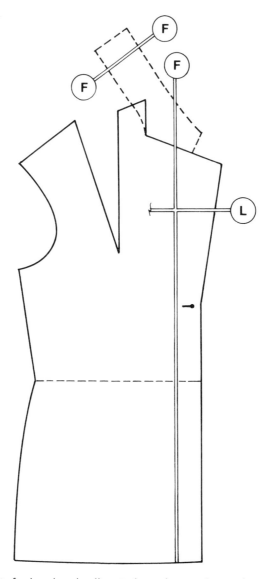

Fig. 10.6. Grading increments for lapel and collar static neck-to-waist grade.

GENERAL

All of the other grades previously demonstrated in this section can be simply adapted to the static neck-to-waist method by applying the specific axes for the length grades. The width grade detail is exactly the same in all cases.

APPLICATIONS

Apart from being used for regular sizes, the static neck-to-waist grade is very often used to grade outsize garments.

Grading instructions: THE ONE-LENGTH BACK

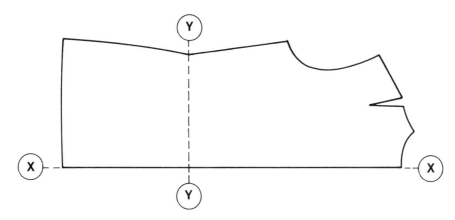

Fig. 10.7. Grading axes for back.

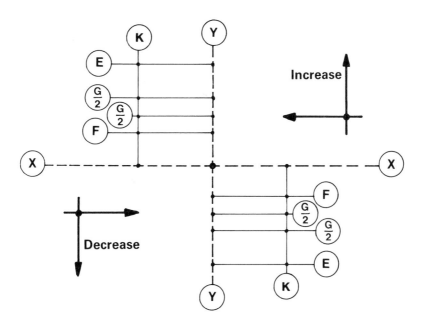

Fig. 10.8. Increment net for back.

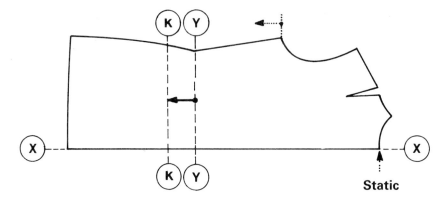

Increasing armhole depth

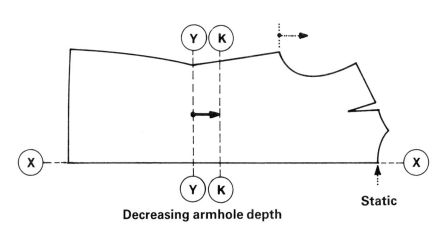

Decreasing armhole depth

The length and waist line position is static for all sizes

Fig. 10.9. The axes of length for the back.

Stage 1: align pattern to X and Y axes (Fig. 10.10)
- Mark part of hem
- Mark centre back
- Mark start of neck.

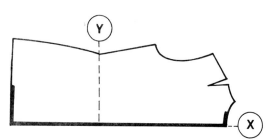

Fig. 10.10.

Stage 2: remain on Y axis (Fig. 10.11)
- Move to F
- Complete neck
- Mark start of shoulder.

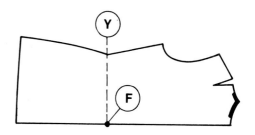

Fig. 10.11.

Stage 3: remain on Y axis (Fig. 10.12)
- Move to first G/2
- Complete first section of shoulder
- Mark dart and start of second section of shoulder.

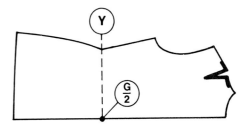

Fig. 10.12.

Stage 4: remain on Y axis (Fig. 10.13)
- Move to second G/2
- Complete shoulder
- Mark armhole to the across back line.

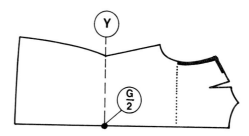

Fig. 10.13.

Stage 5: remain on Y axis (Fig. 10.14)
- Move to E
- Mark side seam from waist to hem only
- Complete hem.

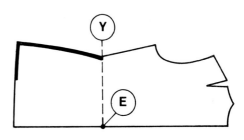

Fig. 10.14.

Stage 6: align Y axis of pattern to relevant K line (Fig. 10.15)
- Move to second G/2
- Mark lower part of armhole.

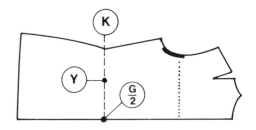

Fig. 10.15.

Stage 7: remain on K line (Fig. 10.16)
- Move to E
- Complete armhole
- Join intersection of armhole and side seam to waist line.

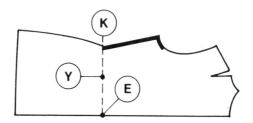

Fig. 10.16.

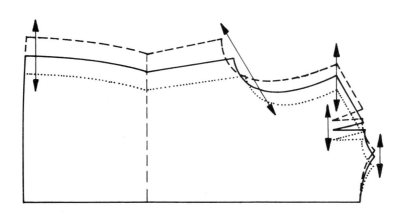

Grade for one-length back

Grading instructions: THE ONE-LENGTH FRONT

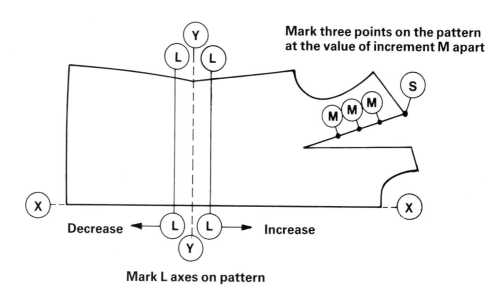

Mark three points on the pattern at the value of increment M apart

Decrease ← L L → **Increase**

Mark L axes on pattern

Fig. 10.17. Grading axes for front.

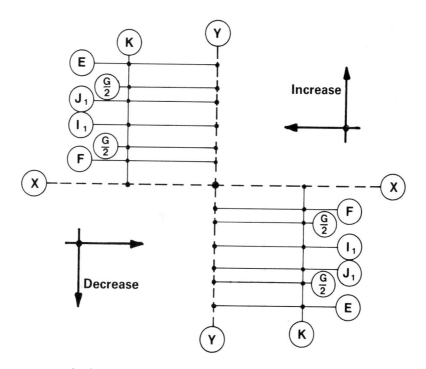

Fig. 10.18. Increment net for front.

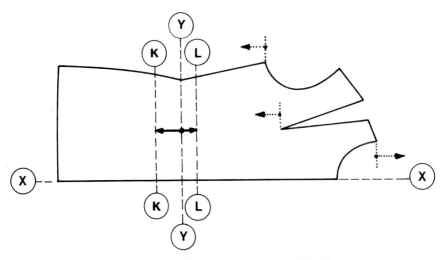

Increase: Armhole and bust point lowered by K
Neck point highered by L

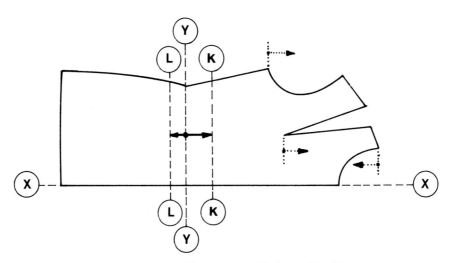

Decrease: Armhole and bust point highered by K
Neck point lowered by L

Fig. 10.19. The axes of length for the front.

Stage 1: align pattern to X and Y axes (Fig. 10.20)
- Mark front edge
- Mark part of hem.

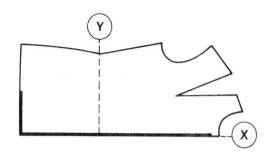

Fig. 10.20.

Stage 2: remain on Y axis (Fig. 10.21)
- Move to J_1
- Mark point S.

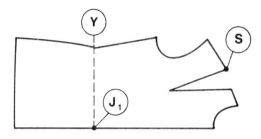

Fig. 10.21.

Stage 3: remain on Y axis (Fig. 10.22)
- Move to second G/2
- Mark part of armhole * (this is a check mark only).

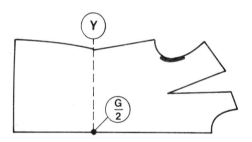

Fig. 10.22.

Stage 4: remain on Y axis (Fig. 10.23)
- Move to E
- Mark side seam from waist to hem only
- Complete hem.

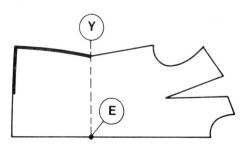

Fig. 10.23.

Stage 5: align Y axis of pattern to relevant K line (Fig. 10.24)
- Move to I_1
- Mark new bust point.

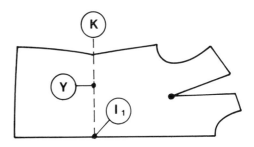

Fig. 10.24.

Stage 6: remain on K line (Fig. 10.25)
- Move to second G/2
- Mark lower section of armhole.

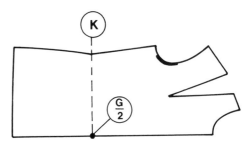

Fig. 10.25.

Stage 7: remain on K line (Fig. 10.26)
- Move to E
- Complete armhole
- Mark start of side seam.

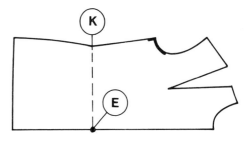

Fig. 10.26.

Stage 8: complete side seam by joining underarm corner to waist (Fig. 10.27).

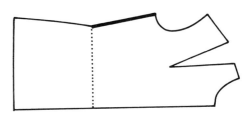

Fig. 10.27.

Stage 9: align Y axis of pattern with relevant L line (Fig. 10.28)
- Complete front edge
- Mark start of neck.

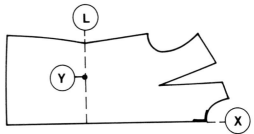

Fig. 10.28.

Stage 10: remain on L axis (Fig. 10.29)
- Move to F
- Complete neck
- Mark start of shoulder.

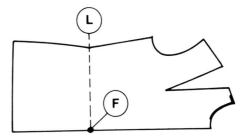

Fig. 10.29.

Stage 11: remain on L axis (Fig. 10.30)
- Move to first G/2
- Complete first part of shoulder
- Mark first corner of dart and connect to new bust point.

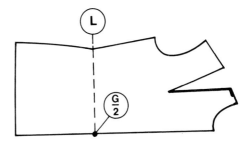

Fig. 10.30.

Stage 12: connect point S to new bust point (Fig. 10.31)
- Align pattern to this line
- Mark relevant M point
- Align to M point
- Mark second side of bust dart and start of shoulder.

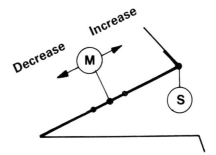

Fig. 10.31.

Stage 13: move distance G/2 parallel to second side of
bust dart (Fig. 10.32)
- Complete shoulder
- Mark central section of armhole.

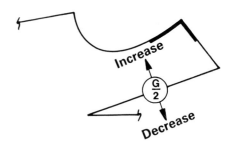

Fig. 10.32.

Stage 14: use pattern to blend armhole (Fig. 10.33).

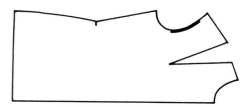

Fig. 10.33.

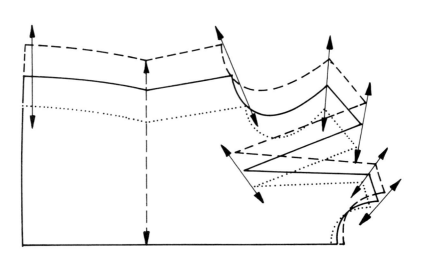

Grade of one-length front

Grading instructions: THE ONE-LENGTH SLEEVE

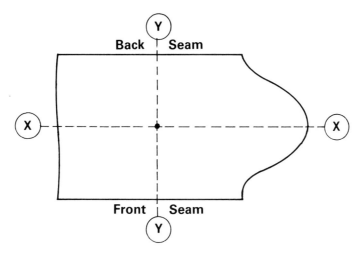

Fig. 10.34. Grading axes for sleeve.

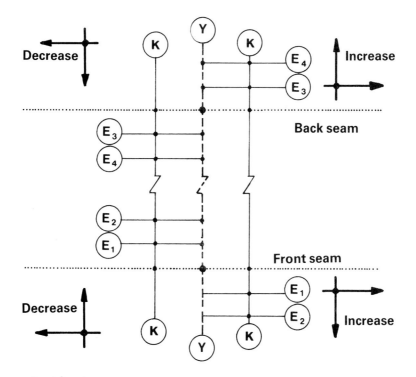

Fig. 10.35. Increment net for sleeve.

Stage 1: front half of sleeve (Fig. 10.36)
- Align pattern to X and Y axes
- Move to E_1
- Mark part of front sleeve.

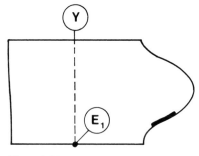

Fig. 10.36.

Stage 2: move to E_2 (Fig. 10.37)
- Complete lower section of sleeve
- Mark part of front underarm seam.

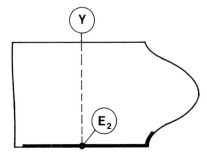

Fig. 10.37.

Stage 3: back half of sleeve (Fig. 10.38)
- Move to E_3
- Mark part of back sleeve.

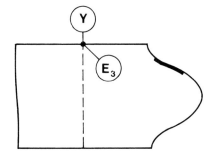

Fig. 10.38.

Stage 4: move to E_4 (Fig. 10.39)
- Complete lower section of sleeve
- Mark part of back underarm seam.

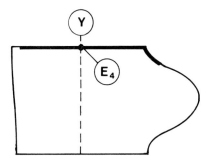

Fig. 10.39.

Stage 5: align Y axis of pattern to relevant K line
(Fig. 10.40)
- Align X axes of pattern and paper
- Mark crown of sleeve and centre nip
- Mark centre of cuff.

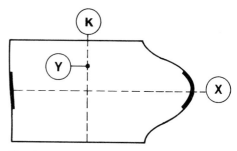

Fig. 10.40.

Stage 6: remain on K line (Fig. 10.41)
- Move to E_2
- Mark seam and hem corner of front sleeve
- Move to E_4
- Mark seam and hem corner of back sleeve.

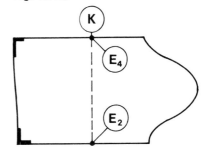

Fig. 10.41.

Stage 7: use pattern to (Fig. 10.42)
- Blend sleeve head
- Blend cuff.

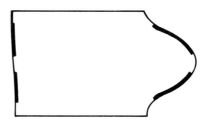

Fig. 10.42.

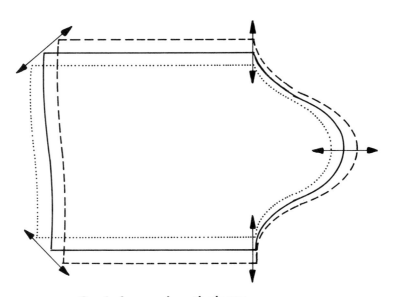

Grade for one-length sleeve

Grading instructions:
LAPEL FOR ONE-LENGTH FRONT

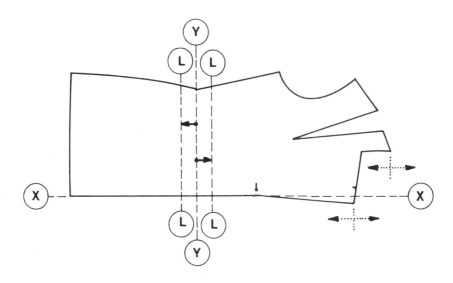

Mark L axes on pattern

Fig. 10.43. Grading axes for lapel.

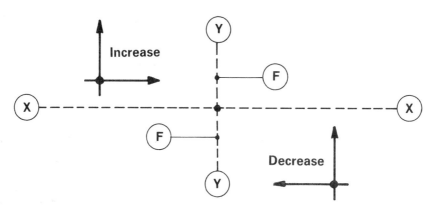

Fig. 10.44. Increment net for lapel.

Stage 1: align pattern on X and Y axes (Fig. 10.45)
- Mark start of hem
- Mark front edge to lapel break.

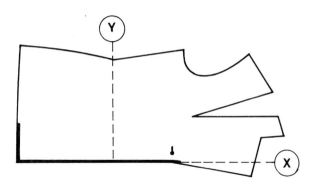

Fig. 10.45.

Stage 2: remain on Y axis (Fig. 10.46)
- Align L axis on pattern to Y
- Mark corner of lapel.

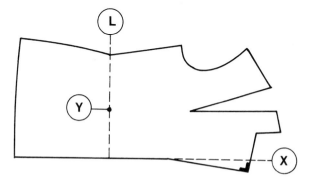

Fig. 10.46.

Stage 3: remain on L axis (Fig. 10.47)
- Move to F
- Mark gorge corner
- Complete neck
- Mark start of shoulder.

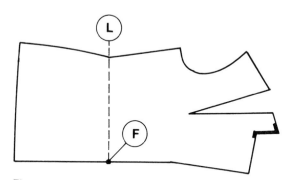

Fig. 10.47.

Stage 4: join gorge corner to lapel corner (Fig. 10.48)
- Mark lapel step nip.

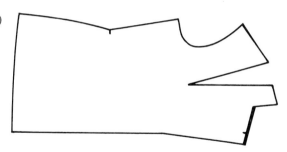

Fig. 10.48.

Stage 5: use pattern to blend lapel from corner to break (Fig. 10.49).

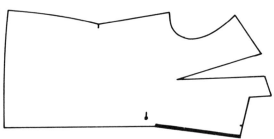

Fig. 10.49.

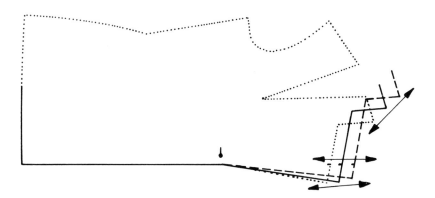

Grade of lapel for one-length front

Grading instructions: COLLAR FOR ONE-LENGTH FRONT

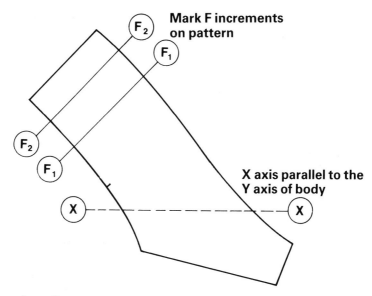

Mark F increments on pattern

X axis parallel to the Y axis of body

Fig. 10.50. Grading axes for collar.

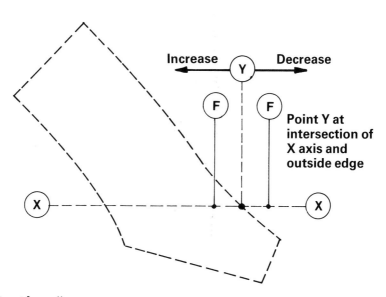

Increase   **Decrease**

Point Y at intersection of X axis and outside edge

Fig. 10.51. Increment net for collar.

Stage 1: align pattern on X axis (Fig. 10.52)
- Mark front step and corners
- Move to F
- Mark gorge corner
- Mark neck seam and nip
- Mark part of outside edge.

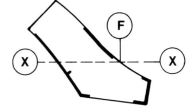

Fig. 10.52.

Stage 2: use neck seam as guide (Fig. 10.53)
- Move to relevant F
- Mark centre back
- Mark neck seam and outside edge corners.

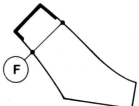

Fig. 10.53.

Stage 3: use pattern to blend outside edge (Fig. 10.54).

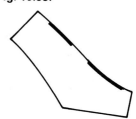

Fig. 10.54.

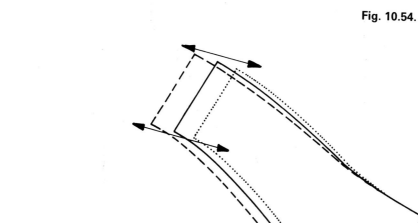

Grade of collar for one-length front

Chapter 11

Skirts and Trousers

The straight skirt

The first example demonstrated is the conventional straight skirt (Fig. 11.1) and it has its own grading method because a skirt which is attached to a bodice would be graded according to the upper sections of the garment.

The grading of this type of skirt must take into account:

(1) The proportions between the back and front sections.
(2) The distribution of the darts around the waistline.

WIDTH GRADE

The first step is to establish the proportions of the back

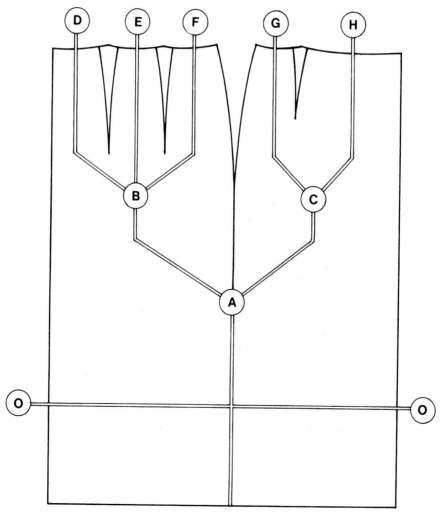

Fig. 11.1. Grading increments for straight skirt.

and front relative to the total hip girth of the pattern as follows:

Stage 1: Measure each section on the hip line, i.e. from the centre back to the side seam and from the centre front to the side seam.

Stage 2: Total them and calculate the percentage that each section is of the total hip girth.

For example:

Measured back hip girth:	27.5 cm
Measured front hip girth:	22.5 cm
Total hip girth of pattern:	50.0 cm

Which gives;

Proportion of back to total girth:	55%
Proportion of front to total girth:	45%

As is the case with the great majority of sizing systems, the size interval is the same for the waist and hip girths, and the allocation per size interval would then be:

Size interval:	4 cm	5 cm	6 cm
A. Total girth grade (100%)	20.0 mm	25.0 mm	30.0 mm
B. Total back grade (55%)	11.0 mm	14.0 mm*	16.5 mm
C. Total front grade (45%)	9.0 mm	11.0 mm*	13.5 mm

(* rounded off)

SUB-DIVISIONS

The proportional distribution of the waist darts (Fig. 11.2) must also be maintained, and this requires the sub-division of increments B and C. These proportions can be calculated, or estimated by eye, which is far simpler. Referring to Fig. 11.1 the dart spacings are:

Back: Approximately three equal sections of one-third each

Front: Approximately one-third and two-thirds of the waist line.

These proportions would give the following increments per size interval.

Location	Size Interval		
	4 cm	5 cm	6 cm
The back			
D: Centre back to first dart:	4.0 mm	5.0 mm	5.5 mm
E: First dart to second dart:	4.0 mm	5.0 mm	5.5 mm
F: Second dart to side seam:	3.0 mm	4.0 mm	5.5 mm
The front			
G: Side seam to dart:	3.0 mm	4.0 mm	4.5 mm
H: Dart to centre front:	6.0 mm	7.0 mm	9.0 mm
A: Total Girth Grade:	20.0 mm	25.0 mm	30.0 mm

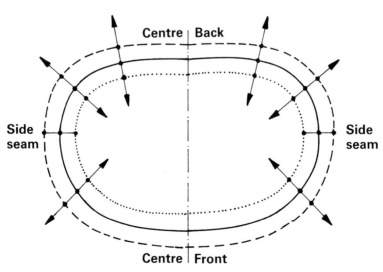

Fig. 11.2. Waist dart grade proportions.

If a length grade is required, then for most purposes increment O can be applied at the hem line.

This method of calculating the allocating of grading increments can be used for most skirts with the exception of fully-flared skirts. These types of skirts have a different grading method and this is demonstrated on p. 245 of this group.

WAIST BANDS

These should be graded according to the alignment detail between the band and the skirt waistline, and this factor can be one of three types:

Type 1: the band has nips at each end and the distance between them is the waist measurement. This

type of waist band is graded by the application of increment A at one end (Fig. 11.3A).

Type 2: apart from having the waist measurement nips, there is also a nip for aligning to the side seams. Accordingly, the back section of the band would receive increment B and the front section, increment C (Fig. 11.3B).

Type 3: where, due to technological and/or design considerations, the waist band has to be matched to a specific point or points on the waist line, then the grade would have the same proportions as that for the relative sections of the body.

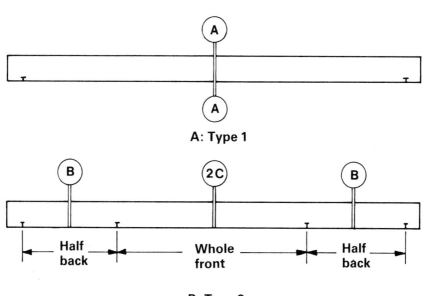

A: Type 1

B: Type 2

Fig. 11.3. Waist band grades.

Grading instructions: THE FRONT SKIRT

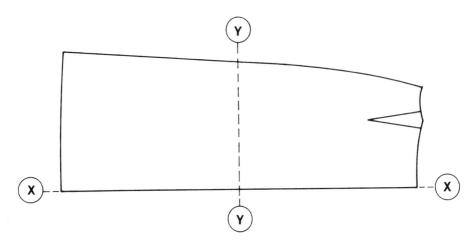

Fig. 11.4. Grading axes for front skirt.

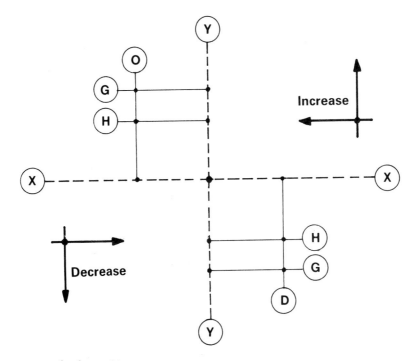

Fig. 11.5. Increment net for front skirt.

Stage 1: align pattern on X and Y axes (Fig. 11.6)
- Mark centre front and start of waist.

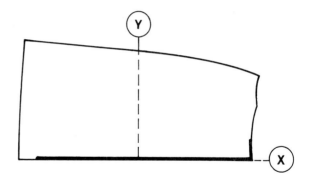

Fig. 11.6.

Stage 2: remain on Y axis (Fig. 11.7)
- Move to H and mark dart.

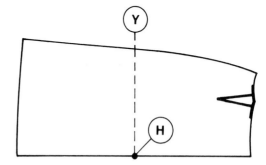

Fig. 11.7.

Stage 3: remain on Y axis (Fig. 11.8)
- Move to G
- Mark side seam.

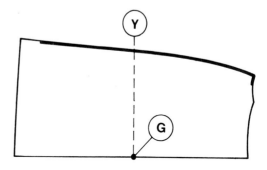

Fig. 11.8.

Stage 4: align pattern on X and relevant O line (Fig. 11.9)
- Mark start of hem.

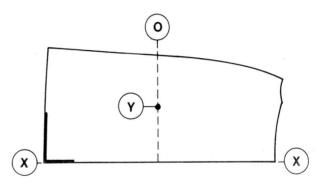

Fig. 11.9.

Stage 5: remain on O line (Fig. 11.10)
● Move to G and complete hem.

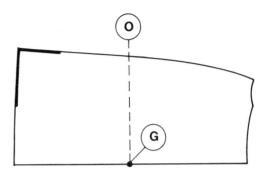

Fig. 11.10.

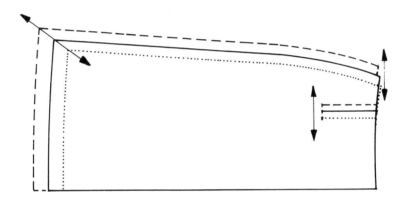

Grade of front skirt

Grading instructions: THE BACK SKIRT

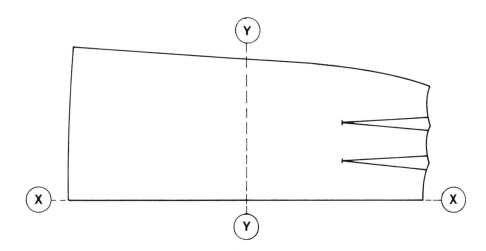

Fig. 11.11. Grading axes for back skirt.

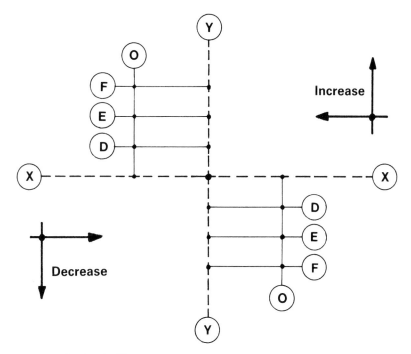

Fig. 11.12. Increment net for back skirt.

Stage 1: align pattern on X and Y axes (Fig. 11.13)
- Mark centre back and start of waist.

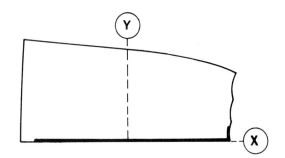

Fig. 11.13.

Stage 2: remain on Y axis (Fig. 11.14)
- Move to D
- Mark part of waist line
- Mark first dart.

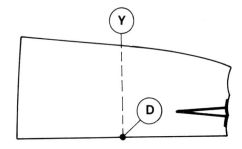

Fig. 11.14.

Stage 3: remain on Y axis (Fig. 11.15)
- Move to E
- Mark part of waist line
- Mark second dart.

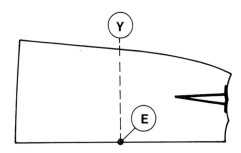

Fig. 11.15.

Stage 4: remain on Y axis (Fig. 11.16)
- Move to F
- Complete waist line
- Mark side seam.

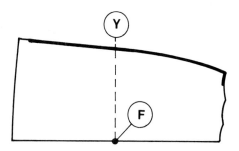

Fig. 11.16.

Stage 5: align pattern on X axis and relevant O line
(Fig. 11.17)
• Mark start of hem.

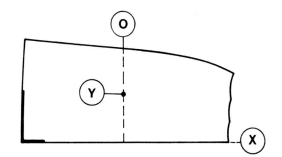

Fig. 11.17.

Stage 6: remain on O line (Fig. 11.18)
• Move to F and complete side seam and hem.

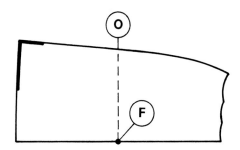

Fig. 11.18.

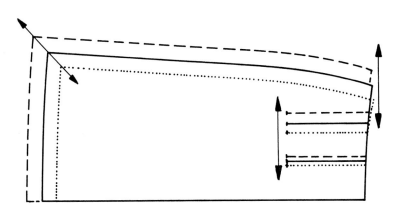

Grade of back skirt

The semi-flared skirt

This type of skirt (Fig. 11.19) is usually comprised of two segments and the waist does not have a true circular shape.

The grading is relatively simple, requiring the addition or subtraction of one quarter of the waist girth interval to each of the four seams. The length is adjusted according to the size chart being used (Fig. 5.4.1.).

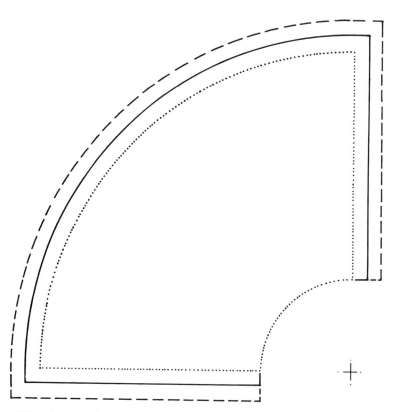

Fig. 11.19. The semi-flared skirt.

The fully flared skirt

CONSTRUCTION

The fully flared skirt in this example is based on a full circle where each panel is one-fourth segment of the circle. When constructing this type of skirt, two measurements are required:

(1) The base size waist girth.
(2) The base size length.

The waist girth is equivalent to a circle having the same circumference, whilst the length is equal to the distance from the waist circle to the hem. This construction is shown in Fig. 11.20 where R_1 is the waist circle radius and R_2 is the hem circle radius, and the panel illustrated is equal to one quarter of the skirt.

GRADING

It would logically follow that the grading of waist girths and lengths would be effected via changes in the radii used to construct the skirt. The two increments used are A for the waist girth and O for the length and the method used to calculate the values of these increments (Fig. 11.21) is as follows:

(1) Waist girth — increment A

$$A = \frac{\text{Half waist girth interval}}{3.14}$$

(2) Length   — increment O
    To lengthen = length interval plus A
    To shorten   = length interval minus A

An example of these two calculations is for a skirt having a waist girth interval of 4 cm and a length interval of 1.5 cm.

Calculation of A: $A = \frac{20\,\text{mm}}{3.14} = 6.5\,\text{mm}\ (0.65)$

Calculation of O: To lengthen = 1.5 + 0.65 = 2.2 cm
                   To shorten = 1.5 − 0.65 = 0.9 cm

These rounded-off figures are sufficiently accurate for grading a skirt of this type and the applicable grading method is demonstrated on the following pages.

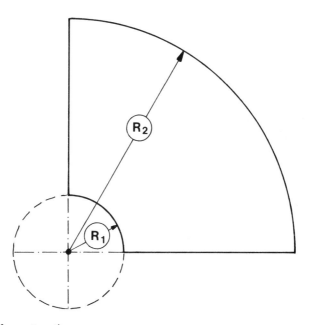

Fig. 11.20. The radii of construction.

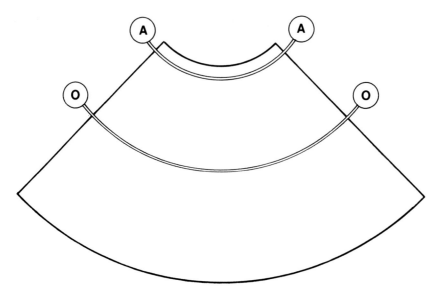

Fig. 11.21. Grading increments for the fully flared skirt.

Grading instructions: THE FULLY FLARED SKIRT WITH FOUR PANELS

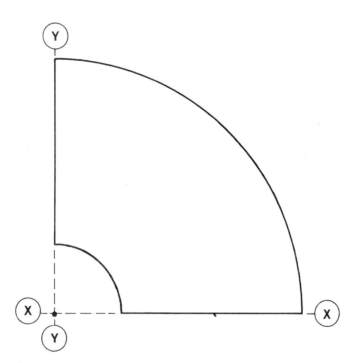

Fig. 11.22. Grading axes.

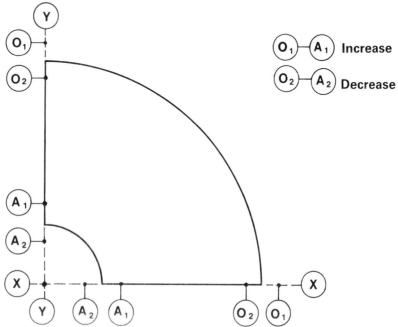

Fig. 11.23. Increment net.

Stage 1: align on X axis (Fig. 11.24)
- Move to relevant A
- Mark part of waist and panel seam.

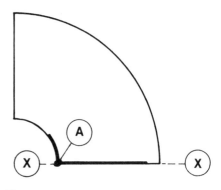

Fig. 11.24.

Stage 2: remain on X axis (Fig. 11.25)
- Move to relevant O
- Complete panel seam
- Mark part of hem.

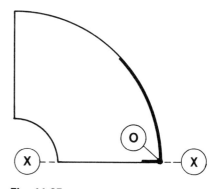

Fig. 11.25.

Stage 3: align on Y axis (Fig. 11.26)
- Move to relevant A
- Mark panel seam and complete waist.

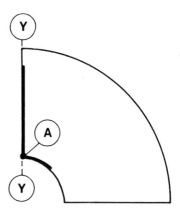

Fig. 11.26.

Stage 4: remain on Y axis (Fig. 11.27)
- Move to relevant O
- Complete panel seam and hem.

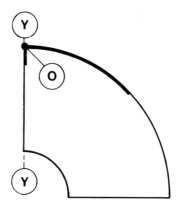

Fig. 11.27.

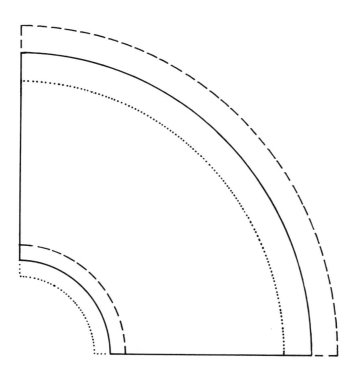

Grade of skirt panel

Trousers

The grading of bifurcated garments, such as trousers and divided skirts (cullottes), is based on the straight skirt grade with the addition of the fork areas. Other than the USA and English surveys, there is very little information available regarding the measurements involved, and as a result the grade development is based on this data only.

The relevant measurements:
No. 6:   thigh girth
No. 32: body rise
No. 57: total crotch length (front and back)
No. 58: front crotch length
and their values for three standard size intervals are given in Table 11.1.

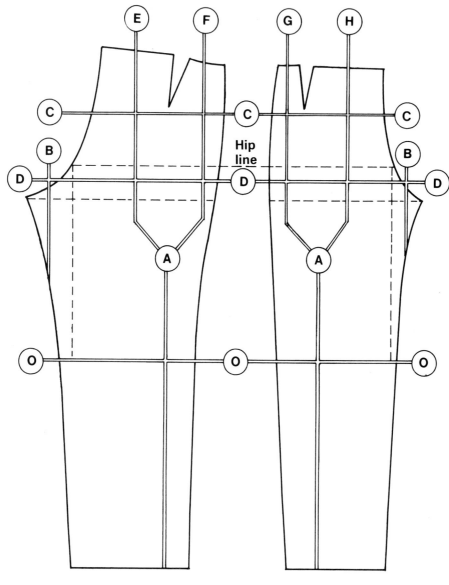

A = hip girth grade
A + B = thigh girth grade

Fig. 11.28. Grading increments for trousers.

Table 11.1.

No.	Measurement	Size interval 4 cm	5 cm	6 cm
6	Thigh girth	25.0 mm	31.0 mm	38.0 mm
32	Body rise	7.5 mm	9.5 mm	11.0 mm
57	Total crotch length	20.0 mm	25.0 mm	30.0 mm
58	Front crotch length	10.0 mm	12.5 mm	15.0 mm

Given these values, the development of the grading increments (Fig. 11.28) is as follows:

Increment A One-quarter of the hip and waist girths interval

Increment B This is the balance of the thigh girth interval remaining after increment A has been applied.

Increment C Applied between the hip and waist lines, this is the major part of the crotch length grade.

Increment D This increment is applied between the hip and fork lines, and is the second part of the crotch length grade. When combined, increments C and D complete the crotch length grade, and they apply similarly to the front and back panels.

Increment O The length grade increment which is applied through the knee line.

These increments per size interval and their notations are given in Table 11.2.

Table 11.2.

Notation	Section	Size interval 4 cm	5 cm	6 cm
A	Waist and hip girths	10.0 mm	12.5 mm	15.0 mm
B	Balance of thigh girth	2.5 mm	3.0 mm	5.0 mm
C	First part of crotch length	7.5 mm	9.5 mm	11.0 mm
D	Second part of crotch length	2.5 mm	3.0 mm	4.0 mm
O	Length	As required		

Increments E and F and increments G and H are sub-divisions of A and are calculated by the same method as that used for the straight skirt (p. 233). The grading of the knee and cuff girths are fashion dependent, and if they are different from increment A, the difference should be applied equally on the side seam and inside leg seam.

The following example is without the dart spacing grade and demonstrates a common line grade, and the grade itself is applicable to the front and back sections of the trouser.

Grading instructions: BASIC TROUSERS

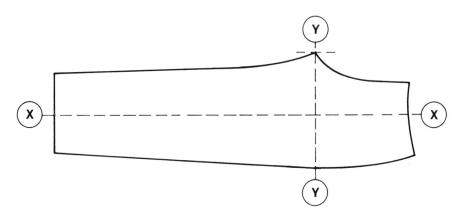

Fig. 11.29. Grading axes.

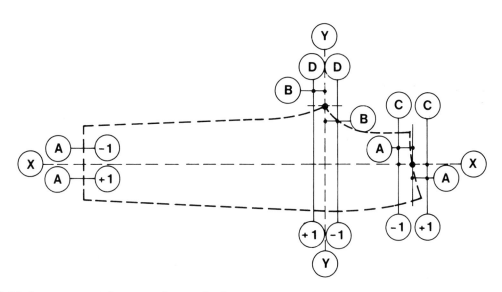

Fig. 11.30. Increment net for centre line method.

Stage 1: align Y axes of pattern and paper (Fig. 11.31)
- Align X axis of pattern to top and bottom A
- Towards outside leg to increase
- Towards inside leg to decrease
- Mark side seam from hip line to hem
- Mark part of hem.

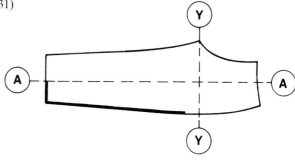

Fig. 11.31.

Stage 2: remain on top and bottom A (Fig. 11.32)
- Move up or down to relevant C mark
- Mark rest of side seam and start of waist.

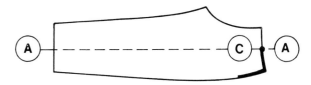

Fig. 11.32.

Stage 3: stay on C line (Fig. 11.33)
- Align pattern with X axis
- Mark seam corner and complete waist.

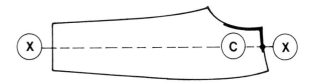

Fig. 11.33.

Stage 4: align Y axis on pattern with relevant D line
(Fig. 11.34)
- Move to B
- Mark crotch point
- Mark start of seam.

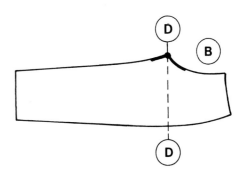

Fig. 11.34.

Stage 5: use pattern (Fig. 11.35)
- Blend crotch point to inside leg seam
- Blend fly line or seat seam.

Fig. 11.35.

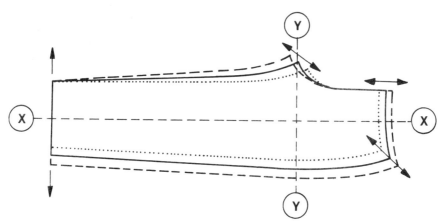

Grade for basic trouser

Basic grading applications

Conclusions

The closer a grading system is related to authentic anthropometric data, the more effective it will be in producing graded patterns with a superior level of sizing quality. Consequently, a fairly complex system has to be used in order to ensure that this important quality factor is integral to the system in all of its applications.

There is no doubt that the system demonstrated in this chapter could be somewhat simplified and thus be made easier to use. However, the resultant 'crude' system would seriously impair the overall effectiveness obtained by degrading what is an essential attribute of garment quality.

In this chapter, the system has been set out with all of its origins and basic principles. This framework provides the pattern grader with the understanding of how to adapt quickly and simply to changing demands without affecting efficiency and quality. There is far more to pattern grading than just moving a pattern around on paper according to a set of fixed rules which have no authoritative basis.

The next section of this book will demonstrate some examples of how the system is applied to styled garments and their major sub-components.

PART 3

APPLICATIONS TO STYLED GARMENTS

Introduction

This chapter contains six examples of the master grades applied to styled garments and fusible and body lining patterns. Each of the examples has been planned to demonstrate the grading of basic design features which, with many variations, are frequently used in the design of women's outerwear.

The step-by-step demonstration grades are for the major components of the garment and combine the two fundamental objectives of effective pattern grading:

(1) The change of size according to anthropometric criteria.
(2) The maintenance of design form and proportions throughout the range of sizes being graded.

The grades demonstrated are based on the dynamic neck-to-waist method but can be equally applied to 'one-length' grades by changing the length grade axes.

Chapter 12

Panelled Jacket

The first example is a classically styled jacket with princess line panels from the shoulder on the back and front (Fig. 12.1). The features of this grade are (Fig. 12.2):

- The grade of the back shoulder dart which has been incorporated into the panel line.

- Pocket position movement in relation to the total grade for the bust panel.
- The grade for a split sleeve with an elbow dart.

The collar grade method is exactly the same as that demonstrated in Chapter 7.

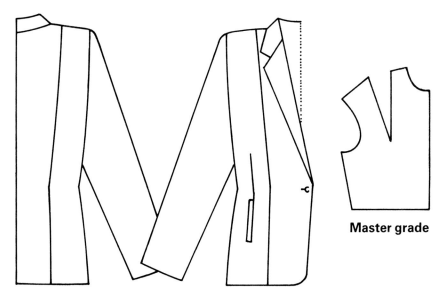

Master grade

Fig. 12.1. Panelled jacket.

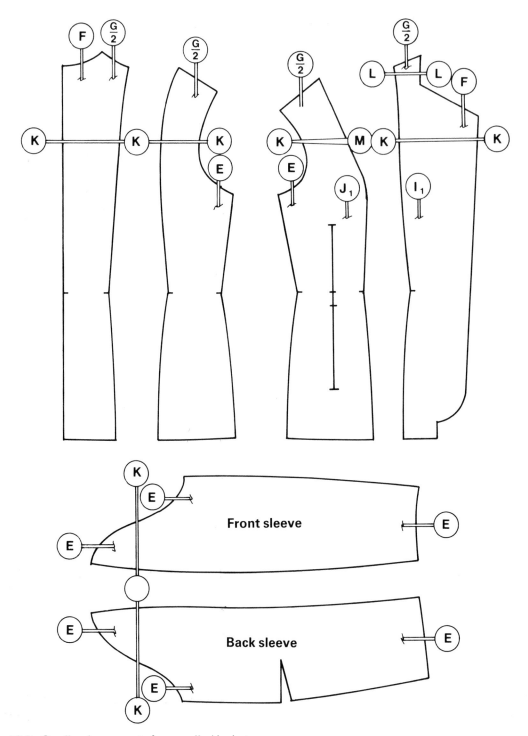

Fig. 12.2. Grading increments for panelled jacket.

Grading instructions: FRONT PANEL

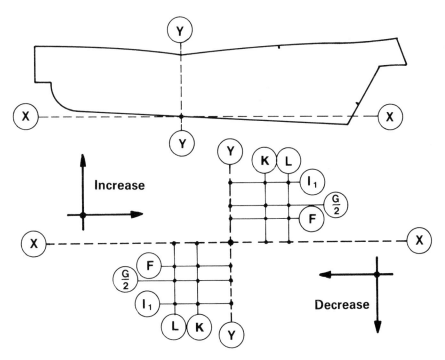

Fig. 12.3. Grading axes and increment net for front panel.

Stage 1: align pattern to X and Y axes (Fig. 12.4)
- Mark part of front edge
- Mark part of hem.

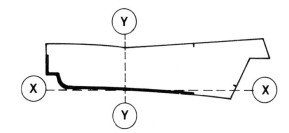

Fig. 12.4.

Stage 2: remain on Y axis (Fig. 12.5)
- Move to I_1
- Mark panel line from bust point to hem
- Complete panel hem.

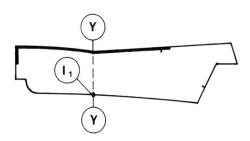

Fig. 12.5.

Stage 3: align pattern to X axis and relevant K line
(Fig. 12.6)
- Mark corner of lapel.

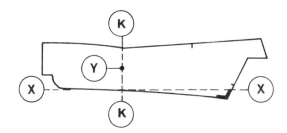

Fig. 12.6.

Stage 4: remain on K line (Fig. 12.7)
- Move to F
- Mark gorge corner.

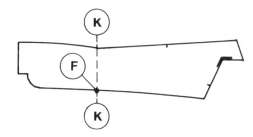

Fig. 12.7.

Stage 5: remain on F (Fig. 12.8)
- Align Y axis of pattern to relevant L line
- Complete neck
- Mark start of shoulder.

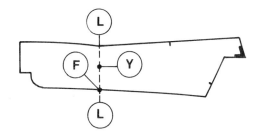

Fig. 12.8.

Stage 6: remain on L line (Fig. 12.9)
- Move to G/2
- Complete shoulder
- Mark panel corner.

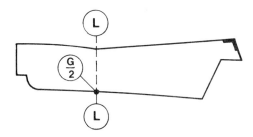

Fig. 12.9.

Stage 7: use pattern to (Fig. 12.10)
- Join panel corner to bust point
- Complete collar seams
- Blend lapel line.

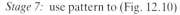

Fig. 12.10.

Grading instructions: BUST PANEL

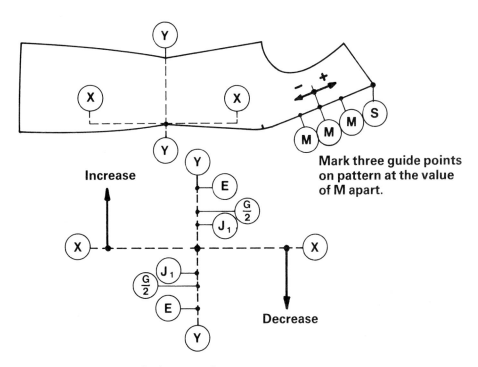

Mark three guide points on pattern at the value of M apart.

Fig. 12.11. Grading axes and increment net for bust panel.

Stage 1: align pattern to X and Y axes (Fig. 12.12)
* Mark panel line from bust point to hem
* Mark part of hem.

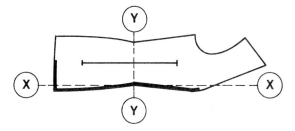

Fig. 12.12.

Stage 2: remain on Y axis (Fig. 12.13)
* Move to J_1
* Mark point S at junction of shoulder and panel lines.

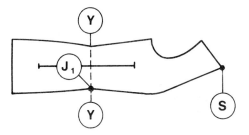

Fig. 12.13.

Stage 3: remain on Y axis (Fig. 12.14)
- Mark part of armhole
- Mark dart (new pocket position).

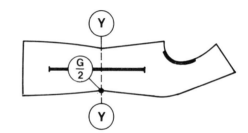

Fig. 12.14.

Stage 4: remain on Y axis (Fig. 12.15)
- Move to E
- Complete lower section of armhole
- Mark side seam
- Complete hem.

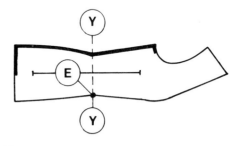

Fig. 12.15.

Stage 5: align bust dart section of pattern from the bust point to point S (Fig. 12.15)
- Mark panel line from bust point to S.

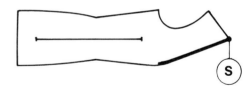

Fig. 12.16.

Stage 6: mark relevant M points on this line (Fig. 12.17)
- Increase: towards shoulder
- Decrease: towards bust point.

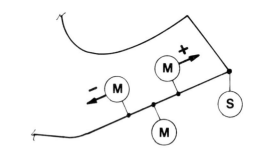

Fig. 12.17.

Stage 7: align bust line of pattern to line marked in Stage 6 (Fig. 12.18)
- Move along this line until the central M point on pattern is aligned to the relevant M point on paper
- Mark start of shoulder.

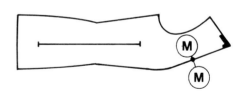

Fig. 12.18.

Stage 8: move panel parallel to bust dart line by distance of G/2 (Fig. 12.19)
- Complete shoulder
- Complete armhole.

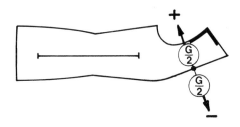

Fig. 12.19.

Grading instructions: CENTRE BACK PANEL

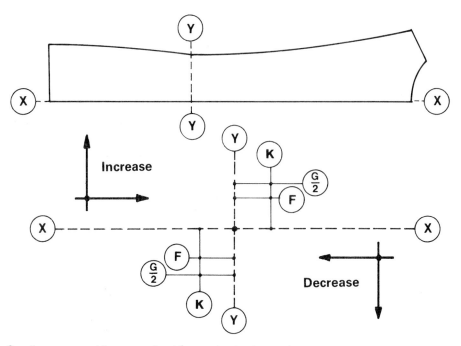

Fig. 12.20. Grading axes and increment net for centre back panel.

Stage 1: align pattern to X and Y axes (Fig. 12.21)
- Mark part of centre back line
- Mark part of hem.

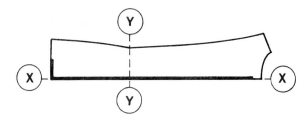

Fig. 12.21.

Stage 2: remain on Y axis (Fig. 12.22)
- Move to G/2
- Mark panel line to about 12 cm from shoulder
- Complete panel hem.

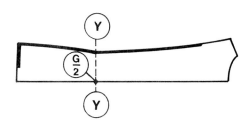

Fig. 12.22.

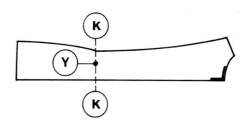

Stage 3: align centre back to X axis (Fig. 12.23)
- Align Y axis of pattern to relevant K line
- Complete centre back line
- Mark start of neck.

Fig. 12.23.

Stage 4: remain on K line (Fig. 12.24)
- Move to F
- Complete neck
- Mark start of shoulder.

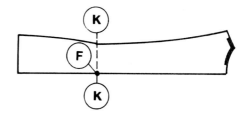

Fig. 12.24.

Stage 5: remain on K line (Fig. 12.25)
- Move to G/2
- Complete shoulder section
- Mark panel corner.

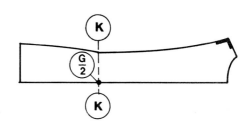

Fig. 12.25.

Stage 6: use pattern to blend panel line from shoulder (Fig. 12.26).

Fig. 12.26.

Grading instructions: SIDE PANEL

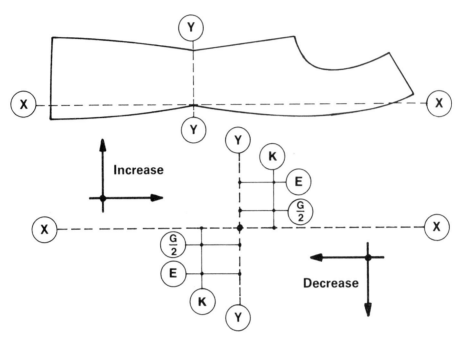

Fig. 12.27. Grading axes and increment net for side panel.

Stage 1: align pattern to X and Y axes (Fig. 12.28)
- Mark panel line to blade
- Mark part of hem.

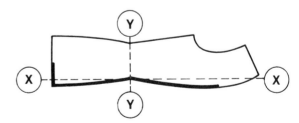

Fig. 12.28.

Stage 2: remain on Y axis (Fig. 12.29)
- Move to G/2
- Mark part of armhole.

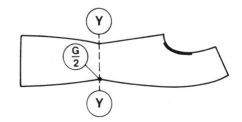

Fig. 12.29.

Stage 3: remain on Y axis (Fig. 12.30)
- Move to E
- Complete lower section of armhole
- Mark side seam
- Complete hem.

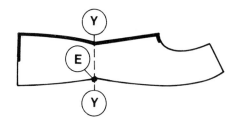

Fig. 12.30.

Stage 4: align pattern to X axis (Fig. 12.31)
- Align Y axis of pattern to relevant K line.

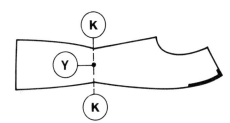

Fig. 12.31.

Stage 5: remain on K line (Fig. 12.32)
- Move to G/2
- Complete shoulder
- Mark start of armhole.

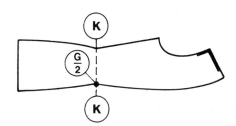

Fig. 12.32.

Stage 6: use pattern to blend panel line and armhole (Fig. 12.33).

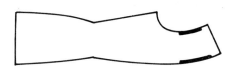

Fig. 12.33.

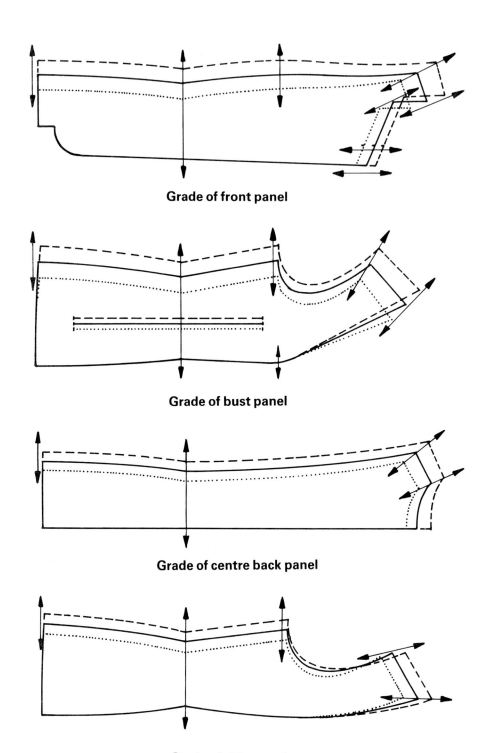

Grade of front panel

Grade of bust panel

Grade of centre back panel

Grade of side panel

Grading instructions: FRONT SLEEVE

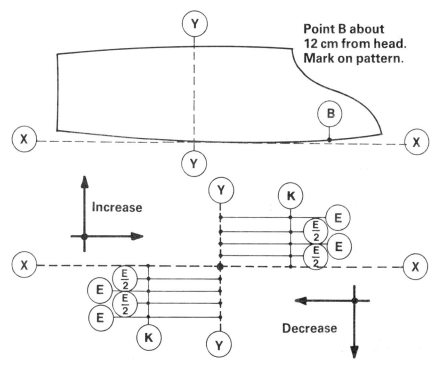

Point B about 12 cm from head. Mark on pattern.

Fig. 12.34. Grading axes and increment net for front sleeve.

Stage 1: align pattern to X and Y axes (Fig. 12.35)
● Mark centre seam from elbow line to point B.

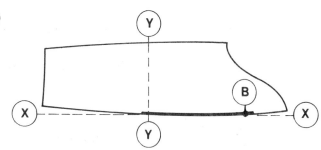

Fig. 12.35.

Stage 2: remain on X axis (Fig. 12.36)
● Align Y axis of pattern to relevant K line
● Complete top section of centre seam
● Mark part of sleeve head.

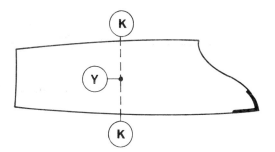

Fig. 12.36.

Stage 3: align Y axis of pattern and paper (Fig. 12.37)
- Move to first E/2
- Mark bottom of centre seam and hem corner.

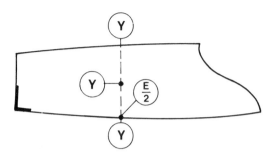

Fig. 12.37.

Stage 4: remain on Y axis (Fig. 12.38)
- Move to first E
- Mark section of sleeve head.

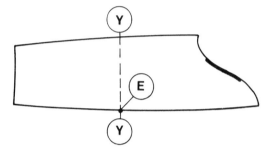

Fig. 12.38.

Stage 5: remain on Y axis (Fig. 12.39)
- Move to second E/2
- Mark underseam corner
- Complete cuff.

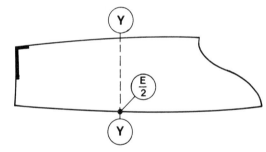

Fig. 12.39.

Stage 6: remain on Y axis (Fig. 12.40)
- Move to second E
- Complete under section of sleeve head
- Mark underseam to elbow line.

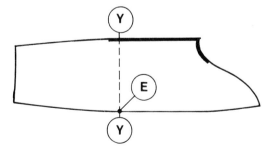

Fig. 12.40.

Stage 7: use pattern to (Fig. 12.41):
- Blend sleeve head
- Blend overarm and underarm seams from elbow line to cuff.

Fig. 12.41.

Grading instructions: BACK SLEEVE

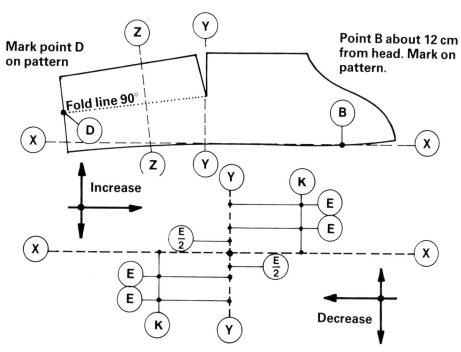

Fig. 12.42. Grading axes and increment net for back sleeve.

Stage 1: align pattern to X and Y axes (Fig. 12.43)
- Mark centre line from point B to elbow line
- Mark part of cuff and point D.

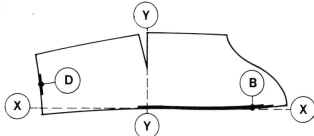

Fig. 12.43.

Stage 2: remain on Y axis (Fig. 12.44)
- Move to E/2
- To increase = below X axis.
- To decrease = above X axis.

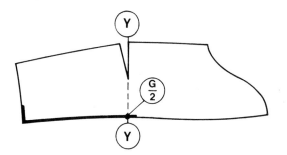

Fig. 12.44.

Stage 3: align pattern to X axis (Fig. 12.45)
- Align Y axis of pattern to relevant K line
- Complete centre seam
- Mark part of sleeve crown.

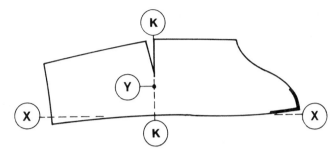

Fig. 12.45.

Stage 4: align Y axes of pattern and paper (Fig. 12.46)
- Move to first E
- Mark section of sleeve head
- Mark dart apex.

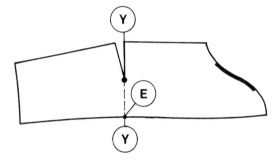

Fig. 12.46.

Stage 5: remain on Y axis (Fig. 12.47)
- Move to second E
- Complete undersection of sleeve head
- Mark underarm seam to elbow dart
- Complete top side of dart.

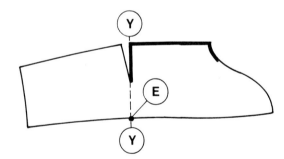

Fig. 12.47.

Stage 6: join point D to new apex of dart (Fig. 12.48)
- Align fold line of pattern to this line
- Mark Z – Z axis and intersection with lower part of
  underseam.

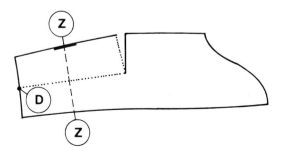

Fig. 12.48.

Stage 7: from this intersection, mark two increments of E/2 on the Z – Z axis (Fig. 12.49)
- To increase: above the intersection
- To decrease: below the intersection.

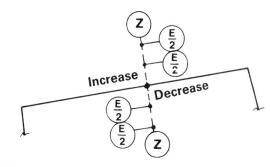

Fig. 12.49.

Stage 8: align fold line of pattern to new fold line (Fig. 12.50)
- Align to origin point on Z – Z axis
- Move to first E/2
- Mark part of cuff and underseam corner.

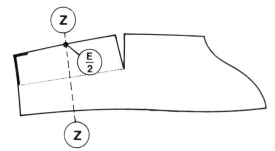

Fig. 12.50.

Stage 9: remain on Z – Z axis (Fig. 12.51)
- Move to second E/2
- Mark corner of dart and underseam.

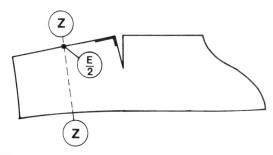

Fig. 12.51.

Stage 10: use pattern to (Fig. 12.52):
- Complete second side of dart
- Join underarm seam from dart to hem.

Fig. 12.52.

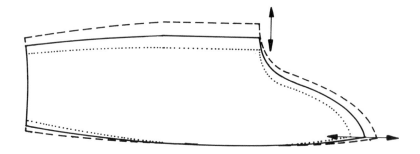

Grade of front sleeve

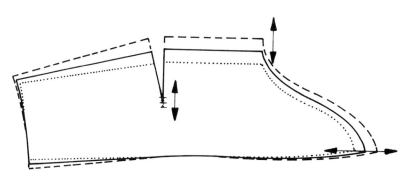

Grade of back sleeve

Chapter 13

Box Jacket with Kimono Sleeve

Both halves of the kimono sleeve in this example have been attached to the back and front side panels respectively (Fig. 13.1). The side panels themselves are not full length, but extend to a horizontal seam at about pocket height level. Thus, the total width grades for the central back and front panels are split into two sections, one for the full length panel and the other for the side panel (Fig. 13.2).

For the front: 1st section $= F + G/2 + I_1$
    2nd section $= J_1 + G/2 + E$
For the back: 1st section $= F + G/2$
    2nd section $= G/2 + E$

Another feature of this example is the grade of the stand collar which is cut in one piece with the central front panel.

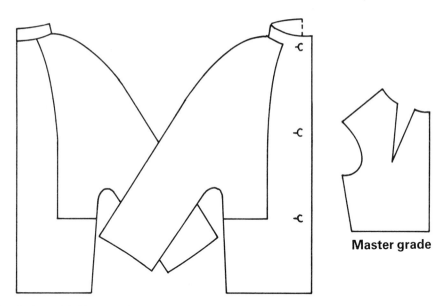

Fig. 13.1. Box jacket with kimono sleeve.

Master grade

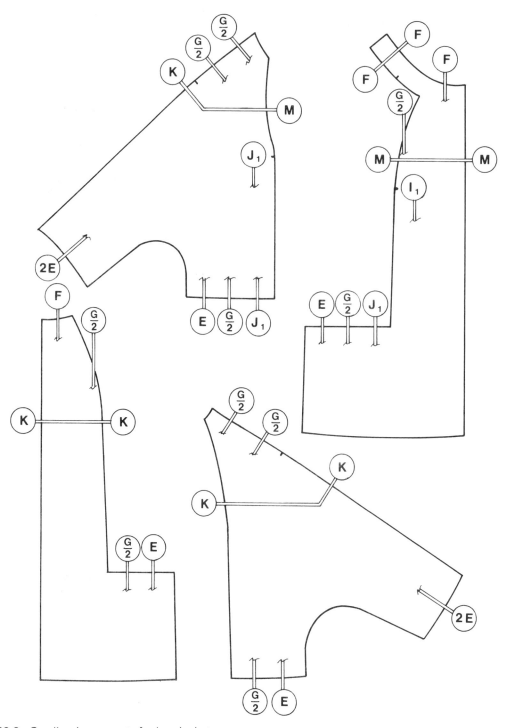

Fig. 13.2. Grading increments for box jacket.

Grading instructions: FRONT PANEL

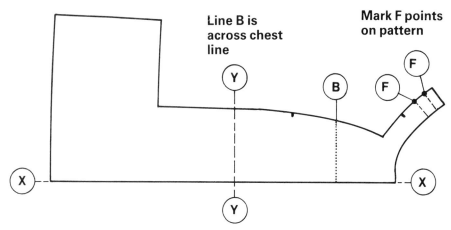

Fig. 13.3. Grading axes for front panel.

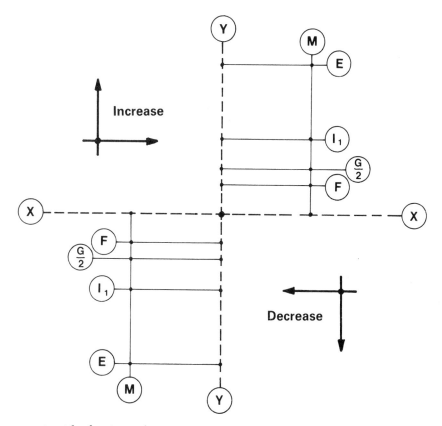

Fig. 13.4. Increment net for front panel.

Stage 1: align pattern to X and Y axes (Fig. 13.5)
- Mark part of front edge
- Mark start of hem.

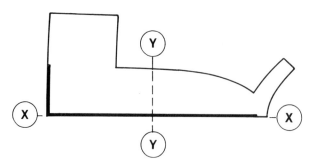

Fig. 13.5.

Stage 2: remain on Y axis (Fig. 13.6)
- Move to I_1
- Mark panel seam from bust point to panel corner
- Mark start of horizontal seam.

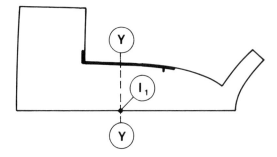

Fig. 13.6.

Stage 3: remain on Y axis (Fig. 13.7)
- Move to E
- Complete horizontal seam
- Mark side seam
- Complete hem.

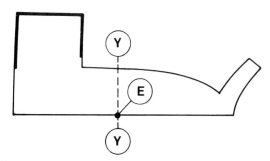

Fig. 13.7.

Stage 4: align pattern to X axis (Fig. 13.8)
- Align Y axis of pattern to relevant M line
- Mark corner of front edge and neck line.

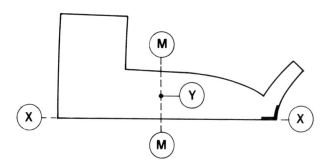

Fig. 13.8.

Stage 5: remain on M line (Fig. 13.9)
- Move to F
- Mark corner of panel line and neck seam
- Mark collar section.

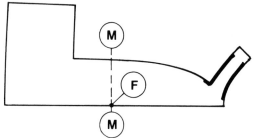

Fig. 13.9.

Stage 6: remain on M line (Fig. 13.10)
- Move to G/2
- Mark small section of panel line on either side of point B (this is a guide point only).

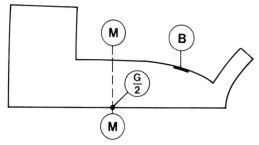

Fig. 13.10.

Stage 7: mark F points on neck seam of collar (Fig. 13.11)
- To increase: mark F_1
- To decrease: mark F_2

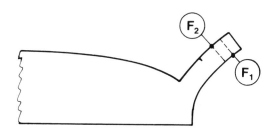

Fig. 13.11.

Stage 8: align F points (Fig. 13.12)
- To increase: F_2 to F_1
- To decrease: F_1 to F_2
- Complete collar seams and end.

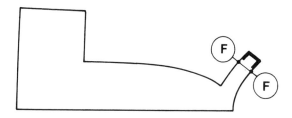

Fig. 13.12.

Stage 9: use pattern to connect panel line from corner, through point B to bust point (Fig. 13.13).

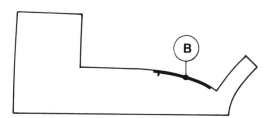

Fig. 13.13.

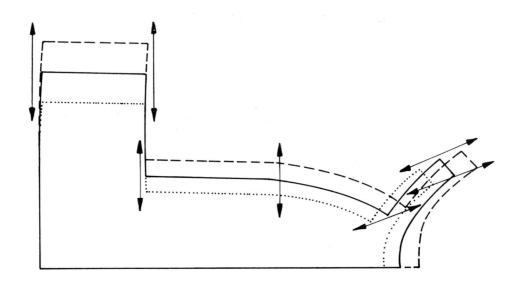

Grade of front panel

Grading instructions: BUST PANEL

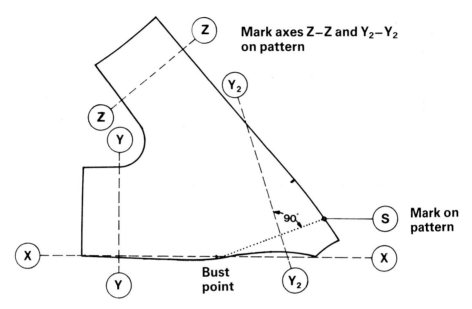

Mark axes Z–Z and Y_2–Y_2 on pattern

Mark on pattern

90°

Bust point

Fig. 13.14. Grading axes for bust panel.

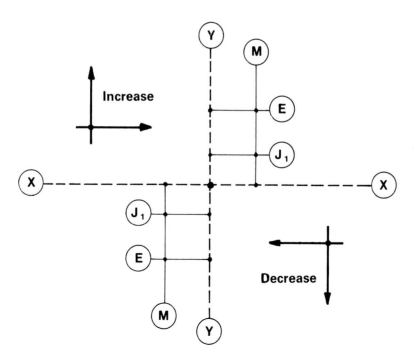

Increase

Decrease

Fig. 13.15 Increment net for bust panel.

Stage 1: align pattern to X and Y axes (Fig. 13.16)
- Mark panel line from bust point to seam corner
- Mark part of horizontal seam.

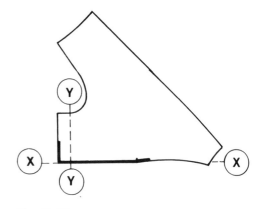

Fig. 13.16.

Stage 2: remain on Y axis (Fig. 13.17)
- Move to J_1
- Mark point S at shoulder.

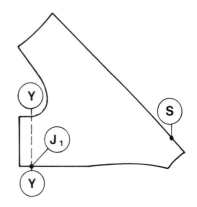

Fig. 13.17.

Stage 3: remain on Y axis (Fig. 13.18)
- Move to E
- Complete horizontal seam
- Mark side seam, underseam and part of cuff
- Mark Z – Z axis
- Mark intersection of overarm seam with Z – Z axis.

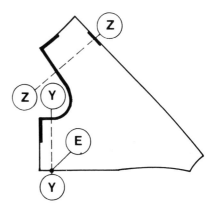

Fig. 13.18.

Stage 4: mark increment 2E from intersection of overarm seam and Z – Z axis (Fig. 13.19)
- To increase — above seam
- To decrease — below seam.

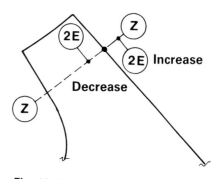

Fig. 13.19.

Stage 5: align Z – Z axes of pattern and paper (Fig. 13.20)
- Move to 2E
- Complete cuff
- Mark corner of cuff and overseam.

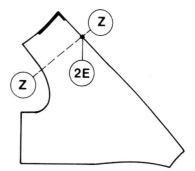

Fig. 13.20.

Stage 6: on paper, join bust point to point S (Fig. 13.21)
- Align bust points of pattern and paper
- Align pivot lines of pattern and paper
- Mark intersection of pattern shoulder line and pivot line.

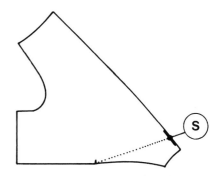

Fig. 13.21.

Stage 7: mark increment M from the intersection of the pivot and shoulder lines (Fig. 13.22)
- To increase — above shoulder line
- To decrease — below shoulder line.

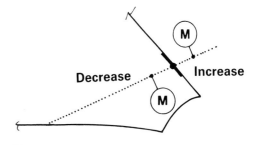

Fig. 13.22.

Stage 8: align pivot lines of pattern and paper
(Fig. 13.23)
- Move pattern along pivot line to point M
- Mark axis $Y_2 - Y_2$
- Mark intersection of panel line and Y_2 axis.

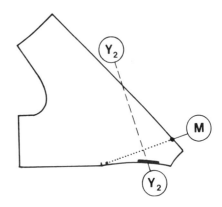

Fig. 13.23.

Stage 9: mark increments G/2A and G/2B on either side of intersection point (Stage 8) (Fig. 13.24).

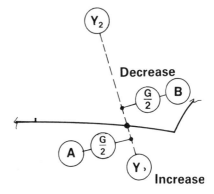

Fig. 13.24.

Stage 10: align Y_2 axes of pattern and paper
(Fig. 13.25)
- To increase: move to G/2A
- To decrease: move to G/2B
- Mark neck point, neck section and start of panel line.

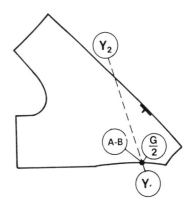

Fig. 13.25.

Stage 11: remain on Y_2 axis (Fig. 13.26)
- To increase: move to G/2B
- To decrease: move to G/2A
- Mark shoulder point and part of shoulder line.

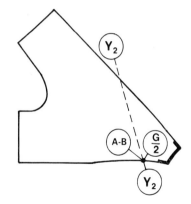

Stage 12: use pattern to (Fig. 13.27)
- Complete panel line
- Complete shoulder and overarm seam.

Fig. 13.26.

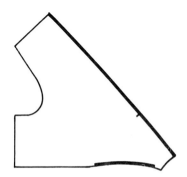

Fig. 13.27.

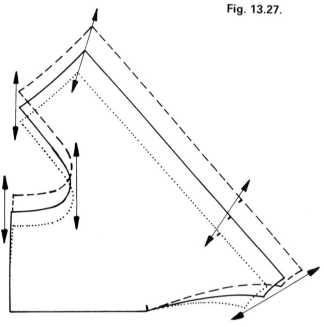

Grade of bust panel

Grading instructions: CENTRE BACK PANEL

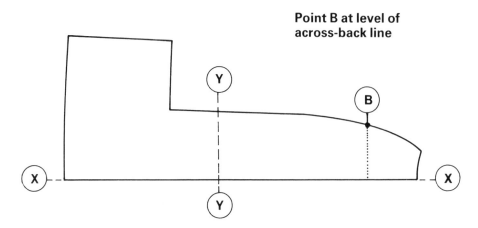

Point B at level of across-back line

Fig. 13.28. Grading axes for centre back panel.

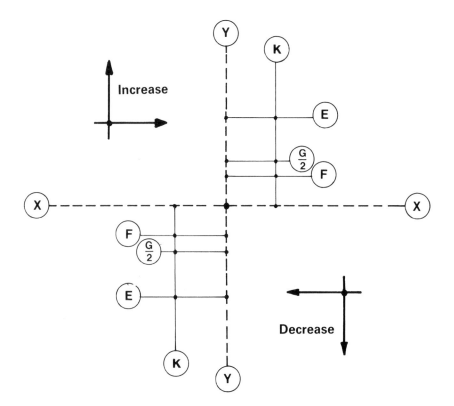

Fig. 13.29. Increment net for centre back panel.

Stage 1: align pattern to X and Y axes (Fig. 13.30)
- Mark part of centre seam
- Mark part of hem.

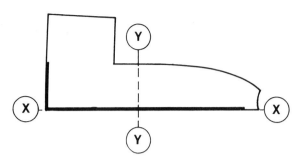

Fig. 13.30.

Stage 2: remain on Y axis (Fig. 13.31)
- Move to G/2
- Mark straight section of panel line
- Mark corner of horizontal seam.

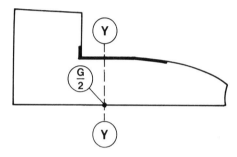

Fig. 13.31.

Stage 3: remain on Y axis (Fig. 13.32)
- Move to E
- Complete horizontal seam
- Mark side seam
- Complete hem.

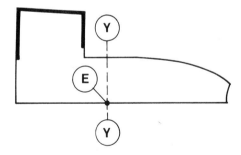

Fig. 13.32.

Stage 4: align pattern to X axis (Fig. 13.33)
- Align Y axis of pattern to relevant K line
- Complete centre back seam
- Mark start of neck.

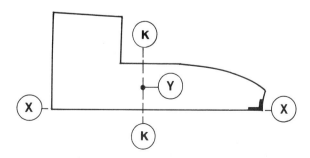

Fig. 13.33.

288

Stage 5: remain on K line (Fig. 13.34)
- Move to F
- Complete neck section
- Mark corner of panel line.

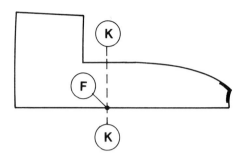

Fig. 13.34.

Stage 6: remain on K line (Fig. 13.35)
- Move to G/2
- Mark point B (guide point only).

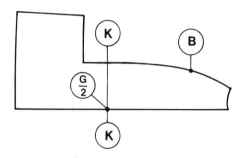

Fig. 13.35.

Stage 7: use pattern to connect neck point, through point B to panel line (Fig. 13.36).

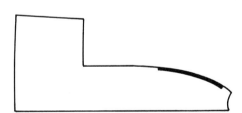

Fig. 13.36.

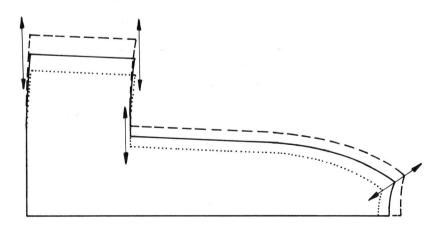

Grade for centre back panel

Grading instructions: SIDE PANEL

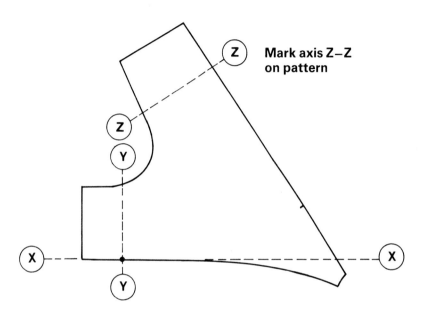

Fig. 13.37. Grading axes for side panel.

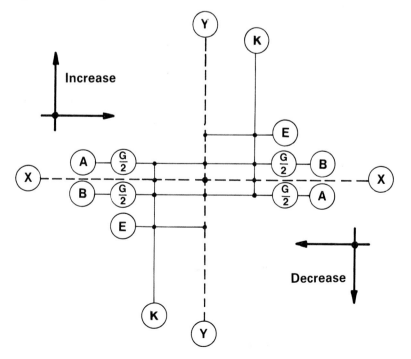

Fig. 13.38. Increment net for side panel.

Stage 1: align pattern to X and Y axes (Fig. 13.39)
- Mark straight section of panel seam
- Mark part of horizontal seam.

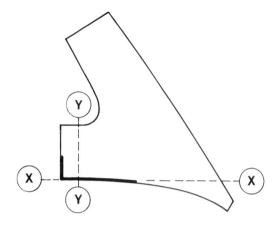

Fig. 13.39.

Stage 2: remain on Y axis (Fig. 13.40)
- Move to E
- Complete horizontal seam
- Mark side and underarm seam to cuff
- Mark Z axis
- Mark part of overarm seam at intersection with Z axis.

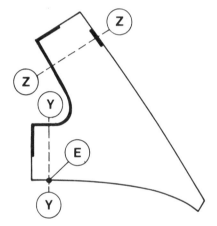

Fig. 13.40.

Stage 3: mark increment 2E from intersection of overarm seam and Z axis (Fig. 13.41)
- To increase: mark above seam
- To decrease: mark below seam.

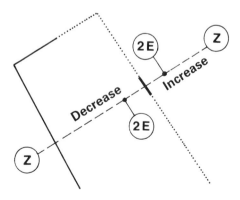

Fig. 13.41.

Stage 4: align Z axes of pattern and paper (Fig. 13.42)
- Move to 2E
- Complete cuff
- Mark corner of overarm seam.

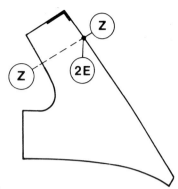

Fig. 13.42.

Stage 5: align pattern to X axis (Fig. 13.43)
- Align Y axis of pattern to relevant K line
- To increase: move to G/2A
- To decrease: move to G/2B.

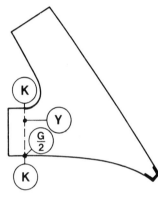

Fig. 13.43.

Stage 6: remain on K line (Fig. 13.44)
- To increase: move to G/2B
- To decrease: move to G/2A
- Complete shoulder section to shoulder nip.

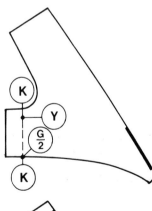

Fig. 13.44.

Stage 7: use pattern to (Fig. 13.45)
- Complete overarm seam from shoulder point to cuff
- Cuff panel line.

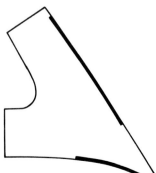

Fig. 13.45.

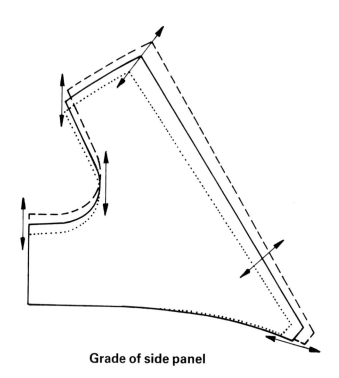

Grade of side panel

Chapter 14

Blouse with Tie Collar and Cuffed Sleeve

The design features of this example are (Fig. 14.1):

- A button cuff sleeve where the vent position is graded to maintain its position on the back draping line of the sleeve.
- The tie collar set into a lowered neckline which can be graded by one of two methods:

Method 1: By applying increment M below the collar end on the centre front. By using this method, the front neck depth remains unchanged for all sizes and this is the method demonstrated.

Method 2: By applying increment M above the collar end on the centre front which changes the front neck depth from size to size.

The back and front have side body panels with the bust dart coming from the front side body panel seam. Both of the side panels receive increment E only (Fig. 14.2).

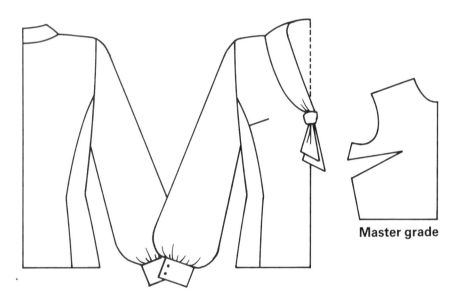

Master grade

Fig. 14.1. Blouse with tie collar.

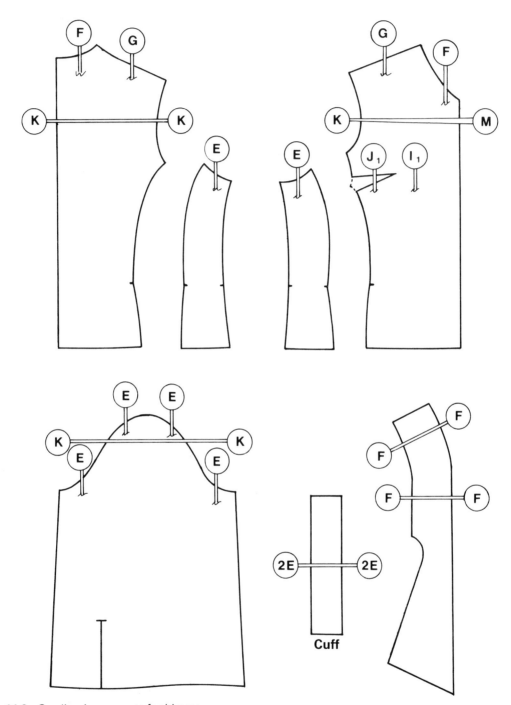

Fig. 14.2. Grading increments for blouse.

Grading instructions: BLOUSE FRONT

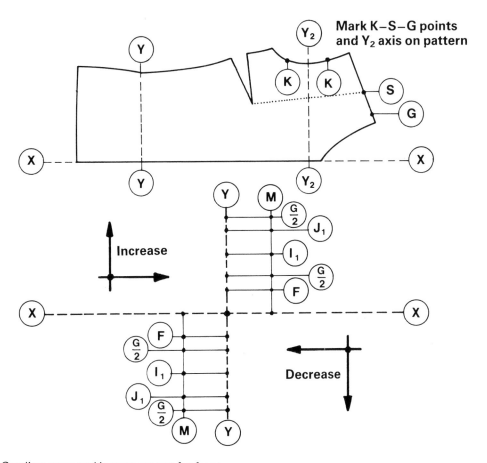

Mark K–S–G points
and Y₂ axis on pattern

Increase

Decrease

Fig. 14.3. Grading axes and increment net for front.

Stage 1: align pattern to X and Y axes (Fig. 14.4)
- Mark front edge
- Mark part of hem.

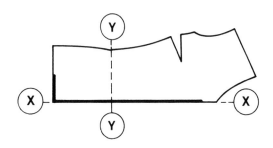

Fig. 14.4.

Stage 2: remain on Y axis (Fig. 14.5)
- Move to first G/2
- Mark point S
- Mark part of shoulder line on either side of point S.

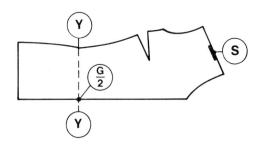

Fig. 14.5.

Stage 3: remain on Y axis (Fig. 14.6)
- Move to I_1
- Mark new bust point.

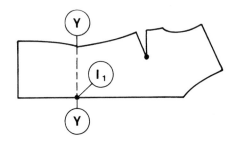

Fig. 14.6.

Stage 4: remain on Y axis (Fig. 14.7)
- Move to second G/2
- Mark lower corner of dart
- Mark panel seam
- Complete hem.

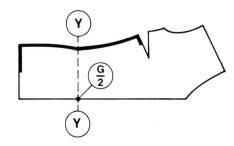

Fig. 14.7.

Stage 5: align pattern to X axis (Fig. 14.8)
- Align Y axis of pattern to relevant M line
- Complete front edge
- Mark start of neckline at centre front.

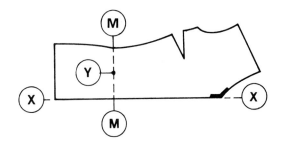

Fig. 14.8.

Stage 6: remain on M line (Fig. 14.9)
- Move to F
- Complete neck
- Mark start of shoulder
- Mark G point.

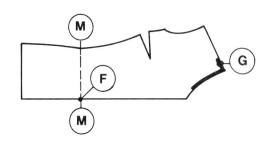

Fig. 14.9.

Stage 7: mark J_1 point from intersection of pivot line and shoulder line (Stage 2) (Fig. 14.10)
- To increase: towards neck.
- To decrease: towards armhole.

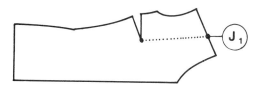

Fig. 14.10.

Stage 8: align the pivot lines of the pattern and paper from the bust point (Fig. 14.11)
- Mark small section of front edge
- Mark axis $Y_2 - Y_2$.

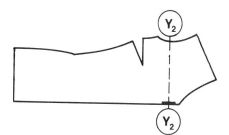

Fig. 14.11.

Stage 9: mark increments J_1 and G/2 on Y_2 axis from intersection with centre front (Fig. 14.12).

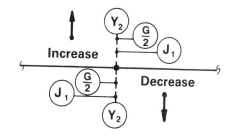

Fig. 14.12.

Stage 10: align pattern to Y_2 axis (Fig. 14.13)
- Move to G/2
- Mark lower section of armhole
- Mark first section of panel line
- Mark top corner of bust dart.

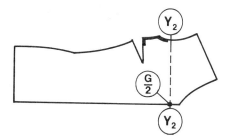

Fig. 14.13.

Stage 11: mark relevant K point (Fig. 14.14)
- To increase: towards shoulder line
- To decrease: towards bust line.

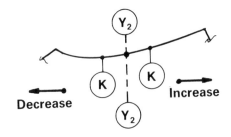

Fig. 14.14.

Stage 12: align pattern to relevant K and G points (Fig. 14.15)
- Complete shoulder and armhole.

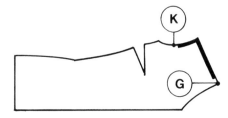

Fig. 14.15.

Stage 13: use pattern to blend neckline and armhole (Fig. 14.16)
- Complete bust dart.

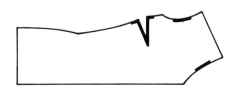

Fig. 14.16.

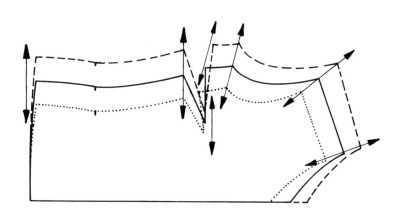

Grade for front

Grading instructions: FRONT SIDE BODY

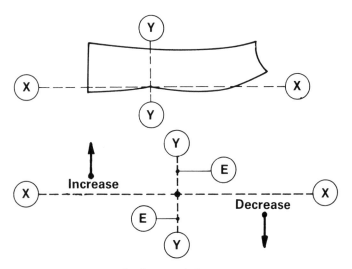

Fig. 14.17. Grading axes and increment net for front side body.

Stage 1: align pattern X and Y axes (Fig. 14.18)
- Mark first section of armhole
- Mark panel line
- Mark part of hem.

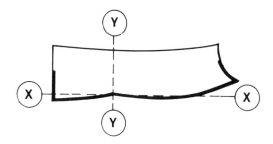

Fig. 14.18.

Stage 2: remain on Y axis (Fig. 14.19)
- Move to E
- Complete armhole
- Mark side seam
- Complete hem.

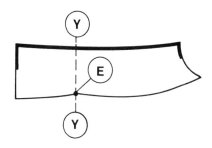

Fig. 14.19.

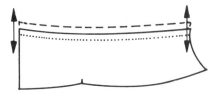

Grade for front side body

Grading instructions: CENTRE BACK PANEL

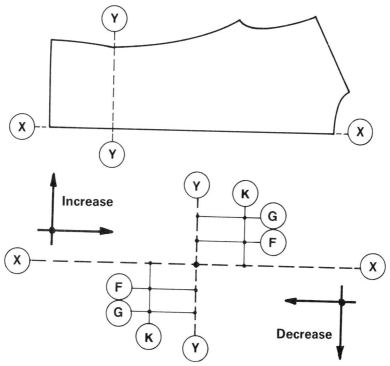

Fig. 14.20 Grading axes and increment net for centre back panel.

Stage 1: align pattern to X and Y axes (Fig. 14.21)
- Mark centre back seam
- Mark part of hem.

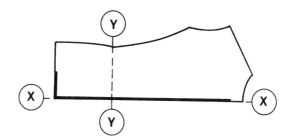

Fig. 14.21.

Stage 2: remain on Y axis (Fig. 14.22)
- Move to G
- Mark part of armhole
- Mark panel seam
- Complete hem.

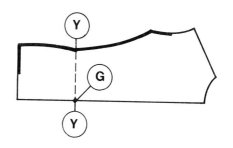

Fig. 14.22.

Stage 3: align Y axis of pattern to relevant K line
(Fig. 14.23)
● Align pattern to X axis
● Complete centre back seam
● Mark start of neck.

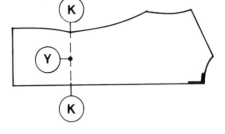

Fig. 14.23.

Stage 4: remain on K line (Fig. 14.24)
● Move to F
● Complete neck
● Mark start of shoulder.

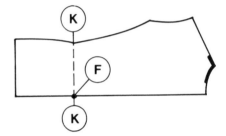

Fig. 14.24.

Stage 5: remain on K line (Fig. 14.25)
● Move to G
● Complete shoulder
● Complete armhole.

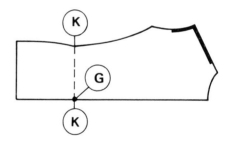

Fig. 14.25.

Grading instructions: SIDE PANEL

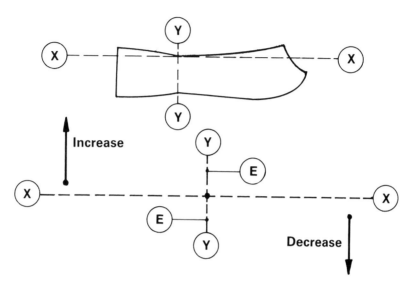

Fig. 14.26. Grading axes and increment net for side panel.

Stage 1: align pattern to X and Y axes (Fig. 14.27)
- Mark panel seam
- Mark part of armhole
- Mark part of hem.

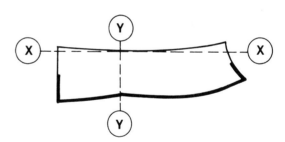

Fig. 14.27.

Stage 2: remain on Y axis (Fig. 14.28)
- Move to E
- Complete armhole
- Mark side seam
- Complete hem.

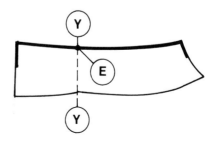

Fig. 14.28.

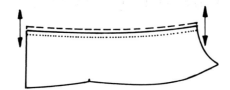

Grade for side panel

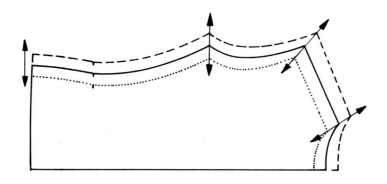

Grade for centre back panel

Grading instructions: BLOUSE SLEEVE

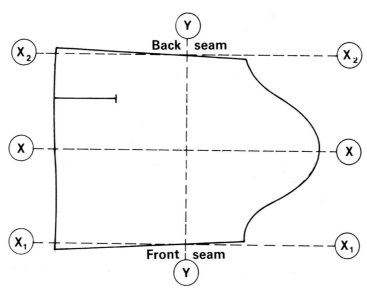

Fig. 14.29. Grading axes for sleeve.

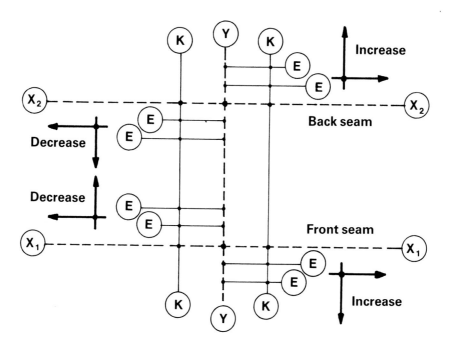

Fig. 14.30. Increment net for sleeve.

Stage 1: align pattern to central X axis (Fig. 14.31)
● Align Y axis of pattern to relevant K line
● Mark part of crown and centre nip.

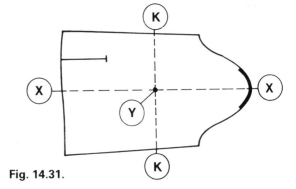

Fig. 14.31.

Stage 2: front section grade (Fig. 14.32)
● Align pattern to Y and X_1 axes
● Move to first E
● Mark section of sleeve head.

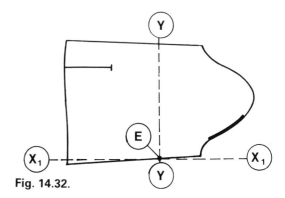

Fig. 14.32.

Stage 3: remain on Y axis (Fig. 14.33)
● Move to second E
● Complete undersection of sleeve head
● Mark underseam
● Mark front half of cuff.

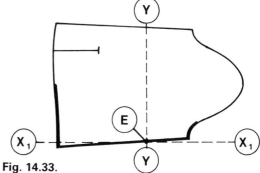

Fig. 14.33.

Stage 4: back section grade (Fig. 14.34)
● Align pattern to Y and X_2 axes
● Move to first E
● Mark section of sleeve head
● Mark cuff vent and part of hem.

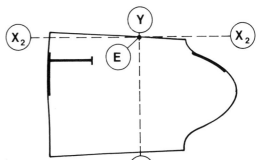

Fig. 14.34.

Stage 5: remain on Y axis (Fig. 14.35)
- Move to second E
- Complete undersection of sleeve head
- Mark underseam
- Mark back half of cuff.

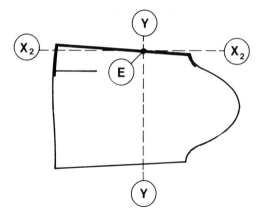

Fig. 14.35.

Stage 6: use pattern to blend sleeve head run
(Fig. 14.36).

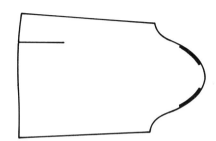

Fig. 14.36.

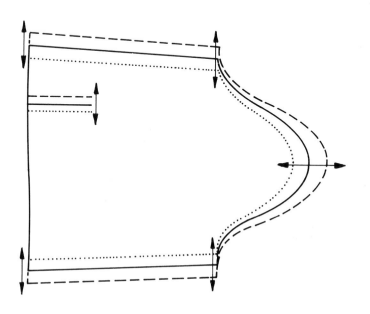

Grade for blouse sleeve

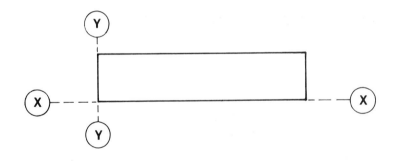

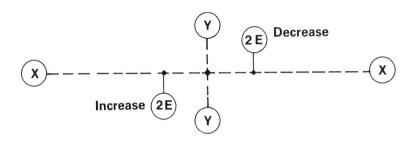

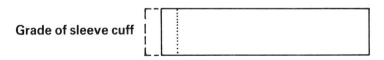

Fig. 14.37. Grading axis and increments for sleeve cuff.

Grading instructions: TIE COLLAR

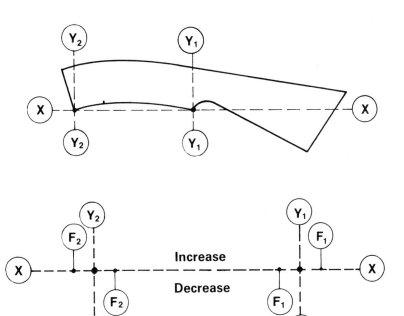

Fig. 14.38. Grading axes and increment net for tie collar.

Stage 1: align pattern to X axis and Y origins
(Fig. 14.39)
- Mark centre section of neck and edge seams
- Mark nip.

Fig. 14.39.

Stage 2: front section (Fig. 14.40)
- Move along X axis to F_1
- Complete front section and tie.

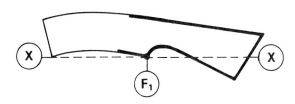

Fig. 14.40.

Stage 3: back section (Fig. 14.41)
● Move along X axis to F_2
● Complete back section.

Fig. 14.41.

Stage 4: use pattern to blend neck and edge seams
(Fig. 14.42).

Fig. 14.42.

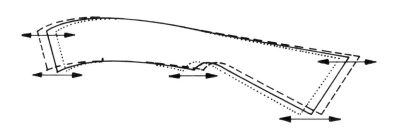

Grade for tie collar

Chapter 15

Double Breasted Jacket

This example (Fig. 15.1) includes the following grading features:

- A waisted, centre back seam.
- Back and front panels which start in the armhole at about the level of the across back and front lines. The front panel line runs through the bust point.
- 'Grown-on' half sleeves connected to the side panels of the back and front.

- A roll-collar with all of the component parts including the facing, extended neck piece and under-collar (Fig. 15.2).

The body and sleeve grades follow the respective master grades and the roll collar grade is based on the demonstration on p. 138 in Chapter 7. In this grade, the collar and lapel widths remain static for all of the sizes graded.

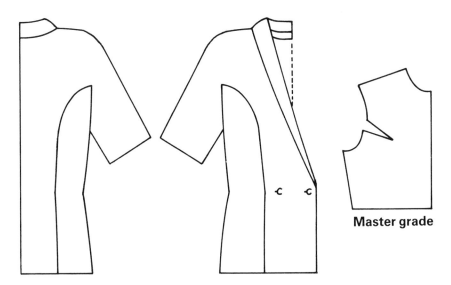

Master grade

Fig. 15.1. Double breasted jacket.

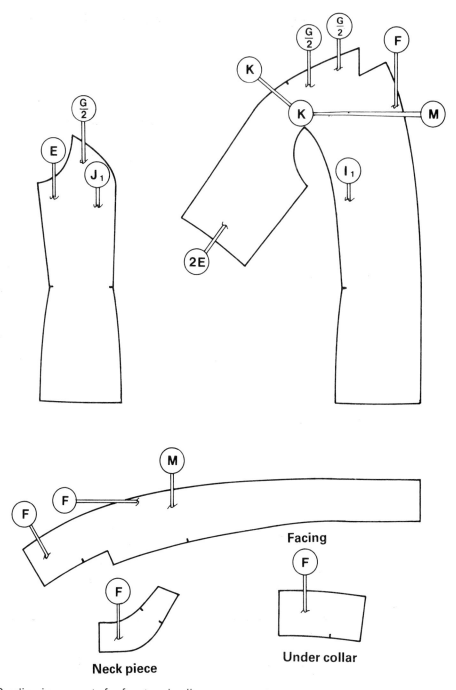

Fig. 15.2. Grading increments for front and collar components.

Grading instructions: FRONT PANEL

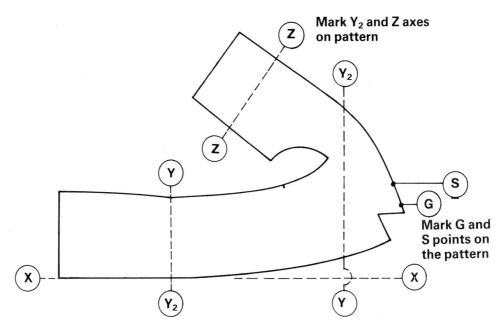

Fig. 15.3. Grading axes for front panel.

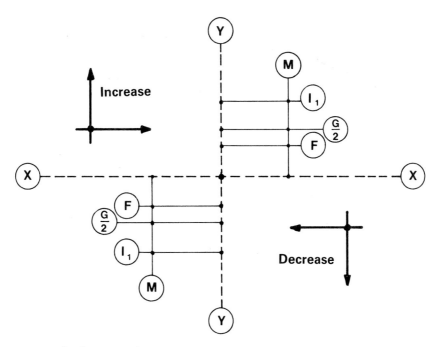

Fig. 15.4. Increment net for front panel.

314

Stage 1: align pattern to X and Y axes (Fig. 15.5)
- Mark front edge and start of lapel
- Mark part of hem.

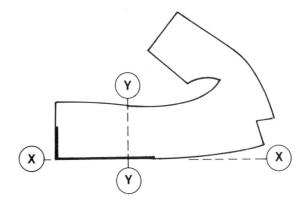

Fig. 15.5.

Stage 2: remain on Y axis (Fig. 15.6)
- Move to G/2
- Mark part of shoulder line
- Mark point S.

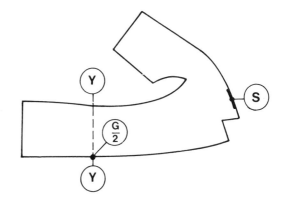

Fig. 15.6.

Stage 3: remain on Y axis (Fig. 15.7)
- Move to I_1
- Mark panel line from bust point down
- Complete hem.

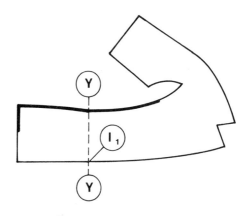

Fig. 15.7.

Stage 4: align Y axis of pattern to relevant M line (Fig. 15.8)
- Move to F
- Mark corner of collar seam (*)
- Mark neck and start of shoulder
- Mark G point.

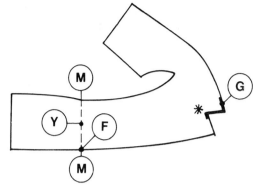

Fig. 15.8.

Stage 5: align neck and collar seam of pattern to the same corner (*) marked in Stage 4 (Fig. 15.9)
- Pivot pattern from this corner until lower lapel edge touches the start of the lapel section
- Mark new collar seam and lapel line.

Fig. 15.9.

Stage 6: join new bust point to S point (pivot line) (Fig. 15.10)
- Mark increment J_1 from the intersection of the shoulder and pivot lines
- To increase: mark towards neck
- To decrease: mark towards armhole.

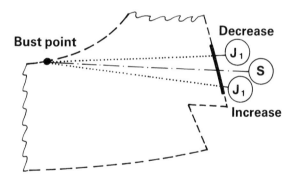

Fig. 15.10.

Stage 7: align the bust points and pivot lines of the pattern and paper (Fig. 15.11)
- Mark $Y_2 - Y_2$ axis
- Mark small section of front edge.

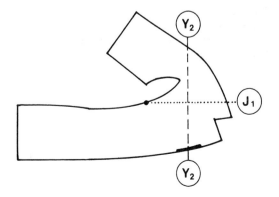

Fig. 15.11.

Stage 8: mark increments J_1 and G/2 from intersection of Y_2 axis and front edge (Fig. 15.12)
- To increase: mark outside of front edge
- To decrease: mark inside of front edge.

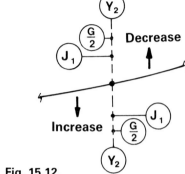

Fig. 15.12.

Stage 9: align the Y_1 axes of pattern and paper (Fig. 15.13)
- Move to G/2
- Mark panel corner and part of sleeve
- Mark Z – Z axis
- Mark intersection of Z axis with overarm and underarm seams.

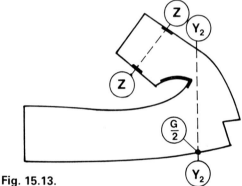

Fig. 15.13.

Stage 10: mark two increments of E on Z axis for the sleeve width grade (Fig. 15.14)
- To increase: mark outside of seam marks.
- To decrease: mark inside of seam marks.

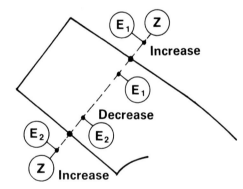

Fig. 15.14.

Stage 11: underarm seam (Fig. 15.15)
- Align Z – Z axes of pattern and paper
- Move to E_2
- Complete under section of sleeve head
- Mark underseam
- Mark part of cuff.

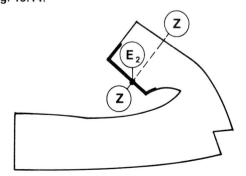

Fig. 15.15.

Stage 12: overarm seam (Fig. 15.16)
- Remain on Z axis
- Move to E_1
- Mark overarm seam to shoulder point
- Complete cuff.

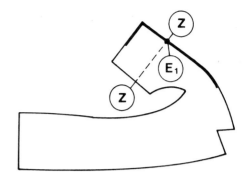

Fig. 15.16.

Stage 13: align neck point of pattern to G point (Fig. 15.17)
- Connect shoulder line to overarm seam.

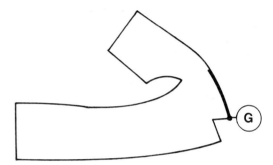

Fig. 15.17.

Stage 14: use pattern to complete upper section of panel line from the bust point to the corner marked in Stage 9 (Fig. 15.18)

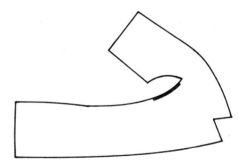

Fig. 15.18.

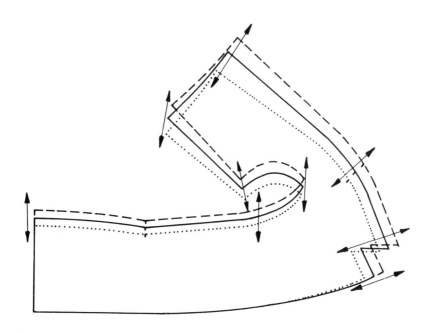

Grade for front panel

Grading instructions: BUST PANEL

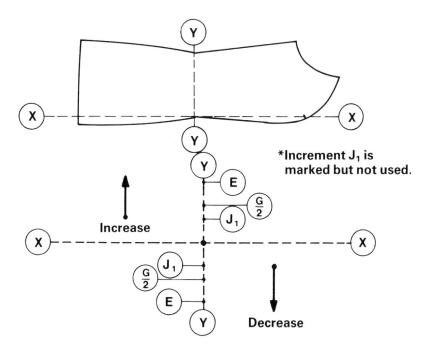

Fig. 15.19 Grading axes and increment net for bust panel.

Stage 1: align pattern to X and Y axes (Fig. 15.20)
- Mark panel line from bust point to hem
- Mark part of hem.

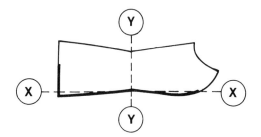

Fig. 15.20.

Stage 2: remain on Y axis (Fig. 15.21)
- Move to G/2
- Mark corner of panel and armhole line
- Mark section of armhole.

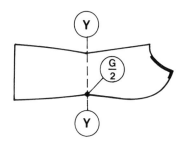

Fig. 15.21.

320

Stage 3: remain on Y axis (Fig. 15.22)
- Move to E
- Complete armhole
- Mark side seam
- Complete hem.

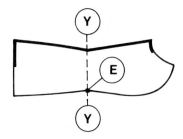

Fig. 15.22.

Stage 4: use pattern to complete panel line from armhole to bust point (Fig. 15.23).

Fig. 15.23.

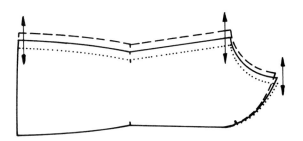

Grade for bust panel

Grading instructions: CENTRE BACK PANEL

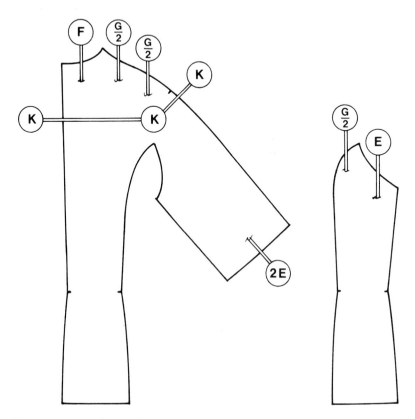

Fig. 15.24. Grading increments for back.

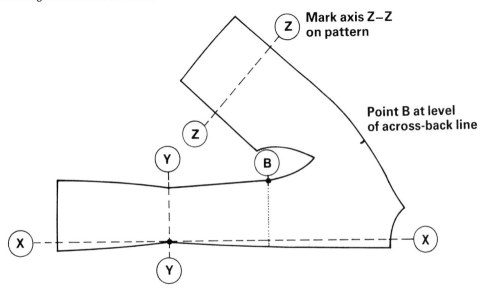

Fig. 15.25. Grading axes for centre back panel.

322

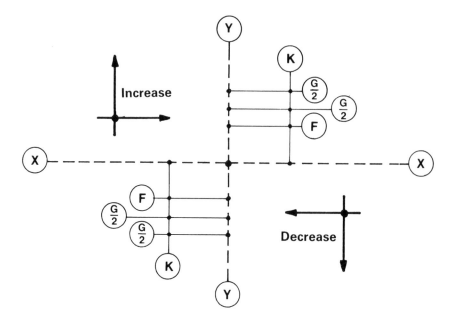

Fig. 15.26. Increment net for centre back panel.

Stage 1: align pattern to X and Y axes (Fig. 15.27)
- Mark part of centre back seam
- Mark part of hem.

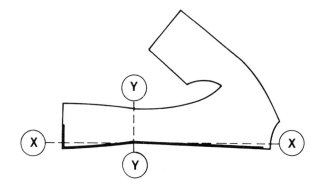

Fig. 15.27.

Stage 2: remain on Y axis (Fig. 15.28)
- Move to first G/2
- Mark panel line from point B to hem.

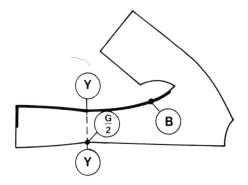

Fig. 15.28.

Stage 3: remain on Y axis (Fig. 15.29)
- Move to second G/2
- Mark panel corner and section of sleeve
- Mark Z – Z axis
- Mark intersections of Z axis with overarm and underarm seams.

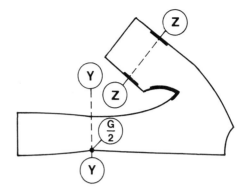

Fig. 15.29.

Stage 4: align Y axis of pattern with relevant K line (Fig. 15.30)
- Mark corner of centre back seam and neck seam.

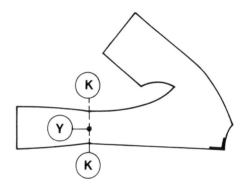

Fig. 15.30.

Stage 5: remain on K line (Fig. 15.31)
- Move to F
- Complete neck line
- Mark start of shoulder.

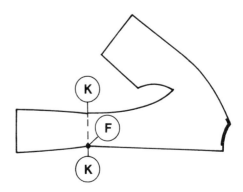

Fig. 15.31.

Stage 6: remain on K line (Fig. 15.32)
- Move to second G/2
- Complete shoulder and mark shoulder nip.

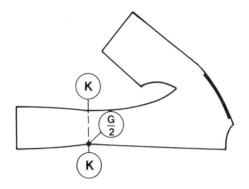

Fig. 15.32.

Stage 7: mark two increments of E for the sleeve width grade (Fig. 15.33)
- To increase: outside of seam marks
- To decrease: inside of seam marks.

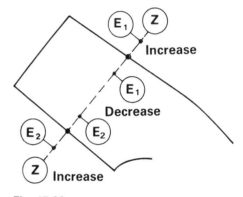

Fig. 15.33.

Stage 8: (Fig. 15.34)
- Align Z – Z axes of pattern and paper
- Move to E_2
- Complete under section of sleeve head
- Mark underarm seam
- Mark part of hem.

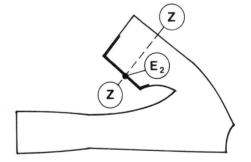

Fig. 15.34.

Stage 9: overarm seam (Fig. 15.35)
- Remain on Z axis
- Move to E_1
- Mark overarm seam to shoulder point
- Complete cuff.

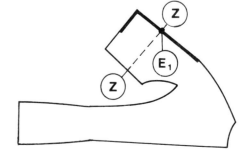

Fig. 15.35.

Stage 10: use pattern to (Fig. 15.36)
- Connect overarm seam to shoulder line
- Complete panel line from corner (Stage 3) to point B.

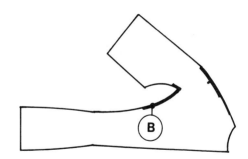

Fig. 15.36.

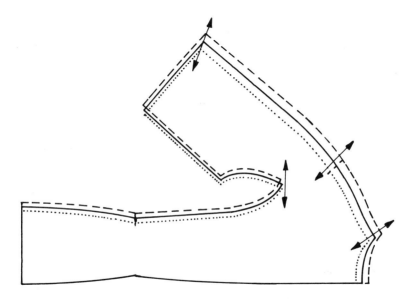

Grade for centre back panel

Grading instructions: SIDE PANEL

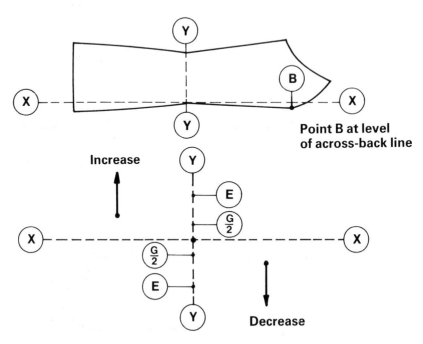

Fig. 15.37. Grading axes and increment net for side panel.

Stage 1: align pattern to X and Y axes (Fig. 15.38)
- Mark panel line from point B to hem
- Mark part of hem.

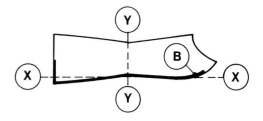

Fig. 15.38.

Stage 2: remain on Y axis (Fig. 15.39)
- Move to G/2
- Mark panel corner
- Mark start of armhole section.

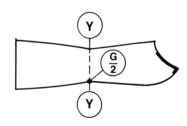

Fig. 15.39.

Stage 3: remain on Y axis (Fig. 15.40)
- Move to E
- Complete armhole
- Mark side seam
- Complete hem.

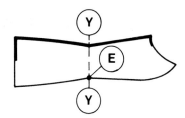

Fig. 15.40.

Stage 4: use pattern to connect panel corner (Stage 2) to point B (Fig. 15.41).

Fig. 15.41.

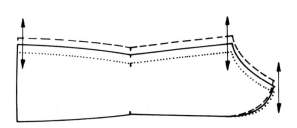

Grade for side panel

Grading instructions: ROLL COLLAR FACING

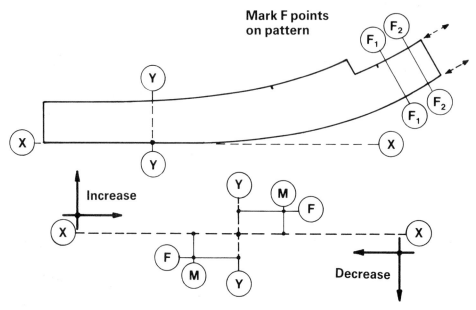

Fig. 15.42. Grading axes and increment net for facing.

Stage 1: align pattern to X and Y axes (Fig. 15.43)
- Mark front edge to start of lapel section
- Mark hem
- Mark inside edge to bust point.

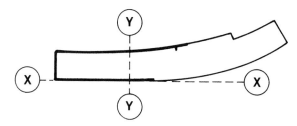

Fig. 15.43.

Stage 2: align Y axis of pattern to relevant M line (Fig. 15.44)
- Move to F
- Mark corner of neck and neck piece seams.

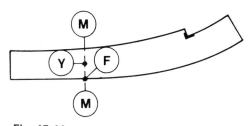

Fig. 15.44.

Stage 3: pivot from corner (Stage 2) until edge of pattern touches the start of the lapel section (Fig. 15.45)
- Mark outside edge
- Mark inside edge
- Mark neck seam and shoulder nip.

Fig. 15.45.

Stage 4: back neck length grade (Fig. 15.46)
- Mark two lines, F_1 and F_2 at a distance apart of increment F.

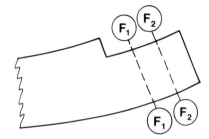

Fig. 15.46.

Stage 5: use neck seam as guide (Fig. 15.47)
- To increase: move F_1 to align with F_2
- To decrease: move F_2 to align with F_1
- Complete neck seam
- Complete centre back section of facing.

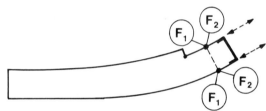

Fig. 15.47.

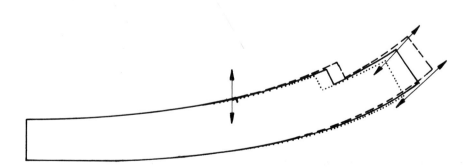

Grade for roll collar facing

Grading instructions: UNDER COLLAR

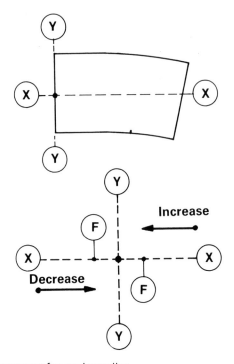

Fig. 15.48. Grading axis and increment for under collar.

Stage 1: align pattern to X and Y axes (Fig. 15.49)
- Mark part of outside edge
- Mark part of neck seam
- Mark shoulder nip.

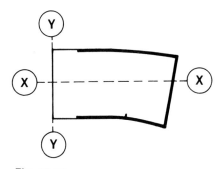

Fig. 15.49.

Stage 2: remain on X axis (Fig. 15.50)
- Move to F
- Complete centre back section of under collar.

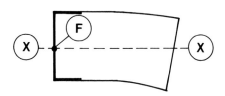

Fig. 15.50.

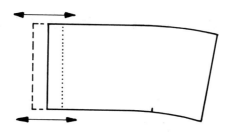

Grade for under-collar

Grading instructions: NECK PIECE

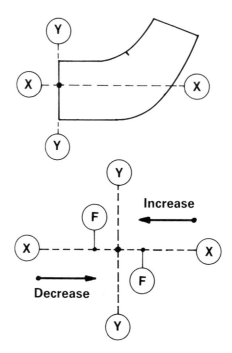

Fig. 15.51. Grading axis and increment for neck piece.

Stage 1: align pattern to X and Y axes (Fig. 15.52)
- Mark part of neck seam and shoulder nip
- Mark part of inside seam
- Mark facing from seam.

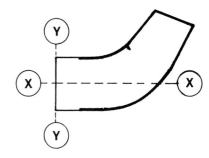

Fig. 15.52.

Stage 2: remain on X axis (Fig. 15.53)
● Move to F
● Complete centre back section of neck piece.

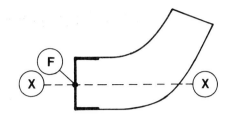

Fig. 15.53.

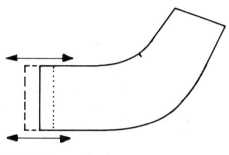

Grade for neck piece

Chapter 16

Front Fusibles for Blazer

The grading of patterns for auxiliary materials is no less important than the grading of top cloth components. This example demonstrates the grade for the fully fused front and patch pocket of a classic blazer jacket (Figs 16.1 and 16.2).

- The front fusibles have the same basic form as the top cloth components for the front, with the bust suppression coming from the lateral seam which is covered by the pocket.

- The width grade of the patch is proportionate to the total width grade between the bust dart and the side seam.

All fusibles which are related to a specific style can be graded by exactly the same method as that used for the top cloth components.

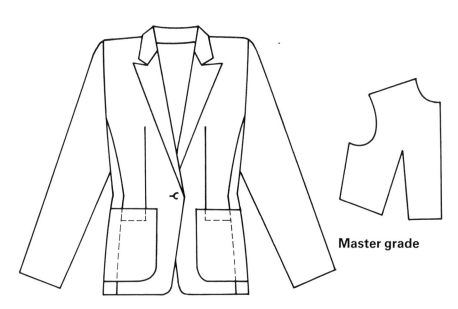

Master grade

Fig. 16.1. Front fusibles.

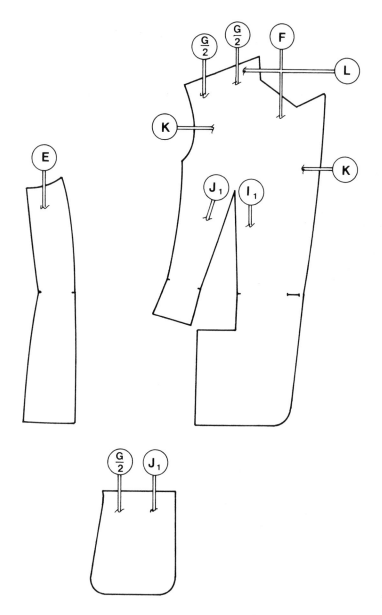

Fig. 16.2. Grading increments for front fusibles.

Grading instructions: FRONT FUSIBLE

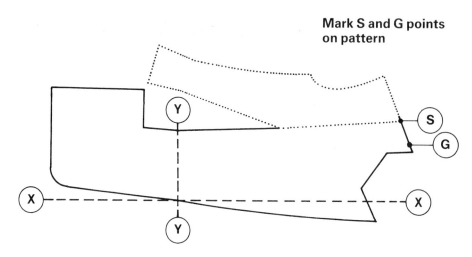

Fig. 16.3. Grading axes for front panel.

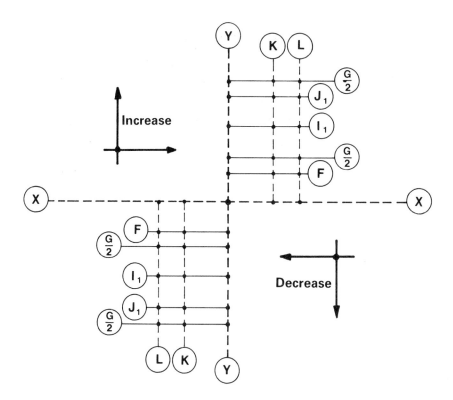

Fig. 16.4. Increment net for front panel.

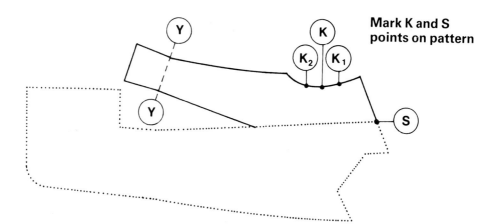

Fig. 16.5. Grading axes for bust panel.

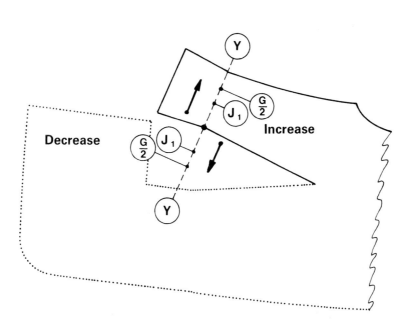

Fig. 16.6. Increment net for bust panel.

Stage 1: align pattern to X and Y axes (Fig. 16.7)
- Mark front edge and start of lapel
- Mark part of hem.

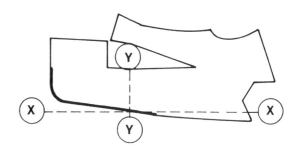

Fig. 16.7.

Stage 2: remain on Y axis (Fig. 16.8)
- Move to first G/2
- Mark point S
- Mark small section of shoulder line on either side of point S.

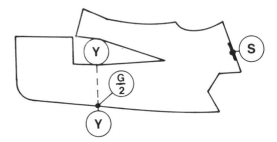

Fig. 16.8.

Stage 3: remain on Y axis (Fig. 16.9)
- Move to I_1
- Mark first side of bust dart
- Mark start of horizontal seam.

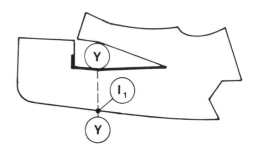

Fig. 16.9.

Stage 4: remain on Y axis (Fig. 16.10)
- Move to second G/2
- Complete horizontal seam
- Mark panel seam
- Complete hem.

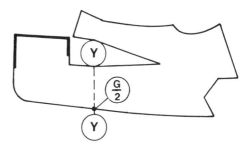

Fig. 16.10.

Stage 5: align Y axis of pattern to relevant K line
(Fig. 16.11)
- Align front edge to X axis
- Mark lapel point and start of gorge seam.

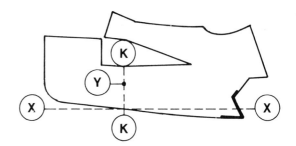

Fig. 16.11.

Stage 6: remain on K line (Fig. 16.12)
- Move to F
- Mark gorge seam corner and start of neck.

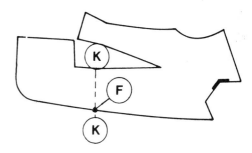

Fig. 16.12.

Stage 7: remain on F increment (Fig. 16.13)
- Align Y axis of pattern to relevant L line
- Complete gorge seam
- Mark start of shoulder and G point.

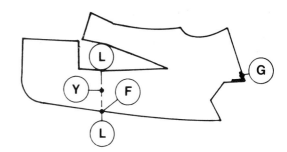

Fig. 16.13.

Stage 8: mark increment J_1 from intersection of
shoulder line and point S (Fig. 16.14)
- To increase: mark towards neck
- To decrease: mark towards armhole.

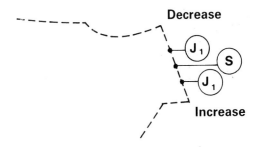

Fig. 16.14.

Stage 9: connect J_1 mark to new bust point (Fig. 16.15). This is the new pivot line.

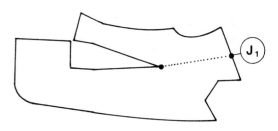

Fig. 16.15.

Stage 10: align the bust points and pivot lines of pattern and paper (Fig. 16.16)
- Mark second side of bust dart
- Mark corner of seam
- Mark new Y axis.

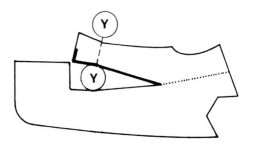

Fig. 16.16.

Stage 11: mark increment J from intersection of bust dart line and Y axis (Increment $J = J_1 + G/2$) (Fig. 16.17).

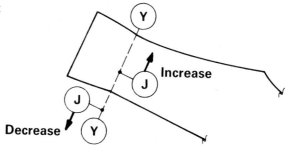

Fig. 16.17.

Stage 12: align Y axis of pattern to Y axis marked in Stage 10 (Fig. 16.18)
- Move to J
- Mark corner of panel seam
- Mark panel seam
- Mark section of armhole and relevant K point.

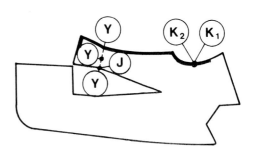

Fig. 16.18.

Stage 13: align neck point to G point (Fig. 16.19)
- Align K mark on pattern to relevant K point
- To increase: align K to K_1
- To decrease: align K to K_2
- Complete shoulder and armhole.

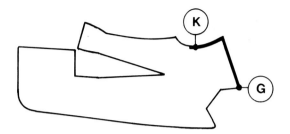

Fig. 16.19.

Stage 14: use pattern to (Fig. 16.20)
- Blend lapel edge
- Complete gorge seam.

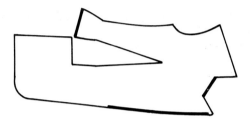

Fig. 16.20.

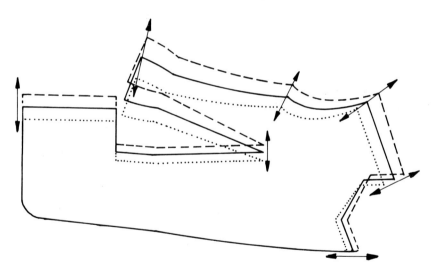

Grade for front fusible

Grading instructions: FRONT SIDE BODY

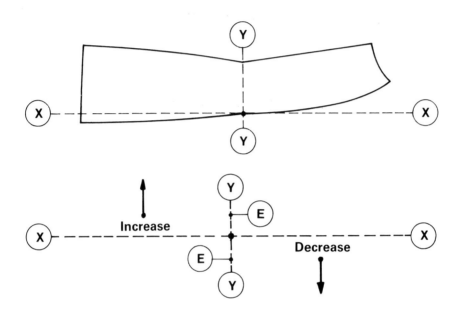

Fig. 16.21 Grading axes and increment for side body.

Stage 1: align pattern to X and Y axes (Fig. 16.22)
- Mark panel seam
- Mark start of armhole
- Mark part of hem.

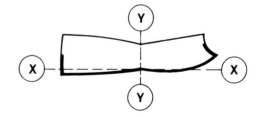

Fig. 16.22.

Stage 2: remain on Y axis (Fig. 16.23)
- Move to E
- Complete lower section of armhole
- Mark side seam
- Complete hem.

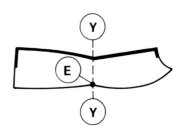

Fig. 16.23.

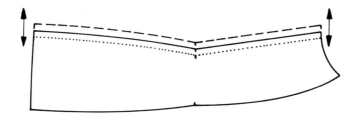

Grade for front side body

Grading instructions: PATCH POCKET

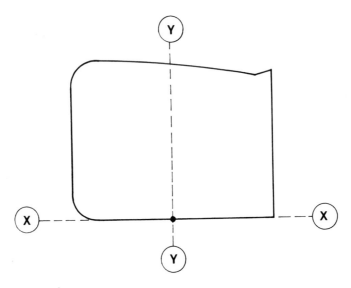

Fig. 16.24. Grading axes for patch pocket.

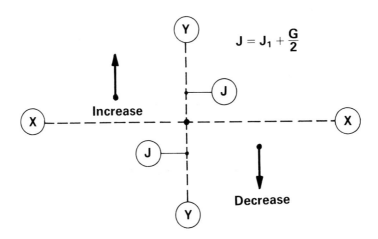

$$J = J_1 + \frac{G}{2}$$

Fig. 16.25. Increment for patch pocket.

Stage 1: align pattern to X and Y axes (Fig. 16.26)
● Mark front half of patch.

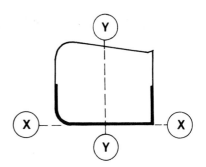

Fig. 16.26.

Stage 2: remain on Y axis (Fig. 16.27)
● Move to J
● Complete side section of patch.

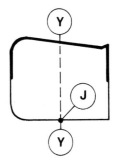

Fig. 16.27.

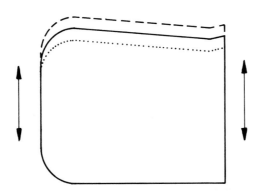

Grade for patch pocket

Chapter 17

Body Lining for Jacket

In general, the body lining for a garment does not have the same seaming etc. as the top cloth components for the same garment (Fig. 17.1). Lining patterns are simpler, and the pattern forms used are more related to a block pattern rather than to a developed pattern.

This example demonstrates the grades for a typical form of body lining where (see Fig. 17.2):

- The back is graded in exactly the same way as the master grade for a basic back (p. 56).

- The bust suppression for the front is incorporated

into a folded off dart coming from the inside edge of the facing and extending to the bust point.

Most professional pattern makers have a block lining pattern for each type of block pattern, which saves considerable time as against preparing each lining pattern from scratch. If this method is used, then a permanent master grade of the block lining pattern would also be called for as an additional time-saver in grading.

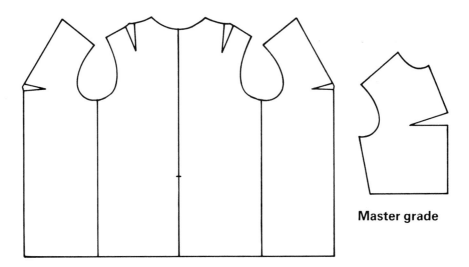

Master grade

Fig. 17.1. Body lining for jacket.

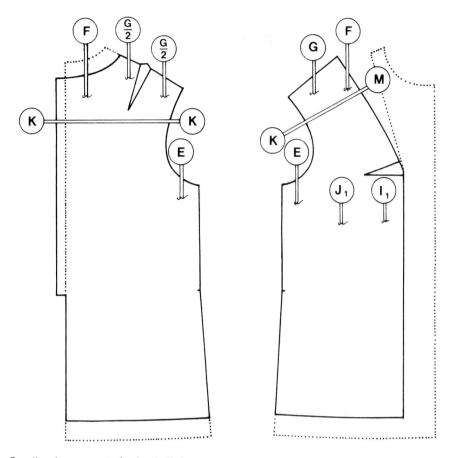

Fig. 17.2. Grading increments for body lining.

Grading instructions: FRONT LINING

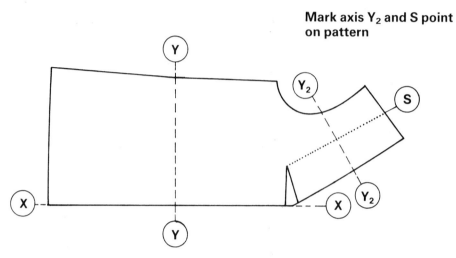

Mark axis Y_2 and S point on pattern

Fig. 17.3. Grading axes for front.

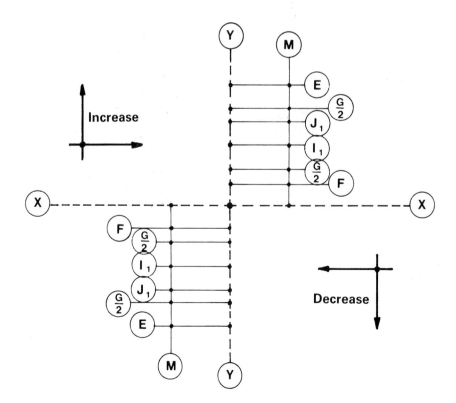

Increase

Decrease

Fig. 17.4. Increment net for front.

Stage 1: align pattern to X and Y axes (Fig. 17.5)
- Mark front edge to lower corner of bust pleat
- Mark start of hem.

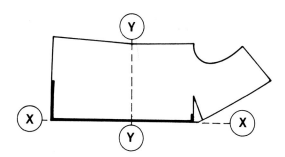

Fig. 17.5.

Stage 2: remain on Y axis (Fig. 17.6)
- Move to I_1
- Mark new bust point.

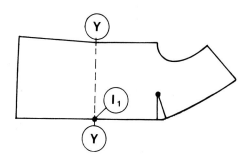

Fig. 17.6.

Stage 3: remain on Y axis (Fig. 17.7)
- Move to J_1
- Mark point S and small section of shoulder line.

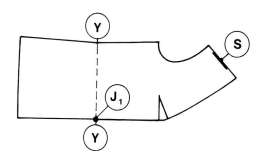

Fig. 17.7.

Stage 4: remain on Y axis (Fig. 17.8)
- Move to second G/2
- Mark lower section of armhole.

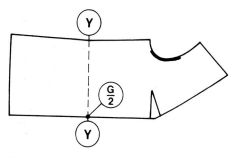

Fig. 17.8.

Stage 5: remain on Y axis (Fig. 17.9)
- Move to E
- Complete armhole
- Mark side seam
- Complete hem.

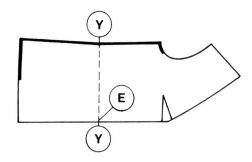

Fig. 17.9.

Stage 6: join new bust point to point S marked in Stage 3 (Fig. 17.10).

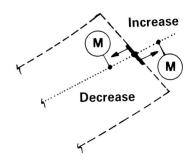

Fig. 17.10.

Stage 7: align the bust points and pivot lines of pattern and paper (Fig. 17.11)
- Mark intersection of shoulder line and pivot line
- Mark increment M from the intersection point
- To increase: mark above the intersection
- To decrease: mark below the intersection.

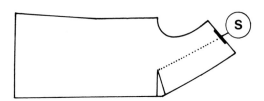

Fig. 17.11.

Stage 8: align pivot lines of pattern and paper (Fig. 17.12)
- Move pattern along pivot line until the shoulder line touches the M mark
- Mark centre section of shoulder
- Mark Y_2 axis
- Mark intersections of front edge and armhole with Y_2 axis.

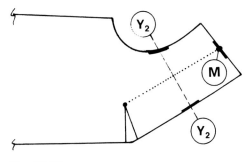

Fig. 17.12.

Stage 9: mark G/2 increments on Y_2 axis (Fig. 17.13)
- To increase: mark outside front edge and armhole
- To decrease: mark inside front edge and armhole.

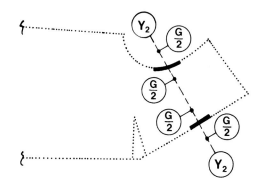

Fig. 17.13.

Stage 10: align pattern to Y_2 axis (Fig. 17.14)
- Move to G/2 at armhole
- Complete armhole
- Mark start of shoulder.

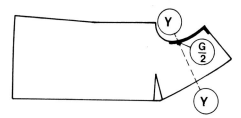

Fig. 17.14.

Stage 11: remain on Y_2 axis (Fig. 17.15)
- Move to G/2 at front edge
- Mark neck point corner.

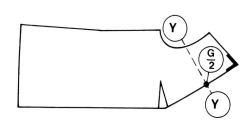

Fig. 17.15.

Stage 12: align the bust points and pivot lines of pattern and paper (Fig. 17.16)
- Mark upper nip of bust dart fold
- Mark part of front edge
- Connect bust point to upper nip.

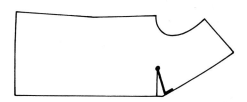

Fig. 17.16.

352

Stage 13: mark increment I from intersection of bust dart fold line and front edge (increment I = F + G/2 + I₁) (Fig. 17.17)
- To increase: mark outside of intersection
- To decrease: mark inside of intersection.

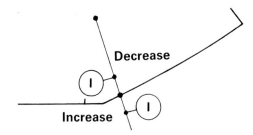

Fig. 17.17.

Stage 14: align dart fold line of pattern with fold line marked in Stage 12 (Fig. 17.18)
- Align front edge to I
- Mark fold nip and fold allowance.

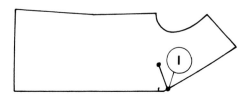

Fig. 17.18.

Stage 15: use pattern to join neck point to upper fold nip (Fig. 17.19).

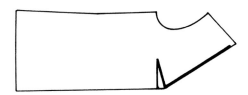

Fig. 17.19.

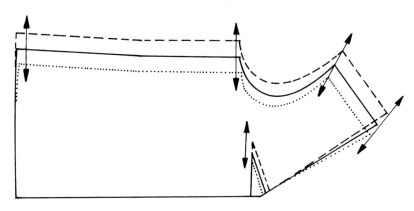

Grade for lining front

Grading instructions: BACK LINING

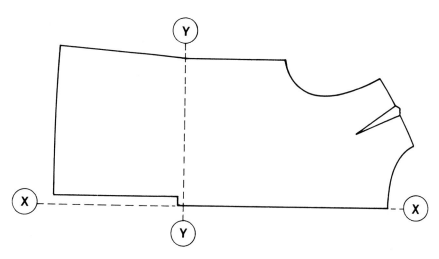

Fig. 17.20. Grading axes for lining back.

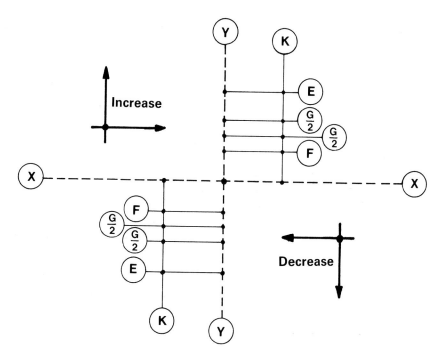

Fig. 17.21. Increment net for lining back.

Stage 1: align pattern to X and Y axes (Fig. 17.22)
- Mark centre back
- Mark part of hem.

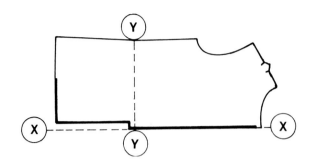

Fig. 17.22.

Stage 2: remain on Y axis (Fig. 17.23)
- Move to second G/2
- Mark lower section of armhole.

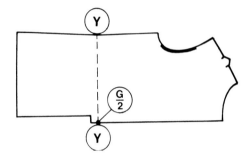

Fig. 17.23.

Stage 3: remain on Y axis (Fig. 17.24)
- Move to E
- Complete lower section of armhole
- Mark side seam
- Complete hem.

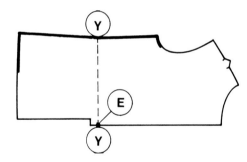

Fig. 17.24.

Stage 4: align Y axis of pattern to relevant K line (Fig. 17.25)
- Mark centre back and start of neck.

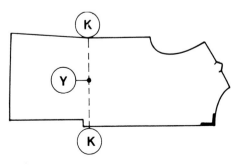

Fig. 17.25.

Stage 5: remain on K line (Fig. 17.26)
- Move to F
- Complete neck
- Mark start of shoulder.

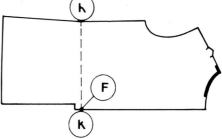

Fig. 17.26.

Stage 6: remain on K line (Fig. 17.27)
- Move to first G/2
- Mark shoulder dart nips.

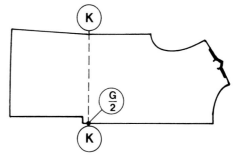

Fig. 17.27.

Stage 7: remain on K line (Fig. 17.28)
- Move to second G/2
- Complete shoulder
- Complete armhole.

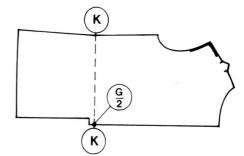

Fig. 17.28.

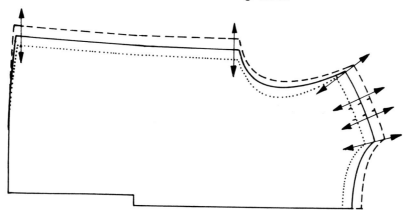

Grade for lining back

PART 4

COMPUTERISED GRADING TECHNOLOGY
AND
APPENDICES

Chapter 18

Computerised Grading Technology

Computerised pattern grading can be said to have started in 1964 with the invention of a computerised digitiser by Dr H.J. Gerber. Through this invention, it became possible to replace the routine aspects of manual grading by automation. By 1968, computerised pattern grading and marker planning systems had become commercially available and since then, this technology has become a basic tool of clothing industries throughout the world. The following is a general description of the typical systems available and whilst operational procedures, hardware and programme options can differ from system to system, the basic functions are the same for all of them.

Information flow

Computerised pattern grading is, in effect, graphic data processing applied to pattern grading and like all data processing requires three steps.

STEP 1: DATA COLLECTION

This starts at the same point as manual grading with a finished master pattern of the garment to be graded. The master pattern is converted, via the digitising process, to a format of numbers which the computer can recognise and process. At this stage, there is also the input of alphanumeric data which includes:

(1) The range and intervals of the sizes required.
(2) The grade points of the pattern components.
(3) The grade rules which are to be applied to these points
(4) The output form required, i.e. a drawing or cut-out patterns.

During this input process, the computer must be instructed in precise terms, what it is expected to accomplish. Thus, the generally allowable imprecisions of manual grading are eliminated and are replaced by defined commands.

STEP 2: DATA PROCESSING

This is where all of the routine and unique manual grading procedures are carried out by the system.

Many manual grading techniques which require great skill and craftsmanship on the part of the pattern grader, become simple and direct when performed by automation.

STEP 3: DATA PRESENTATION

The principal output at this stage is the graded patterns and these are drawn out by the plotter according to requirements. The graded components can be presented as individual components or nested in full size or miniature scale (Figs 18.1 and 18.2). Alternatively, the patterns can be cut out, notched, and annotated in pattern paper, in full sized or miniature scales. Operational data is also generated at this phase via the line printer which produces hard copy reports and statistics for records and management information.

These three foregoing stages convert the master pattern into a set of graded patterns which can be used to plan cutting markers for manual or computerised cutting.

System description

A typical system (Fig. 18.3) usually consists of five hardware units operating in conjunction with a central processing unit, and these units are described below.

CENTRAL PROCESSING UNIT (CPU) (Fig. 18.4)

This is the unit of the computer which includes the circuits controlling the interpretation and execution of instructions. The CPU is generally referred to as the main frame.

DISC DRIVE UNIT (Fig. 18.5)

This includes the magnetic disc which is a mass storage device with real time recall, and interfaces directly with the CPU. This unit primarily provides data storage for on-going operations and information can be transferred from the disc to a magnetic tape or floppy disc for temporary or permanent storage.

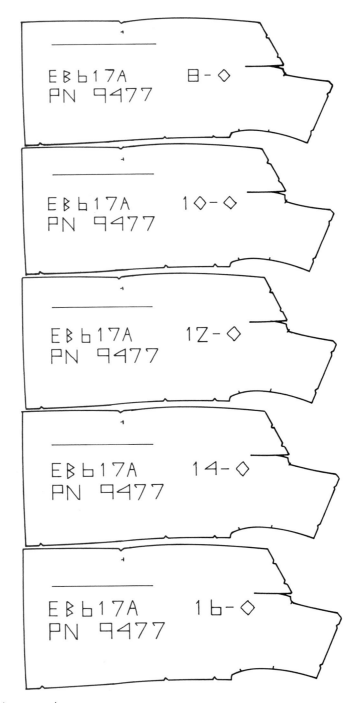

Fig. 18.1 Individual part grade.

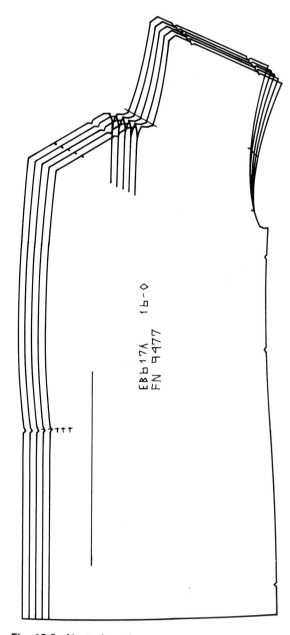

Fig. 18.2. Nested grade.

Fig. 18.3. Typical system.

Fig. 18.4. Central processing unit (CPU).

Fig. 18.5. Disc and tape unit.

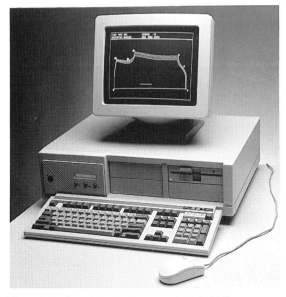

Fig. 18.6. Graphic display terminal (VDU).

GRAPHIC DISPLAY TERMINAL (Fig. 18.6)

This is the basic work station of the system and provides the means to implement and visually monitor functions relating to pattern grading and marker planning. The unit itself consists of:

(1) The cathode ray tube display screen on which the operator can view the contents of files and the graphic display of stored pattern pieces and markers. Most systems have the option of regular or coloured displays.
(2) The keyboard (Fig. 18.7) which interfaces with the CPU and through which the operator is enabled

Fig. 18.8. Data tablet and pen.

to input commands for data processing and manipulation routines.
(3) The terminal's data tablet and pen (Fig. 18.8) which are used to position pattern pieces during the marker planning process or for manipulatory routines when creating patterns via the system.
(4) The graphic display terminal can also be configured with an on-line printer (Fig. 18.9) which prints out commands and system responses.

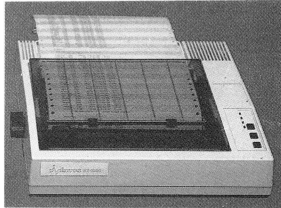

Fig. 18.9. On-line printer.

THE DIGITISER (Fig. 18.10)

This unit consists of a digitising work table and a free-floating cursor which are used to convert pattern shapes into a format understood by the computer system. This format is basically a description of the lines of the pattern according to sets of X and Y coordinates.

Fig. 18.10. Digitising table.

Under the plastic surface of the digitising table, there is a fine network of wires similar to that of graph paper which provides an extremely high resolution grid for identifying any position on the table's surface.

The cursor (Fig. 18.11) has two hair lines engraved onto the viewing glass and the intersection of these

Fig. 18.11. Multi function cursor.

lines is used as the registering point. The cursor is placed on a line and when a button is pressed, the X and Y coordinates of the location of the cursor register point is inputed to the system. This process is repeated on a number of points on a line segment so that the computer can then determine the curve to be used which would precisely represent the original pattern line segment for grading.

Apart from the entry of grading instructions, the cursor's buttons are used to input other information which has positional characteristics such as notches and drill holes.

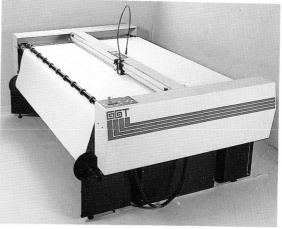

Fig. 18.12. Flat bed plotter.

THE PLOTTER (Fig. 18.12)

This generates system output in the form of pattern pieces and/or markers. The plotter uses the same type of information as that recorded by the digitiser, namely X and Y coordinate values. These coordinates define the position of the pen on the paper and successive commands provide the necessary instructions to the plotter for the definition of the required line.

The plotter usually has its own CRT terminal which controls the plotting function. In addition, the plotter can be equipped with a knife for cutting out patterns, or alternatively, a laser cutter can be used for this purpose.

SOFTWARE

These are the programmes and procedures which control and co-ordinate the tasks associated with all of the functions of the system.

The pattern grading process

This process automatically generates multiple sizes of a digitised pattern piece according to the inputed data which, amongst others, includes:

(1) The special piece number of the component. Most systems have a piece file or library in which each basic type of component is stored in a separate section. Each section has its own unique coding and this acts as the primary identification for components.
(2) The piece number itself. This is the number of the piece within its particular section of the piece file.
(3) A written piece description. Typical descriptions could be top sleeve or back lining, etc., and this method simplifies piece identification.
(4) The grain line of the piece. Apart from being used to position pieces correctly when planning markers, it also acts as the X axis when digitising the pattern.
(5) The grade points. These are the cardinal external or internal points which have grading rules applied to them: for example, the front neck point or a skirt dart position, etc.
(6) The intermediate points. These are located between grading points and move in accordance with them.
(7) The grade rule data for every grade point. This data defines the movement of a grade point for one size. The grading rule data itself can be derived from one of two methods.

METHOD 1

The actual growth between sizes can be defined by digitising a graded nest. Usually this nest consists of the base size and the largest size required, where all of the peripheral and internal vectors are straight lines between the largest and smallest sizes. Intermediate sizes are only entered when there is a grade break caused by the use of different grading increments for one or more points on the pattern piece, i.e. the vector is no longer a straight line.

METHOD 2

This is based on a previously established grade rule library which is a file containing the measured distances by which a point will change when a specific rule is applied. Each grade rule has a unique number and is not generally restricted in its application to one type of garment only.

PRINCIPLES

Computerised pattern grading is based on an X, Y coordinate grid system which provides the coordinate definition of the position of a point within the grid. The grid itself (Fig. 18.13) has X and Y axes which cross each other perpendicularly and intersect at O. Each of these axes has a negative and positive value in relation to O and these values are:

X axis: to the right of O — positive
to the left of O — negative

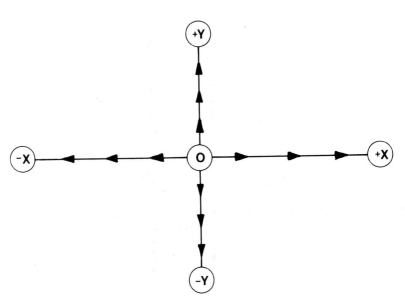

Fig. 18.13. Movement along the X and Y axes.

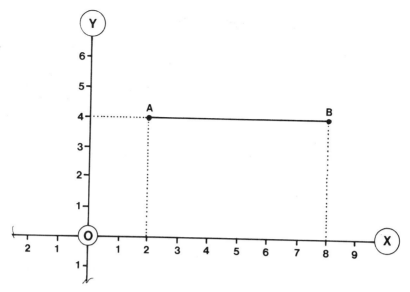

Fig. 18.14. Line segment definition.

Y axis: above O — positive
below O — negative

Thus, any point on the grid can be identified by a set of two coordinates, one X and the other Y. As all line segments are composed of a beginning point and an ending point, a line segment can be identified by two sets of X, Y coordinates, one of which defines the location of the starting point whilst the other defines the location of the ending point. For example, Fig.

18.14 shows line A – B, and by using the scales on the X and Y coordinates, this segment can be defined as (2, 4) (8, 4).

When defining the movement of any point, the starting point is the O intersection of the grid, and the four possibilities of movement are (Fig. 18.15):

(1) +X, +Y: Growth to the right of, and above O
(2) −X, +Y: Growth to the left of, and above O
(3) +X, −Y: Growth to the right of, and below O

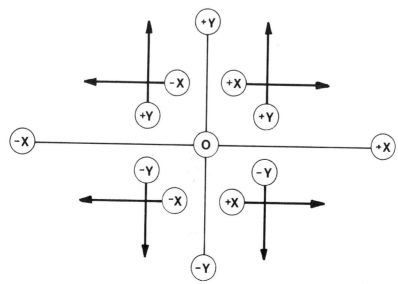

Fig. 18.15. The four areas of movement.

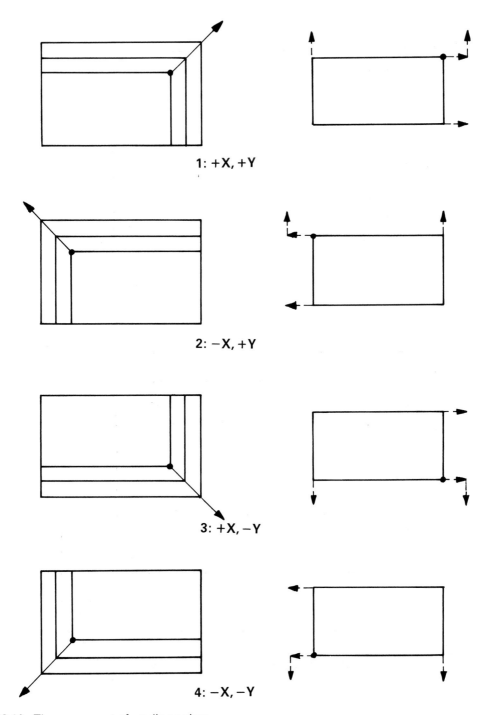

Fig. 18.16. The movement of grading points.

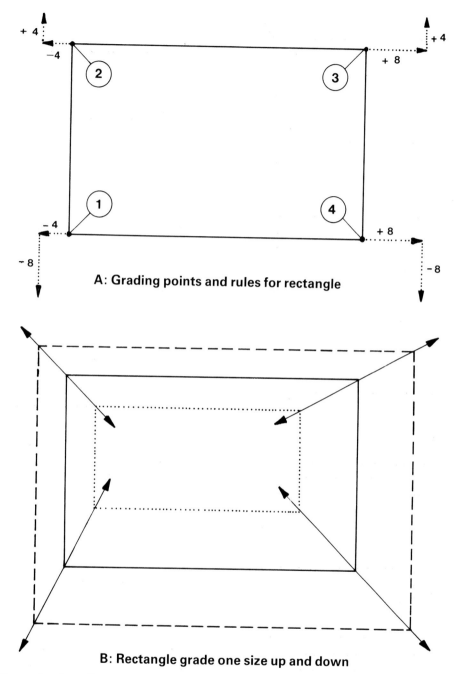

A: Grading points and rules for rectangle

B: Rectangle grade one size up and down

Fig. 18.17. Example of grading rules.

(4) −X, −Y: Growth to the left of, and below O

The effects of these four movements on a plain rectangle are shown in Fig. 18.16 and the related movement of other points is represented by a single arrow.

The applicable grade rule is entered for every

grading point and this defines the actual growth movement of the point. For example, the grade rules for the rectangle shown in Fig. 18.17 would be written as follows:

Point 1: −4 mm in X, and −8 mm in Y
Point 2: −4 mm in X, and +4 mm in Y

368

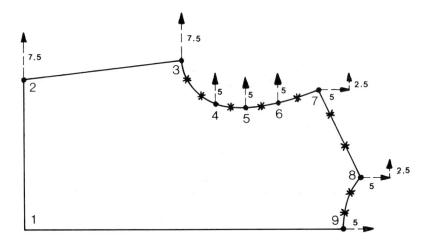

Fig. 18.18. Back of bodice.

STYLE NO	PART NO	BASE SIZE	PIECE DESCRIPTION
1234	*567*	*38*	*BODICE BACK*

RULE NO	AXIS	SIZES							
		36	*38*	*40*	*42*				
1	X	*0*	*0*	*0*	*0*				
	Y	*0*	*0*	*0*	*0*				
2	X	*0*	*0*	*0*	*0*				
	Y	*−75*	*0*	*75*	*75*				
3	X	*0*	*0*	*0*	*0*				
	Y	*−75*	*0*	*75*	*75*				
4	X	*0*	*0*	*0*	*0*				
	Y	*−50*	*0*	*50*	*50*				
5	X	*0*	*0*	*0*	*0*				
	Y	*−50*	*0*	*50*	*50*				
6	X	*0*	*0*	*0*	*0*				
	Y	*−50*	*0*	*50*	*50*				
7	X	*−50*	*0*	*50*	*50*				
	Y	*−25*	*0*	*25*	*25*				
8	X	*−50*	*0*	*50*	*50*				
	Y	*−25*	*0*	*25*	*25*				
9	X	*−50*	*0*	*50*	*50*				
	Y	*0*	*0*	*0*	*0*				
10	X								
	Y								

Fig. 18.19. Grading rules for bodice back.

Point 3: +8 mm in X, and +4 mm in Y
Point 4: +8 mm in X, and −8 mm in Y

(It should be noted that the grading points are entered in a clockwise direction, starting from the bottom left-hand corner.)

Using this principle of grade rule definition, the grade rules for the back bodice shown in Fig. 18.18 would be defined as per the form in Fig. 18.19. The grade points are shown by dots, and the intermediate points by asterisks.

Thus, the growth of any line segment, or series of line segments is achieved by:

(1) Designating the critical points which are to be grade points.
(2) Ascertaining the amount of growth to be applied to each grade point.
(3) Determining in which direction (positive or negative) each grade point is to be moved in the assigned amount.

These are the basic procedures for computerised pattern grading.

TO SUM UP

Computerised pattern grading can be an integral part of sizing technology as long as the actual grading system used is correct. The computer cannot make a good grading system out of a bad one but can, if properly used, complement and enhance an accurate and efficient system.

Appendix A

Size Charts

The detailed statistics and size charts of the surveys are far too numerous to be included in a book of this nature. However, the original reports are usually obtainable from most reference libraries and professional associations. The size charts in this section are:

SURVEY SIZE CHARTS

These charts show the measurements which are common to all of the surveys and cover the three main height groups and the average bust type.

NATIONAL SIZE CHARTS

These are issued by the respective government offices, standards bureaux and professional associations and are useful for comparative purposes.

Finally, a size chart should not be judged by its size or complexity, but rather on the sources from which it was compiled.

SIZE CHART NO. 1
USA* SHORT HEIGHT GROUP — AVERAGE BUST

		Size symbol					
Ref:	Measurement	8 S	10 S	12 S	14 S	16 S	18 S
1	Bust girth	78.7	82.6	86.4	90.2	95.3	100.3
2	Waist girth	58.4	61.0	64.8	68.6	73.7	78.7
3	Hip girth	82.6	86.4	91.4	96.4	101.4	106.4
12	Neck base girth	35.9	36.5	37.2	37.8	38.7	39.7
13	Upper arm (muscle)	23.2	24.8	26.3	27.9	29.8	31.8
24	Height	151.1	152.4	153.7	154.9	156.2	157.5
25	Cervical height	128.3	129.5	130.8	132.1	133.6	134.6
29	Knee height	40.6	41.0	41.3	41.6	41.9	42.2
31	Outside leg	93.0	94.0	94.9	95.9	96.8	97.8
35	Back waist length	35.9	36.2	36.8	39.2	37.8	38.1
36	Across back	29.8	30.8	31.7	32.7	34.0	35.2
39	Shoulder length	10.5	1.8	10.8	11.1	11.1	11.4
49	Cervical to centre front waist	46.4	47.0	47.6	48.3	49.2	50.2
—	Weight: kg	42.7	46.4	50.9	56.4	62.7	69.1

S = Short Height Group
* The USA size charts are reproduced by permission of: US Department of Commerce, Maryland, USA.

SIZE CHART NO. 2
USA REGULAR HEIGHT GROUP — AVERAGE BUST

Ref:	Measurement	Size symbol						
		30 R	32 R	34 R	36 R	38 R	40 R	42 R
1	Bust girth	83.8	85.8	90.8	95.8	100.8	105.8	110.8
2	Waist girth	63.5	68.5	73.5	78.5	85.1	91.4	97.8
3	Hip girth	86.4	91.4	96.4	101.4	106.4	111.4	116.4
12	Neck base girth	36.8	37.5	38.1	38.7	39.7	40.6	41.6
13	Upper arm (muscle)	25.1	27.0	28.9	30.8	32.7	34.6	36.5
24	Height	161.3	162.6	163.8	165.1	166.4	167.6	168.9
25	Cervical height	38.4	139.7	141.0	142.2	143.5	144.8	146.0
29	Knee height	43.5	43.8	44.1	44.4	44.8	45.1	45.4
31	Outside leg	100.6	101.6	102.5	103.5	104.4	105.4	106.3
35	Back waist length	39.4	39.7	40.0	40.3	40.7	41.0	41.3
36	Across back	31.1	32.4	33.7	34.9	36.2	37.5	38.7
39	Shoulder length	11.1	11.1	11.4	11.4	11.8	11.8	12.1
49	Cervical to centre front waist	48.9	49.5	50.2	50.8	51.8	52.7	53.7
—	Weight: kg	50.9	56.4	61.8	69.1	76.4	83.6	90.9

R = Regular Height Group

SIZE CHART NO. 3
USA TALL HEIGHT GROUP — AVERAGE BUST

Ref:	Measurement	Size symbol					
		10 T	12 T	14 T	16 T	18 T	20 T
1	Bust girth	82.6	86.4	90.1	94.0	97.8	101.6
2	Waist girth	61.0	64.8	68.6	72.4	76.2	80.0
3	Hip girth	87.6	91.4	96.4	101.4	106.4	111.4
12	Neck base girth	37.1	37.8	38.4	39.1	39.7	40.3
13	Upper arm (muscle)	24.1	25.7	27.3	28.9	30.5	32.1
24	Height	171.5	172.7	174.0	175.3	176.5	177.8
25	Cervical height	148.6	149.9	151.1	152.4	153.7	154.9
29	Knee height	47.6	47.9	48.2	48.5	48.8	49.1
31	Outside leg	115.6	116.8	118.1	119.4	120.7	121.9
35	Back waist length	41.0	41.62	41.9	42.6	42.9	43.5
36	Across back	31.4	32.3	33.3	34.3	35.2	36.2
39	Shoulder length	11.4	11.4	11.8	11.8	12.1	12.1
49	Cervical to centre front waist	50.5	51.1	51.8	52.4	53.0	53.6
—	Weight: kg	51.8	57.3	62.7	69.1	75.5	81.8

T = Tall Height Group

SIZE CHART NO. 4
ENGLAND — SHORT HEIGHT GROUP — AVERAGE BUST

Ref:	Measurement	Size symbol					
		34	36	38	40	42	44
1	Bust girth	81.3	86.3	91.3	96.3	101.3	106.3
2	Waist girth	59.7	64.7	69.7	74.7	79.7	84.7
3	Hip girth	86.3	91.3	96.3	101.3	106.3	111.3
12	Neck base girth	34.9	36.2	37.5	38.7	40.0	41.2
13	Upper arm (muscle)	25.1	27.0	28.9	30.8	32.7	34.6
24	Height	153.7	154.3	155.0	155.6	156.2	157.8
25	Cervical height	132.7	133.0	133.4	133.7	134.0	134.3
29	Knee height	41.0	41.0	41.3	41.3	46.1	41.6
31	Outside leg	97.5	98.1	98.8	99.4	100.0	100.7
35	Back waist length	37.1	37.5	37.8	38.1	38.4	38.7
36	Across back	31.4	32.7	34.0	35.2	36.5	37.8
39	Shoulder length	11.1	11.1	11.4	11.4	11.7	11.7
49	Cervical to centre front waist	47.3	47.9	48.6	49.2	49.9	50.5
—	Weight: kg	44.5	50.9	57.3	63.6	70.0	76.4
Nearest British Standard Size		8 S	12 S	14 S	16 S	18 S	20 S

S = Short Height Group
* The English size charts are reproduced by permission of Her Majesty's Stationery Office, Norwich, England.

SIZE CHART NO. 5
ENGLAND — MEDIUM HEIGHT GROUP — AVERAGE BUST

Ref:	Measurement	Size symbol					
		34	36	38	40	42	44
1	Bust girth	81.3	86.3	91.3	96.3	101.3	106.3
2	Waist girth	58.4	63.4	68.4	73.4	78.4	83.4
3	Hip girth	86.3	91.3	96.3	101.3	106.3	111.3
12	Neck base girth	35.6	36.8	38.1	39.4	40.6	41.9
13	Upper arm (muscle)	35.6	36.5	37.5	38.4	39.4	40.3
24	Height	161.3	161.9	162.6	163.2	163.9	164.5
25	Cervical height	139.1	139.4	139.7	140.0	140.3	140.7
29	Knee height	43.5	43.5	43.8	43.8	44.1	44.1
31	Outside leg	102.9	103.5	104.2	104.8	105.4	106.1
35	Back waist length	38.7	39.1	39.4	39.7	40.0	40.3
36	Across back	31.8	33.0	34.3	35.6	36.8	38.1
39	Shoulder length	11.4	11.4	11.8	11.8	12.1	12.1
49	Cervical to centre front waist	48.9	49.5	50.2	50.8	51.5	52.1
—	Weight: kg	47.3	53.6	60.0	66.4	72.7	79.1
Nearest British Standard Size		8	12	14	16	18	20

Medium height — numerical size symbol only

SIZE CHART NO. 6
ENGLAND — TALL HEIGHT GROUP — AVERAGE BUST

Ref:	Measurement	34	36	38	40	42	44
				Size symbol			
1	Bust girth	81.3	86.3	91.3	96.3	101.3	106.3
2	Waist girth	57.1	62.1	67.1	72.1	77.1	82.1
3	Hip girth	86.3	91.3	96.3	101.3	106.3	111.3
12	Neck base girth	36.2	37.5	38.7	40.0	41.3	42.5
13	Upper arm (muscle)	23.8	25.7	27.6	29.5	31.4	33.3
24	Height	168.9	169.6	170.2	170.8	171.5	172.5
25	Cervical height	145.5	145.7	146.1	146.4	147.7	147.0
29	Knee height	46.0	46.0	46.4	46.4	46.7	46.7
31	Outside leg	108.3	108.9	109.5	110.2	110.8	111.5
35	Back waist length	40.3	40.6	41.0	41.3	41.6	41.9
36	Across back	32.1	33.3	34.6	35.9	37.1	38.4
39	Shoulder length	11.7	11.7	12.1	12.1	12.4	12.4
49	Cervical to centre front waist	50.5	51.1	51.8	52.4	53.0	53.7
—	Weight: kg	50.0	56.4	62.7	69.1	75.5	81.8
	Nearest British Standard Size	8 T	12 T	14 T	16 T	18 T	20 T

T = Tall Height Group

BRITISH STANDARD 3666:1982

Size codes	Hips From cm	Hips To cm	Bust From cm	Bust To cm
8	83	87	78	82
10	87	91	82	86
12	91	95	86	90
14	95	99	90	94
16	100	104	95	99
18	105	109	100	104
20	110	114	105	109
22	115	119	110	114
24	120	124	115	119
26	125	129	120	124
28	130	134	125	129
30	135	139	130	134
32	140	144	135	139

Reproduced by permission of the British Standards Institution, London, England.

West German sizing system

The West German sizing nomenclature uses a numerical system and it is of great interest because of its logic and simplicity. This system has been widely adopted by both retailers and manufacturers in West Germany and it operates as follows:

(1) The base size is for average height and a regular hip girth in relation to the bust girth. Thus the base size 38 would have the following measurements:

Height: 168 cm
Bust Girth: 88 cm
Hip Girth: 94.5 cm

(2) The size symbol for a short fitting (160 cm height) with the same girth measurements would be half of the base size symbol, e.g. 38 ÷ 2 = size 19.
(3) The size symbol for a tall fitting (176 cm height) with the same girth measurements would be double the base size symbol, e.g. 38 × 2 = size 76.
(4) Where the hip girth is smaller than the regular hip girth then the size symbol for the height is prefixed

by 0. Thus a size 19 with a small hip fitting would carry the symbol 019.

(5) Where the hip girth is larger than the regular hip girth, then the size symbol for the height is prefixed by 5. For example, a tall fitting size 76 with a large hip girth would be a size 576.

The principles of this nomenclature system are shown in the following charts which, together with the main size charts, are reproduced by permission of Dob-Verband, Cologne, West Germany.

Bust girth	Hip girth	Size symbol		
		160 cm	168 cm	176 cm
84	85	018	036	—
88	88.5	019	038	076
92	92	020	040	080
96	95.5	021	042	084
100	99	022	044	088
104	102.5	023	046	092

B: size symbols for small hip girth

Bust girth	Hip girth	Size symbol		
		160 cm	168 cm	176 cm
84	91.0	18	36	72
88	94.5	19	38	76
92	98.0	20	40	80
96	101.5	21	42	84
100	105.0	22	44	88
104	108.5	23	46	92

A: size symbols for regular hip girth

Bust girth	Hip girth	Size symbol		
		160 cm	168 cm	176 cm
84	97	518	536	572
88	100.5	519	538	576
92	104	520	540	580
96	107.5	521	542	584
100	111	522	544	588
104	114.5	523	546	592

C: size symbols for large hip girth

SIZE CHART NO. 7
WEST GERMANY — SHORT HEIGHT GROUP — AVERAGE BUST

Ref:	Measurement	Size symbol					
		18	19	20	21	22	23
1	Bust girth	84.0	88.0	92.0	96.0	100.0	104.0
2	Waist girth	64.5	69.0	73.5	78.0	82.5	87.0
3	Hip girth	90.0	94.0	98.0	102.0	106.0	110.0
12	Neck base girth	33.9	34.6	35.3	36.0	36.7	37.4
13	Upper arm (muscle)	26.0	27.3	28.6	29.9	31.2	32.5
24	Height	156.0	156.0	156.0	156.0	156.0	156.0
25	Cervical height	134.5	134.9	135.3	135.7	136.1	136.5
29	Knee height	44.0	44.0	44.0	44.0	44.0	44.0
31	Outside leg	98.5	98.8	99.1	99.4	99.7	100.0
35	Back waist length	38.0	38.0	38.0	38.0	38.0	38.0
36	Across back	34.0	35.0	36.0	37.0	38.0	39.0
39	Shoulder length	12.0	12.1	12.2	12.3	12.4	12.5
49	Cervical to centre front waist	48.5	49.2	49.9	50.6	51.3	52.0
—	Weight: kg	48.0	52.2	56.4	60.6	64.8	69.0

SIZE CHART NO. 8
WEST GERMANY — REGULAR HEIGHT GROUP — AVERAGE BUST

Ref:	Measurement	Size symbol					
		36	38	40	42	44	46
1	Bust girth	84.0	88.0	92.0	96.0	100.0	104.0
2	Waist girth	63.5	68.0	72.5	77.0	81.5	86.0
3	Hip girth	90.0	94.0	98.0	102.0	106.0	110.0
12	Neck base girth	33.9	34.6	35.3	36.0	36.7	37.4
13	Upper arm (muscle)	26.0	27.3	28.6	29.9	31.2	32.5
24	Height	164.0	164.0	164.0	164.0	164.0	164.0
25	Cervical height	141.0	141.4	141.8	142.2	142.6	143.0
29	Knee height	46.0	46.0	46.0	46.0	46.0	46.0
31	Outside leg	103.5	103.8	104.1	104.4	104.7	105.0
35	Back waist length	40.0	40.0	40.0	40.0	40.0	40.0
36	Across back	34.0	35.0	36.0	37.0	38.0	39.0
39	Shoulder length	12.0	12.1	12.2	12.3	12.4	12.5
49	Cervical to centre front waist	49.9	50.6	51.3	52.0	52.7	53.4
—	Weight: kg	49.8	54.0	58.2	62.4	66.6	70.8

SIZE CHART NO. 9
WEST GERMANY — TALL HEIGHT GROUP — AVERAGE BUST

Ref:	Measurement	Size symbol					
		72	76	80	84	88	92
1	Bust girth	84.0	88.0	92.0	96.0	100.0	104.0
2	Waist girth	62.5	67.0	71.5	76.0	80.5	85.0
3	Hip girth	90.0	94.0	98.0	102.0	106.0	110.0
12	Neck base girth	33.9	34.6	35.3	36.0	36.7	37.4
13	Upper arm (muscle)	26.0	27.3	28.6	29.9	31.2	32.5
24	Height	172.0	172.0	172.0	172.0	172.0	172.0
25	Cervical height	147.5	147.9	148.3	148.7	149.1	149.5
29	Knee height	48.0	48.0	48.0	48.0	48.0	48.0
31	Outside leg	108.5	108.8	109.1	109.4	109.7	110.0
35	Back waist length	42.0	42.0	42.0	42.0	42.0	42.0
36	Across back	34.0	35.0	36.0	37.0	38.0	39.9
39	Shoulder length	12.0	12.1	12.2	12.3	12.4	12.5
49	Cervical to centre front waist	51.3	52.0	52.7	53.4	54.1	54.8
—	Weight: kg	51.6	55.8	60.0	64.2	68.4	72.6

SIZE CHART NO. 10
WEST GERMANY 1983
SHORT HEIGHT GROUP — AVERAGE BUST

Ref:	Measurement	Size symbol			
		18	19	20	21
1	Bust girth	84.0	88.0	92.0	96.0
2	Waist girth	67.0	71.0	75.0	79.0
3	Hip girth	91.0	94.5	98.0	101.5
12	Neck base girth	36.0	36.6	37.2	37.8
13	Upper arm (muscle)	27.0	28.2	29.4	30.6
24	Height	160.0	160.0	160.0	160.0
25	Cervical height	138.9	139.3	139.7	140.1
31	Outside leg	101.0	101.0	101.0	101.0
35	Back waist length	39.0	39.2	39.4	39.6
36	Across back	34.5	35.5	36.5	37.5
39	Shoulder length	12.5	12.5	12.5	12.5
49	Cervical to centre front waist	48.3	49.2	50.1	51.0
—	Weight: kg	51.0	55.0	59.0	63.0

SIZE CHART NO. 11
WEST GERMANY 1983
REGULAR HEIGHT GROUP — AVERAGE BUST

Ref:	Measurement	Size symbol					
		36	38	40	42	44	46
1	Bust girth	84.0	88.0	92.0	96.0	100.0	104.0
2	Waist girth	66.0	70.0	74.0	78.0	82.0	86.0
3	Hip girth	91.0	94.5	98.0	101.5	105.0	108.5
12	Neck base girth	36.0	36.6	37.2	37.8	38.4	39.0
13	Upper arm (muscle)	27.0	28.2	29.4	30.6	31.8	33.0
24	Height	168.0	168.0	168.0	168.0	168.0	168.0
25	Cervical height	145.4	145.8	146.2	146.6	147.0	147.4
31	Outside leg	106.0	106.0	106.0	106.0	106.0	106.0
35	Back waist length	41.0	41.2	41.4	41.6	41.8	42.0
36	Across back	34.5	35.5	36.5	37.5	38.5	39.5
39	Shoulder length	12.5	12.5	12.5	12.5	12.5	12.5
49	Cervical to centre front waist	49.7	50.6	51.5	52.4	53.3	54.2
—	Weight: kg	53.0	57.0	61.0	65.0	69.0	73.0

SIZE CHART NO. 12
WEST GERMANY 1983
TALL HEIGHT GROUP — AVERAGE BUST

Ref:	Measurement	Size symbol					
		72	76	80	84	88	92
1	Bust girth	84.0	88.0	92.0	96.0	100.0	104.0
2	Waist girth	65.0	69.0	73.0	77.0	81.0	85.0
3	Hip girth	91.0	94.5	98.0	101.5	105.0	108.5
12	Neck base girth	36.0	36.6	37.2	37.8	38.4	39.0
13	Upper arm (muscle)	27.0	28.2	29.4	30.6	31.8	33.0
24	Height	176.0	176.0	176.0	176.0	176.0	176.0
25	Cervical height	151.9	152.3	152.7	153.1	153.5	153.9
31	Outside leg	111.0	111.0	110.0	110.0	110.0	110.0
35	Back waist length	43.0	43.2	43.4	43.6	43.8	44.0
36	Across back	34.5	35.5	36.5	37.5	38.5	39.5
39	Shoulder length	12.5	12.5	12.5	12.5	12.5	12.5
49	Cervical to centre front waist	51.1	52.0	52.9	53.8	54.7	55.6
—	Weight: kg	55.0	59.0	63.0	67.0	71.0	75.0

COMPARISON OF BOTH WEST GERMAN SURVEYS
(All Measurements)

Base size 38

Measurement	Short size 19		Regular bust fitting Regular size 38		Tall-size 76	
	1973	1983	1973	1983	1973	1983
Height	156.0	160.0	164.0	168.0	172.0	176.0
Bust girth	88.0	88.0	88.0	88.0	88.0	88.0
Waist girth	69.0	71.0	68.0	70.0	67.0	69.0
Hip girth	94.0	94.5	94.0	94.5	94.0	94.5
Back waist length	38.0	39.2	40.0	41.2	42.0	43.2
Front shoulder to waist	41.6	41.9	43.0	43.3	44.4	44.7
Across back	35.0	35.5	35.0	35.5	35.0	35.5
Cervical height	134.9	139.3	141.4	145.8	147.9	152.3
Cervical to knee	90.9	95.9	95.4	100.4	99.9	104.9
Waist to hip (side)	19.4	20.6	20.2	21.4	21.0	22.2
Shoulder length	12.1	12.5	12.1	12.5	12.1	12.5
Acromion point to elbow	33.6	34.7	34.6	35.7	35.6	36.7
Acromion point to wrist	56.7	57.8	59.1	60.2	61.5	62.6
Upper arm (muscle)	27.3	28.2	27.3	28.2	27.3	28.2
Wrist girth	15.9	15.9	15.9	15.9	15.9	15.9
Neck base girth	34.6	36.6	34.6	36.6	34.6	36.6
Front neck point to bust point	23.7	27.0	23.7	27.0	23.7	27.0
Cervical to centre waist	49.2	49.2	50.6	50.6	52.0	52.0
Waist height from soles	98.8	101.0	103.8	106.0	108.8	111.0
Inside leg	72.4	74.0	76.8	78.4	81.2	82.8
Weight: kg	52.2	55.0	54.0	57.0	55.8	59.0

Some conclusions regarding the comparison between the 1973 and 1983 size charts which affect the grading of regular sizes:

- The bust grade interval of 4 cm is unchanged.
- The waist grade interval for the 1973 charts was 4.5 cm, and according to the 1983 survey, this is now 4 cm.
- The hip grade interval is now 3.5 cm instead of the 4 cm interval of the 1973 survey.
- Noticeably, the neck-to-waist grade is dynamic in the 1983 charts as against the static grade given in the earlier survey.
- The waist to hip grade for the 1973 charts was static whilst it is now dynamic.
- The latest charts show static shoulder length grade whereas in the 1973 charts, this grade was dynamic.
- The inside leg grade for the 1973 charts was dynamic as against the static grade given in the later survey.

There are also a few other intervals which have slightly changed but these changes are relatively unimportant and can be safely ignored.

SIZE CHART NO. 13
FRANCE — SHORT HEIGHT GROUP — AVERAGE BUST

		Proposed European size symbol						
Ref:	Measurement	80 84 152	84 88 152	88 92 152	92 96 152	96 100 152	100 104 152	104 108 152
1	Bust girth	80.0	84.0	88.0	92.0	96.0	100.0	104.0
2	Waist girth	58.6	61.8	65.2	68.8	72.6	76.0	80.7
3	Hip girth	84.0	88.0	92.0	96.0	100.0	104.0	108.0
12	Neck base girth	29.8	31.2	32.3	33.3	34.1	34.8	35.4
13	Upper arm (muscle)	23.5	25.8	27.6	29.2	30.5	31.7	32.7
24	Height	152.0	152.0	152.0	152.0	152.0	152.0	152.0
25	Cervical height	130.2	130.2	130.2	130.2	130.2	130.2	130.2
29	Knee height	40.2	40.2	40.2	40.2	40.2	40.2	40.2
31	Outside leg	94.9	94.9	94.9	94.9	94.9	94.9	94.9
35	Back waist length	38.1	38.1	38.1	38.1	38.1	38.1	38.1
36	Across back	32.4	33.9	35.2	36.2	37.1	37.9	38.6
39	Shoulder length	13.4	13.4	13.4	13.4	13.4	13.4	13.4
49	Cervical to centre front waist	47.8	49.2	50.4	51.3	52.1	52.9	53.5
—	Weight: kg	37.9	45.4	51.6	56.7	61.6	65.0	68.5

* The French charts are reproduced by permission of CITHE, Paris, France.

SIZE CHART NO. 14
FRANCE — MEDIUM HEIGHT GROUP — AVERAGE BUST

		Proposed European size symbol						
Ref:	Measurement	80 84 160	84 88 160	88 92 160	92 96 160	96 100 160	100 104 160	104 108 160
1	Bust girth	80.0	84.0	88.0	92.0	96.0	100.0	104.0
2	Waist girth	58.6	61.8	65.2	68.8	72.6	76.0	80.7
3	Hip girth	84.0	88.0	92.0	96.0	100.0	104.0	108.0
12	Neck base girth	29.8	31.2	32.3	33.3	34.1	34.8	35.4
13	Upper arm (muscle)	23.5	25.8	27.6	29.2	30.5	31.7	32.7

SIZE CHART NO. 14 (cont.)

Ref:	Measurement	*Proposed European size symbol*						
		80 84 160	84 88 160	88 92 160	92 96 160	96 100 160	100 104 160	104 108 160
24	Height	160.0	160.0	160.0	160.0	160.0	160.0	160.0
25	Cervical height	137.6	137.6	137.6	137.6	137.6	137.6	137.6
29	Knee height	42.5	42.5	42.5	42.5	42.5	42.5	42.5
31	Outside leg	100.4	100.4	100.4	100.4	100.4	100.4	100.4
35	Back waist length	39.7	39.7	39.7	39.7	39.7	39.7	39.7
36	Across back	32.4	33.9	35.2	36.2	37.1	37.9	38.6
39	Shoulder length	13.8	13.8	13.8	13.8	13.8	13.8	13.8
49	Cervical to centre front waist	47.8	49.2	50.4	51.3	52.1	52.9	53.5
—	Weight: kg	37.9	45.4	51.6	56.7	61.1	65.0	68.5

SIZE CHART NO. 15
FRANCE — TALL HEIGHT GROUP — AVERAGE BUST

Ref:	Measurement	*Proposed European size symbol*						
		80 84 168	84 88 168	88 92 168	92 96 168	96 100 168	100 104 168	104 108 168
1	Bust girth	80.0	84.0	88.0	92.0	96.0	100.0	104.0
2	Waist girth	58.6	61.8	65.2	68.8	72.6	76.0	80.7
3	Hip girth	84.0	88.0	92.0	96.0	100.0	104.0	108.0
12	Neck base girth	29.8	31.2	32.3	33.3	34.1	34.8	35.4
13	Upper arm (muscle)	23.5	25.8	27.6	29.2	30.5	31.7	32.7
24	Height	168.0	168.0	168.0	168.0	168.0	168.0	168.0
25	Cervical height	144.9	144.9	144.9	144.9	144.9	144.9	144.9
29	Knee height	44.8	44.8	44.8	44.8	44.8	44.8	44.8
31	Outside leg	105.8	105.8	105.8	105.8	105.8	105.8	105.8
35	Back waist length	41.3	41.3	41.3	41.3	41.3	41.3	41.3
36	Across back	32.4	33.9	35.2	36.2	37.1	37.9	38.6
39	Shoulder length	14.2	14.2	14.2	14.2	14.2	14.2	14.2
49	Cervical to centre front waist	47.8	49.3	50.4	51.3	52.1	52.9	53.5
—	Weight: kg	37.9	45.4	51.6	56.7	61.1	65.0	68.5

SIZE CHART 16A
SWITZERLAND   SHORT STATURE — HEIGHT 160 CM

	36	38	40	42	44	46	48	50	52
Bust girth	84	88	92	96	100	104	110	116	122
Waist girth	66	70	74	78	82	86	92	98	104
Hip girth	90	94	98	102	106	110	116	122	128
Arm length	58	58	58	58	58	58	58	58	58
Inside leg	76	76	76	76	76	76	76	76	76

SIZE CHART 16B
SWITZERLAND   REGULAR STATURE — HEIGHT 168 CM

	36	38	40	42	44	46	48	50	52
Bust girth	84	88	92	96	100	104	110	116	122
Waist girth	66	70	74	78	82	86	92	98	104
Hip girth	90	94	98	102	106	110	116	122	128
Arm length	60	60	60	60	60	60	60	60	60
Inside leg	80	80	80	80	80	80	80	80	80

SIZE CHART 16C
SWITZERLAND   TALL — HEIGHT 176 CM

	36	38	40	42	44	46	48	50	52
Bust girth	84	88	92	96	100	104	110	116	122
Waist girth	66	70	74	78	82	86	92	98	104
Hip girth	90	94	98	102	106	110	116	122	128
Arm length	62	62	62	62	62	62	62	62	62
Inside leg	84	84	84	84	84	84	84	84	84

Although no back neck-to-waist measurement is provided in these charts, it can be assumed that the static neck-to-waist grade would be applicable. The charts have two size intervals, a 4 cm interval from sizes 36 to 46, whilst a 6 cm interval is used for the outsizes from size 46 to 52.

Reproduced by permission of The Swiss Clothing Industry Association, Zurich, Switzerland.

SIZE CHART NO. 17
HOLLAND — VARYING HEIGHTS — AVERAGE BUST

Measurement	34	36	38	40	42	44	46	48	50	52
Waist girth	64	68	72	76	80	84	88	96	104	112
Hip girth	98	100	103	106	110	114	118	124	132	140
Bust girth	92	95	98	101	104	108	112	120	128	136

Height									
From:	152	156	160	164	167	Not given			
To:	157	161	165	169	173				
Back neck to waist:	35.5	37.5	39.5	41.5	43.5	Not given			

This size chart does not relate size to height.
Reproduced by permission of the Dutch Clothing Manufacturers Association, Amsterdam, Holland.

Canadian standard sizes

These standards which were issued by the Canadian Government Specifications Board in 1987 and are very comprehensive, covering Children's, Teenage and Women's sizes. The Women's size charts are distinguished by the height group divisions which are based on the relationship between the back neck to waist and leg length measurements. These divisions are:

A: Short waist — short leg
B: Short waist — long leg
C: Long waist — short leg
D: Long waist — long leg

An example of these length relationships for one hip and bust girth is shown in the following chart:

	Short waist short leg Size: $14\frac{1}{2}$	Short waist long leg Size: $14\frac{1}{2}$	Long waist short leg Size: 34	Long waist long leg Size: 34
Height	154.0	161.0	161.0	169.0
Bust girth	94.0	94.0	94.0	94.0
Hip girth	96.5	96.5	96.5	96.5
Back neck to waist	39.0	39.0	42.0	42.0
Leg length	95.5	103.0	95.5	103.0

The following example size chart is reproduced by permission of the Canadian General Standards Board, Ottawa, Canada.

SIZE CHART NO. 18
CANADA: SHORT WAIST — SHORT LEG

					Size symbol					
Measurement	$10\frac{1}{2}$	$12\frac{1}{2}$	$14\frac{1}{2}$	$16\frac{1}{2}$	$18\frac{1}{2}$	$20\frac{1}{2}$	$22\frac{1}{2}$	$24\frac{1}{2}$	$26\frac{1}{2}$	$28\frac{1}{2}$
Bust girth	86	90	94	99	104	109	114	119	124	129
Waist girth	67	71	76	82	88	94	99	105	111	117
Hip girth	86	91	96	101	106	111	116	121	126	131
Neck base girth	37.8	38.4	39.1	39.9	40.9	41.7	42.7	43.4	44.2	45.2
Upper arm (muscle)	25.9	27.7	29.2	31.2	33.3	35.3	37.1	39.1	41.1	43.2
Height	154	154	154	154	154	154	154	154	154	154
Cervical height	131	131	131	131	131	131	131	131	131	131
Knee height	42	42	42	42	42	42	42	42	42	42
Waist height	95.5	95.5	95.5	95.5	95.5	95.5	95.5	95.5	95.5	95.5
Back waist length	38.9	39.0	39.1	39.4	39.7	39.7	39.9	40.1	40.3	40.3
Across back	32.8	33.8	34.5	35.6	36.8	37.8	39.1	40.1	41.1	42.4
Shoulder length	11.4	11.7	11.7	11.9	12.2	12.4	12.4	12.7	13.0	13.0
Cervical to centre front waist	47.0	47.2	47.7	48.5	49.0	49.8	50.3	51.1	51.6	52.3

SIZE CHART NO. 19
AUSTRALIA — AVERAGE WOMEN

					Size symbol					
Measurement	8	10	12	14	16	18	20	22	24	26
Bust girth	75	80	85	90	95	100	105	110	115	120
Waist girth	55	60	65	70	75	80	85	90	95	100
Hip girth	80	85	90	95	100	105	110	115	120	125
Neck base girth	35	36	37	38	39	40	41	41	42	43
Upper arm (muscle)	23	24	26	28	29	31	33	35	37	38
Height	160	161	163	164	165	166	168	168	169	169
Cervical height	137	138	140	141	142	144	145	145	146	146
Knee height	43	43	44	44	44	45	45	45	45	—
Outside leg	99	100	101	102	103	104	105	106	106	106
Back waist length	38	39	39	40	40	41	41	42	42	42
Across back	30	31	32	33	34	35	37	38	39	40

SIZE CHART NO. 19 (cont.)

Measurement	Size symbol									
	8	10	12	14	16	18	20	22	24	26
Shoulder length	11.0	11.0	11.0	11.5	11.5	11.5	11.5	11.5	12.0	12.0
Weight: kg	45	49	54	59	65	73	80	84	91	—

The above is an extract from the size charts issued by the Standards Association of Australia. These standards are based on three height groups plus one for variable fittings in the bust/hip girths relationships. Reproduced by permission of the Standards Association of Australia, Sydney, NSW, Australia.

SIZE CHART NO. 20
ISRAEL: STATIC HEIGHT — AVERAGE BUST

Measurement	Size symbol					
	32	34	36	38	40	42
Height	164	164	164	164	164	164
Bust girth	76	80	84	88	92	96
Waist girth	61	63	65	67	70	74
Hip girth	83	87	90	94	98	102
Neck base girth	32.9	33.7	34.5	35.3	36.1	36.9
Upper arm (muscle)	25	25.5	26	27.3	28.6	29.9
Back waist length	39.5	39.5	40	40	40.5	40.5
Across back	30	31	32	33	34	35
Shoulder length	11.6	11.8	12	12.2	12.4	12.6

SIZE CHART NO. 21
ISRAEL: DYNAMIC HEIGHT — AVERAGE BUST

Measurement	Size symbol					
	36	38	40	42	44	46
Height	160	162	164	166	168	170
Bust girth	84	88	92	96	100	104
Waist girth	65	67	70	74	78	82
Hip girth	90	94	98	102	106	110
Neck base girth	34	35	36	37	38	39
Back waist length	40	40.5	41	41.4	42	42.5
Across back	31.6	32.7	33.8	34.9	36	36.8
Shoulder length	32	12.2	12.4	12.6	12.8	13.0

Reproduced by permission of The Ministry of Labour, Jerusalem, Israel.

Appendix B

Glossary of Technical Terms

Acromion — The highest point on the distal part of the spine of the scapula.

Allometry — Differential growth of one part of the body to the remainder.

Anterior — To the front.

Biotypology — The distinguishing of groups of people with common physiques or physical proportions.

Block pattern — A template of the basic pattern/ shape upon which design details can be superimposed.

Cervical — The seventh of the cervical vertebrae.

Distal — Belonging to the back, directed backwards.

Gorge — The neckline of the front to which the collar is joined.

Gorge seam — The seam joining the collar to the front.

Inter- — Between.

Intra — Within or inside.

Lapel break — The lower end of the lapel which is usually a small distance above the highest or first buttonhole.

Median — In the centre, nearer or towards the centre or middle.

Morpho — Shape, form.

Parameter — The construction of a convenient variable in which other variables can be expressed.

Photogrammetry — Photographic methods used in anthropometry.

Post — Behind or after

Scye — The armhole of a garment. Derived from the words 'Arms eye'.

Sleeve crown — The top section of the sleeve head which extends approximately 6 cm on either side of a central shoulder seam.

Somatotype — Body type, figure type.

Appendix C

Bibliography

SURVEY REPORTS

(a) US Department of Commerce, Office of Technical Services, Washington, D.C., USA. "Body Measurements for the Sizing of Women's Patterns and Apparel". CS 215-58.

(b) Her Majesty's Stationery Office, London, England. 'Women's Measurements and Sizes'.

(c) Hohenstein Institute, Bonningheim, W. Germany. 'Body Measurements and Sizes for Women's and Girls' Clothing'. (1972 and 1983)

(d) Technical Centre for Clothing, Paris, France. 'Women's Measurements'.

REFERENCES

(1) Alceqa (1589) *Tailors Pattern Book*. Republished 1979. Ruth Bean, Bedford, England.

(2) Beever (Ed), No date. *Clothing Terms and Definitions*. The Clothing Institute, London, England.

(3) Cooklin (1986). *Introduction to Anthropometry* The Ministry of Education, Jerusalem, Israel.

(4) Cooklin (1988). *Grading Technology* The Ministry of Labour, Jerusalem, Israel.

(5) Croney (1980). *Anthropometry for Designers*. Batsford Academic and Educational Ltd, London.

(6) Defty (1984). *The Art of Grading Patterns*. Butterworths, Durban, South Africa.

(7) Greenburg (1981). *Pattern Construction and Grading*. The Ministry of Labour, Tel-Aviv, Israel.

(8) Hrdlcka (1939). *Practical Anthropometry*. The Wister Institute of Anatomy and Biology, Philadelphia, USA.

(9) Krigsfeld (1969). *Basic Patterns for Ready Made Clothing*. The Ministry of Labour, Tel-Aviv, Israel.

(10) Kunick (1967). *Sizing, Pattern Construction and Grading for Women's and Children's Garments*. Phillip Kunick, London, England.

(11) Laver (1982). *Costume and Fashion*. Thames and Hudson. England.

(12) Liming (1982). *Mathematics for Computer Graphics*. Aero Publishers, California, USA.

(13) Moroney (1976). *Facts from Figures*. Penguin Books, England.

(14) Morris (1952). *Ladies' Garment Cutting and Making*. The New Era Publishing Co., London, England.

(15) Muller, no date. *Grading of Women's and Misses Patterns*. M. Muller and Sohn, Munich, W. Germany.

(16) Price and Zamkoff (1974). *Grading Techniques for Modern Design*. Fairchild Publications, New York.

(17) Rohr (1974). *Pattern Drafting and Grading*. Rohr Publishing Co, Connecticut, USA.

(18) Scheier (1974). *The ABC's of Grading*. Murray Sheier, New York, USA.

(19) Sichel (1980). *Costumes of the Classical World*. Batsford Academic and Educational, London, England.

(20) Taylor and Shoben (1987). *Grading for the Fashion Industry*. Hutchinson and Co., London, England.

(21) Thompson, Barden, Kirk, Mitchelson and Ward (1973). *Anthropometry of British Women*. University of Technology, Loughborough, England.

BLACKWELL SCIENCE LTD
List of Available Books

'An exceptional collection of publications for the apparel industry' Apparel International

Pattern cutting

Metric Pattern Cutting
Third Edition
Winifred Aldrich
The number one, best-selling book on pattern cutting for women's wear, including a new section on computerised pattern cutting and numerous blocks.
192 pages, illustrated hardback.
0 632 03612 5

Metric Pattern Cutting for Menswear Including Computer Aided Design
Third Edition
Winifred Aldrich
In the third edition of this standard work on the subject, sizing charts have been updated and the chapter devoted to computer-aided design has been updated and extended. An extra section on workwear has been added.
160 pages, illustrated hardback.
0 632 04113 7

Metric Pattern Cutting for Children's Wear From 2–14 years
Second Edition
Winifred Aldrich
Another bestseller by Winifred Aldrich, providing a simple but comprehensive system of pattern cutting for children's wear. Highly illustrated with hundreds of stylish diagrams and clear, concise instructions, it features basic blocks which can be adapted for creative design and includes illustrated grading instructions.
165 pages, illustrated hardback.
0 632 03057 7

Pattern Cutting for Lingerie, Beachwear and Leisurewear
Ann Haggar
This comprehensive text takes the reader through the whole process from the initial planning stages to finished pattern pieces. It is illustrated by numerous examples, working diagrams and drawings and contains patterns for stretch fabrics.
250 pages, illustrated paperback.
0 632 02033 4

Pattern Cutting for Women's Outerwear
Gerry Cooklin
Highly illustrated with clear stage-by-stage instructions, this innovative book emphasises the technological aspects of pattern development for women's mass-produced clothing. A simple, integrated system of drafting block patterns is described, followed by a wide-ranging toolbox of professional pattern cutting techniques with many examples of their applications. Patterns for linings and fusibles and computerised pattern design systems are also described.
192 pages, illustrated paperback.
0 632 03797 0

Dress Pattern Designing The Basic
Principles of Cut and Fit
Fifth Edition
Natalie Bray
With Fashion Supplement by Ann
Haggar
This classic and well-known textbook
now includes instructions on recent
fashion shapes. The book contains
over 100 basic diagrams and 40
plates, combined with clear and
detailed instructions.
192 pages, illustrated paperback.
0 632 01881 X

More Dress Pattern Designing
Fourth Edition
Natalie Bray
With Fashion Supplement by Ann
Haggar
This text expands the basic course,
showing the applications of the basic
principles and methods to more
advanced styles and specialist cutting
techniques. Lingerie, tailoring and
children's patterns are included.
208 pages, illustrated paperback.
0 632 01883 6

Dress Fitting
Second Edition
Natalie Bray
Fitting can cause problems for
dressmakers and students. Natalie
Bray discusses these problems,
outlining techniques for better fit;
problems of figure, posture and
pattern adjustment; and how to
identify a defect and choose the best
method of dealing with it.
120 pages, illustrated paperback.
0 632 01879 8

**Pattern Grading for Women's
Clothes**
Gerry Cooklin
A comprehensive text on pattern
grading setting out a simple and
effective grading system, which can be
applied to most size charts used for
women's clothing. Over 50
demonstrations of master and basic
garment grades are provided,
accompanied by simple and clear
instructions. Includes 200 illustrations
and 30 detailed size charts of
international sizing systems.
400 pages, illustrated paperback.
0 632 02295 7

**Pattern Grading for Children's
Clothes**
Gerry Cooklin
This thoroughly practical guide
includes demonstration grades broken
down into easy-to-follow illustrated
stages with simple and clear
instructions, and children's size charts
from 22 countries and leading retailers
in Europe and the USA.
320 pages, illustrated paperback.
0 632 02612 X

Pattern Grading for Men's Clothes
Gerry Cooklin
An up-to-date, profusely illustrated
and comprehensive manual setting out
the practical principles and
applications of pattern grading for the
whole range of men's clothing,
including computerised grading, the
latest developments in fully automatic
grading and grades for linings, fusibles
and pockets.
304 pages, illustrated paperback.
0 632 03305 3

**Fabric, Form and Flat Pattern
Cutting**
Winifred Aldrich
The relationship between garment cut
and fabric potential is probably the
most important feature of present
design skill. This book is based on an
appraisal of the fabric and the body
form to help students develop an
intuitive and practical approach.
208 pages, illustrated paperback.
0 632 03917 5

Master Patterns and Grading for Women's Outsizes
Gerry Cooklin
Improved foundation garments and greater fashion awareness make it imperative for an entirely new approach to the construction and sizing of garment patterns for outsizes. This new textbook is a specialized and up-to-date treatment of the subject, and provides pattern cutters and graders with a wealth of practical information.
128 pages, illustrated paperback.
0 632 03915 9

Clothing production

The Technology of Clothing Manufacture
Second Edition
Harold Carr and Barbara Latham
The full range of clothing manufacturing technology is surveyed and discussed, including the processes of modern clothing manufacture; cutting, sewing, alternative methods of joining materials and pressing; manual, mechanical and computer-controlled methods of production; and current applications of computerised techniques and robotics.
288 pages, illustrated paperback.
0 632 03748 2

Fashion Design and Product Development
Harold Carr and John Pomeroy
A new book which sets out the modern, commercial approach to product design in the clothing and fashion market and discusses the practical factors including materials, manufacture, costs, quality and organisation of the process.
192 pages, illustrated paperback.
0 632 02893 9

Introduction to Clothing Manufacture
Gerry Cooklin
This introductory textbook for students and newcomers to the clothing business provides a comprehensive view of the clothing industry. It explains practical aspects of clothing manufacture, from the original design to deliveries to retail customers; describes each of the basic planning and manufacturing technologies; and contains many realistic and practical examples of the day-to-day operation of a clothing factory.
190 pages, illustrated paperback.
0 632 02661 8

Knitted Clothing Technology
Terry Brackenbury
This unique book covers the specific techniques used to convert weft knitted fabric into garments. It examines techniques of shaping and construction, specialist assembly machinery, and future trends in the production of knitted garments.
208 pages, illustrated paperback.
0 632 02807 6

CAD and Design

CAD in Clothing and Textiles
Second Edition
Edited by Winifred Aldrich
A unique insight into the practice of computer aided design. With contributions from experts in the industry, many aspects of CAD in clothing and textiles are discussed including writing of the software, sale of systems, applications, training and education.
192 pages, illustrated paperback.
0 632 03893 4